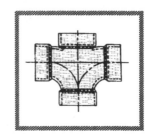

Planning Drain, Waste & Vent Systems

by

Howard C. Massey

Craftsman Book Company
6058 Corte del Cedro, P.O. Box 6500, Carlsbad, CA 92008

Acknowledgments

The author wishes to thank the following for providing material used in the preparation of this book.

International Association of Plumbing and Mechanical Officials
2001 Walnut Drive, South
Walnut, California 91789

Tyler Pipe — Wade Division
P.O. Box 2027
Tyler, Texas 75710

Library of Congress Cataloging-in-Publication Data

Massey, Howard C.
    Planning drain, waste & vent systems / by Howard C. Massey.
      p.   cm.
    ISBN 0-934041-51-2
    1. Plumbing--Handbooks, manuals, etc.   I. Title. II. Title:
Planning drain, waste, and vent systems.
TH6125.M36   1990
696'.1--dc20   90-32521

Contents

Chapter 1

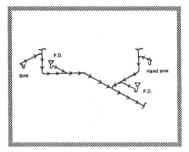

Basic Plumbing Principles

Everyone who designs plumbing systems knows from experience how important it is to follow the code exactly. Even a small mistake can keep a plan from being approved — causing expensive delays. Unfortunately, it's easy to make mistakes. The plumbing code isn't like a cookbook. It doesn't explain what to do step by step. Plumbing codes are complex regulations written to be enforced (like a law) rather than to be understood.

But that doesn't mean you have to understand the code any less. You have to follow the code exactly — every time. That's what this manual will help you do.

This book is written for anyone who wants to avoid mistakes and delays when preparing plans for drain, waste and vent systems in buildings. Whether you're a plumbing engineer, plumbing designer, plumbing contractor or plumber, I think you'll find the design information you're looking for between the covers of this book.

I'm going to assume that you know a little about plumbing materials and how they're installed. But that's all I'm going to assume. Whether you're an experienced professional plumbing designer, or working on your first plumbing plan, this manual will answer your plumbing design questions. If trying to learn the code by reading the code itself has left you frustrated and confused, don't worry. Even those who have worked with the code for years get tripped up sometimes. I intend to explain every point in plain language and offer examples that simplify the learning process.

If you're new to the plumbing trade and need information on basic plumbing principles and installation practice, check the order form at the back of this manual. *Basic Plumbing with Illustrations* explains how to install plumbing materials. *Plumbers Handbook* describes what plumbing installers need to know about the code.

Which Code Do You Need?

Before we go any further, let me identify the plumbing code I'm talking about. It's the Uniform Plumbing Code, published by International

Association of Plumbing and Mechanical Officials, 5032 Alhambra Avenue, Los Angeles, California 90032-3490. Every plumbing designer (and every plumber) working in the western and southwestern states should have a copy. Building departments usually sell copies of the code they enforce. Larger bookstores or technical bookstores also sell code books adapted for use in their area.

There are several major plumbing codes, of course. The **Uniform Plumbing Code** is the most widely used code in the United States. It is co-sponsored by the International Association of Plumbing and Mechanical Officials (IAPMO) and the International Conference of Building Officials (ICBO).

Twenty-four states currently using the Uniform Plumbing Code are Alaska, California, Hawaii, Idaho, Maine, Montana, Nevada, New Hampshire, Oregon, Utah, Washington, and areas of Arizona, Colorado, Iowa, Kansas, Missouri, Nebraska, North Dakota, Oklahoma, Pennsylvania, South Dakota, Texas, West Virginia, and Wyoming.

The second most widely used code in the United States is the **Standard Plumbing Code,** published by Southern Building Code Congress International, Inc., 900 Montclair Road, Birmingham, Alabama 35213-1206. It's used in fourteen southern states: Alabama, Arkansas, Florida, Georgia, Louisiana, Mississippi, North Carolina, South Carolina, Tennessee and some parts of Delaware, Missouri, Oklahoma, Texas and West Virginia.

The remaining states have either adopted their own codes or refer to the **National Standard Plumbing Code** or the **Building Officials and Code Administrators, International** (BOCA). The BOCA Basic Code is widely accepted in the northeastern states.

If your local plumbing code isn't based on the Uniform Plumbing Code, don't be concerned. The differences between these model codes are minor — and with each revision they become less important.

Every plumbing professional should understand how a plumbing code becomes the local law. Here's how it works. Few cities and counties have the resources and time required to create their own plumbing code from scratch. Instead, most cities and counties adopt one of the model

codes published by one of the national code-writing organizations. Your city or county can adopt any code they want to follow, of course. And they can make any changes they feel are necessary when adopting that code. But once adopted, the code (with any changes) becomes a regulation that's enforced like a law in your city or county. That code remains in effect as adopted until it's amended or replaced by the adoption of another code.

Note this very carefully. Even if you know that your city or county follows the Uniform Building Code, it's not safe to assume that they've adopted the current version that's being sold by International Association of Plumbing and Mechanical Officials. Many jurisdictions are still enforcing older versions of the code. And it's common for a city or county to adopt changes or additions to the code that apply only in that community. You can see why it's so important to have a copy of the *current code as adopted* in the city or county where you do business.

How Plans Are Approved

Every plumbing system begins with a plumbing designer, someone who decides what pipes will run where and how each plumbing fixture will be served. In a single-family residence, this plan will be very simple. So simple in fact, that the plumbing plan may be no more than a few lines and notes on the building floor plan. For a large commercial building, the plumbing plan may consist of many plan sheets. Preparing a plan like this is complex work and requires a good understanding of the code.

If you're preparing plans for commercial or industrial buildings or for larger residential buildings, this manual should save you hours of time. It can also prevent expensive mistakes. That's especially true if you prepare plans for use in a community that requires an engineer's review of plumbing plans for commercial buildings. Many building departments won't accept commercial plumbing plans designed by non-engineers (architects, draftspersons) without an engineer's seal of approval stamped on the construction plans. So whether you're a plumbing system designer or an engineer, you'll find this book essential.

When the plumbing plans have been prepared and checked by an engineer (if required), they go to the local building department for approval. A plans examiner will pore over your plan, checking every detail, looking for anything that doesn't comply with the code. If there are discrepancies, and there usually are, the examiner will return the plans to the designer for correction. When corrections have been made, the plans go back to the examiner for approval. This process is repeated again and again until no discrepancies are found. Then the plan is approved and a building permit is issued.

Naturally, it's in your interest to have the plan approved the first time. Making corrections is expensive. And corrected plans usually go to the bottom of the pile on the examiner's desk. That may delay issuing the building permit by days or even weeks. Delays like that are both expensive *and* embarrassing.

What You'll Find Here

This book is intended to help you design plumbing systems that can be approved the first time by any plans examiner. I'm not going to cover the entire code because plumbing designers don't need to understand every sentence in the code. Many parts of the plumbing code are of interest only to material manufacturers and those who install plumbing. But I *will* cover every code section that you need to know to handle any common residential, commercial or industrial job. Most important, the information in this manual applies nearly everywhere in the United States, regardless of which model code is enforced in that area.

Let me offer a little background on myself so you understand my perspective. I started as a plumber and was a plumbing contractor for many years. I'm the author of the two books mentioned earlier in this chapter. For the last fourteen years I've worked as a plans examiner, reviewing more than 20,000 plans a year. I'm very familiar with the mistakes plumbing designers make. Some are minor, some are major. But all are unnecessary.

I've written this book to make your work easier if you prepare plumbing drawings.

A word of caution, however. This book is *not* the plumbing code. You should have the code by your side and refer to it regularly. There's no substitute for having a current copy of the code enforced in your city or county.

Basic Principles of the Plumbing Code

Every plumbing designer should understand why plumbing codes are written and enforced. It's to protect the health, welfare and safety of the public. While details of plumbing design may vary from area to area, the basic principles of sanitation and safety remain the same everywhere.

Everything in the code is intended to carry out the objectives in the code's "Basic Principles" chapter. Obviously, these principles are the foundation on which the plumbing code is based. They define the intent of the code. If you follow the general principles carefully, your plumbing systems will operate safely and efficiently.

I'll use the rest of this chapter to identify the basic concepts on which the plumbing code is built. These broad policy statements explain what the plumbing code is trying to do.

In brief, the purpose of the plumbing code is to ensure that buildings intended for human occupancy have adequate plumbing systems. Plumbing should be designed, installed and maintained to protect human health and safety. The code also requires a minimum number of plumbing fixtures, depending on the occupancy and use of the building.

Here are some examples of fixture requirements:

Residential units:

- ◆ one water closet
- ◆ one bathtub or shower
- ◆ one lavatory
- ◆ one kitchen sink
- ◆ adequate hot water

♦ some codes might require an outlet for a washing machine

Commercial buildings:

♦ adequate sanitary facilities, as occupancy or use may require

♦ no less than one water closet

♦ no less than one lavatory

Construction of standard plumbing fixtures:

♦ from approved non-absorbent material

♦ have smooth surfaces

♦ be free from defects and concealed fouling surfaces

Construction of special-use fixtures:

(Most codes approve the following, but check with the code in your area.)

♦ from stainless steel

♦ from soapstone

♦ from chemical stoneware

♦ from plastic

Job-constructed special-use fixtures:

♦ lined with lead

♦ lined with copper

♦ lined with corrosion-resisting material

♦ lined with other approved materials especially suited to the use for which the fixture is designed

Check with your building department before selecting lining materials for on-the-job construction of special-use fixtures. Local authorities will suggest various kinds of materials acceptable for use under local conditions.

Conditions for Proper Fixture Location

Rooms with plumbing fixtures have to be well-lighted and adequately ventilated. Fixtures must be spaced to allow their intended use.

Fixtures must be located to allow access for repair, maintenance and replacement and can't obstruct normal operation of windows and doors.

Plumbing fixtures in commercial buildings must accommodate the handicapped.

All standard plumbing fixtures that are directly connected to a drainage system should be equipped with a water-seal trap. Some special fixtures, appliances, devices and appurtenances must be indirectly connected to a drainage system.

Only those plumbing fixtures which are provided with an overflow and meet the following code criteria are permitted. These fixtures must be designed by the manufacturer so that standing water in the fixture cannot rise in the overflow when the stopper is in place. Design must also ensure that when the stopper is in the open position and the fixture is empty, no water can be retained in the overflow.

Most codes require that hot water be provided in all dwelling units and certain types of commercial establishments. This is considered a minimum basic requirement to protect health, proper sanitation and personal hygiene.

Fixtures that heat and store hot water must have protective devices installed to avoid overheating and explosion.

The location of a hot water tank must allow easy access for maintenance or replacement. Water heaters can be located *in* an apartment or living unit only when supplying hot water to that one unit. Central hot water facilities which supply hot water for more than one unit must be accessible without entering any individual living unit.

As a rule, codes require that water heaters have devices that keep hot water and steam out of the cold water distribution system.

Materials for Plumbing Systems

As a designer, it isn't enough to follow the code. You have to specify in your plan that only code-approved piping, fittings, valves, fixtures, appliances and appurtenances be used. That just makes good sense. You should also be careful to design for durability, so frequent repairs and replacement aren't needed.

Some areas have highly corrosive water supplies that require special pipe or fixtures. Your building department will be aware of any special requirements in your community. They will also know if external corrosion is likely from local soils, and can also advise you if special protection is required for approved piping materials.

The code doesn't cover special conditions that occur in some areas. Rely on your building department to identify special precautions needed to protect the plumbing systems you design. But always ask before you begin the design process. Asking after your plan is complete may delay plan approval.

Be sure to follow the recommendations of the manufacturers of materials, fixtures, appliances and appurtenances. Use only new materials free of manufacturing defects and damage. If an owner requests that used equipment or material be installed in a new structure (or in an addition to an existing structure), get the approval of your building department before making any commitment.

As a designer of plumbing systems, you need to remember that the purpose of the code is to set *minimum* standards for plumbing systems. The plans you draw can provide more than the minimum, of course. And any requirements imposed by your local building department will take precedence over other sections of the code.

If you're planning a job in an area where you haven't worked before, start by talking to the building department with authority to approve your plan. Ask for any amendments they have to the code and inquire about special requirements to meet local soil or water conditions.

Designing Drainage, Waste and Vent Systems

A sanitary drainage system is needed any time plumbing facilities are required by code. Waste from the plumbing system must be piped to an approved means of disposal.

The drainage system should exclude anything that might obstruct the free flow of waste through the pipes, produce explosive mixtures, destroy piping joints, or interfere with sewage disposal. You do this with interceptors, special traps, piping materials and fittings.

The code takes special care to keep sewage backflow away from food and drinking waster. For example, walk-in coolers need special protection. You do this by connecting fixtures, appliances or floor drainage in a walk-in cooler *indirectly* to the building drainage system.

The code also requires that drainage systems be designed to keep solids and deposits in pipes from stopping normal flow. Cleanouts must be placed where they are accessible for maintenance.

No matter how remote the building, you can never assume that waste can be discharged on the ground surface, or in any lake, pond, stream, ditch, or tidal reservoir. It is *always* necessary to get prior approval from the local authorities.

If a drainage system is subject to backflow of sewage (such as in a basement), the code requires that you have some means of preventing overflow into the building.

We'll discuss the vent system in detail later. For now, you only need to know that vents are used to keep pressure in a waste line from discharging sewer gas into the building. Vent pipes are usually extended through the roof so air can enter or leave the plumbing system freely. All piping in the plumbing system needs a free flow of air.

Vents have to extend full size, upward, through the roof, and have a free opening. In cold climates where frost may form in the vent, special precautions are needed. And the open end of the vent must never be located where sewer gas from the line could pass into a window, door, louvers or air intake. The open vent end should be well away from places where articles might be thrown into the pipe or where water might drain into the opening.

Structural Safety

Avoid any plumbing plan that requires the plumber to weaken the building structure. For example, don't locate a public toilet where installation would require the plumber to put a sleeve or notch in a key part of the foundation. Work with the architect if you see a conflict between your needs and structural requirements. This is especially important in multi-story buildings. Find a way to run supply and waste lines without jeopardizing the building's structure.

This chapter has listed the basic principles of the plumbing code. I'll admit that these are broad, general concepts. But they're what the code is all about: concern for public health, welfare and safety. While details of plumbing designs can vary from code to code, the basic principles of sanitation presented here are common to all codes. But you can't follow the code if you don't understand the words.

The Terminology

Fortunately, the code isn't written in Greek. Most words mean exactly what they mean in everyday conversation. If you don't understand the meaning of some term in the code, look first in any good dictionary.

But sometimes the English language isn't adequate to express the meaning that's intended. That's why the plumbing code has assigned special meanings to key terms. To eliminate misunderstandings, the authors of the code include definitions of these terms. Let's look at some examples.

The words *shall* and *may* appear in every plumbing code. We all know what these words mean in daily conversation. But they have a specialized meaning in the plumbing code. *Shall* means *you must*. It *requires* compliance. Take the example of preventing cross-connection in a potable water supply system. The code states: "All devices installed in a potable water supply system for protection against backflow *shall* be maintained in good working condition." That means that you don't have any choice.

As used in the code, *may* is a permissive term. It means allowable or optional, but not required. For example, "Two fixtures set back-to-back, *may* be served by a single vertical drainage pipe." Thus, a single vertical pipe is *permitted* with a back-to-back fixture arrangement, but not *required*. Other options which meet code specifications are acceptable.

Two other commonly misused code terms are *building drain* and *building sewer*. Many professional designers assume that both terms mean the same part of the drainage system. Not so. Note the code definition of these terms.

A *building drain* is the lowest horizontal collection system which receives the discharge from other drainage pipes within the walls of a building and extends 2 feet beyond the building line. (This distance may vary in some codes.)

A *building sewer* is defined as that part of the horizontal piping of a drainage system which extends from the end of the building drain and conveys the liquid waste to an approved point of disposal.

Before you read the rest of the book, I suggest that you take the time to read the glossary at the back of the book. It includes the definitions from the code, plus some I've added. There are also plenty of illustrations to help you understand the definitions.

I don't recommend that you try to memorize these terms now. Just look over the glossary to get a general idea of what's there. Later, when you're having trouble understanding some explanation, you can look up any terms you don't understand.

Now let's start looking at some of the details of the code.

Chapter 2

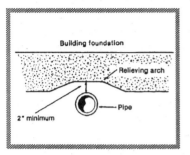

Plumbing Systems: General Regulations

General regulations in the plumbing code are broad principles that explain what's required when designing, installing and maintaining plumbing systems. For example, general regulations require the proper disposal of waste products.

The general regulations also cover such topics as:

♦ Fittings used in direction changes

♦ Fittings that are prohibited

♦ Repairs and alterations to existing buildings

♦ Trenching, excavation and backfill

♦ Structural safety

♦ Protection of pipes

♦ Location of plumbing fixtures

The code always requires that the plumbing design conform to accepted engineering practices. Every plumbing designer needs to understand these general regulations. I'll cover all the regulations that are important to plumbing system designers.

General Instructions and Regulations

Liquid Waste

Liquid waste must drain into an approved drainage system that meets code requirements. All plumbing fixtures, drains, appliances, and appurtenances must be connected properly to the drainage system.

If a public sewer is available, the building sewer must connect to it. If no public sewer is available, you can use a private sewer system —

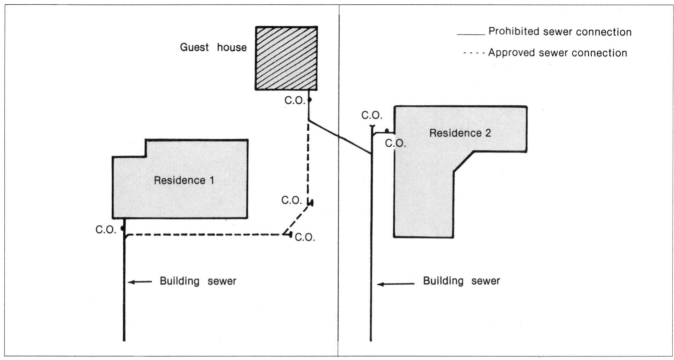

Figure 2-1   Sewer line location

Storm Drainage Systems

Storm drainage systems convey rain water to a legal drain. Storm drainage includes roof drains, area drains, gutters, downspouts, leaders, building storm drains and storm sewers, catch basins and soakage pits. Storm water can't flow into the building drainage system unless approved by the building department. See Chapter 8 for more information on storm drainage.

Industrial Wastes

Industrial wastes can damage a building drainage system, the public sewer, or even the sewage treatment plant. Your building department will decide how industrial waste should be treated. There's more information in Chapter 7.

The code prohibits pollution of surface or subsurface water. Of course, nearly every form of liquid waste can be treated to eliminate contaminants. Check with your building department.

usually a septic tank and drainfield. We'll cover private sewer systems in Chapter 9.

Location

Every part of the plumbing system must be located on the lot with the building that plumbing system serves. Look at Figure 2-1. Even if both lots are owned by the same person, the sewer from the guest house must run entirely within lot 1. This is also true of the water supply, gas lines, wells, and private sewage disposal systems.

Improper Location

Never locate piping, fixtures or equipment where they might interfere with doors, windows or other parts of the building.

Designing Plumbing Systems

Every plumbing system you design must do two things: First, it must conform with accepted engineering practices. Second, it has to actually work the way it's supposed to. Some approved fittings are shown in Figure 2-2.

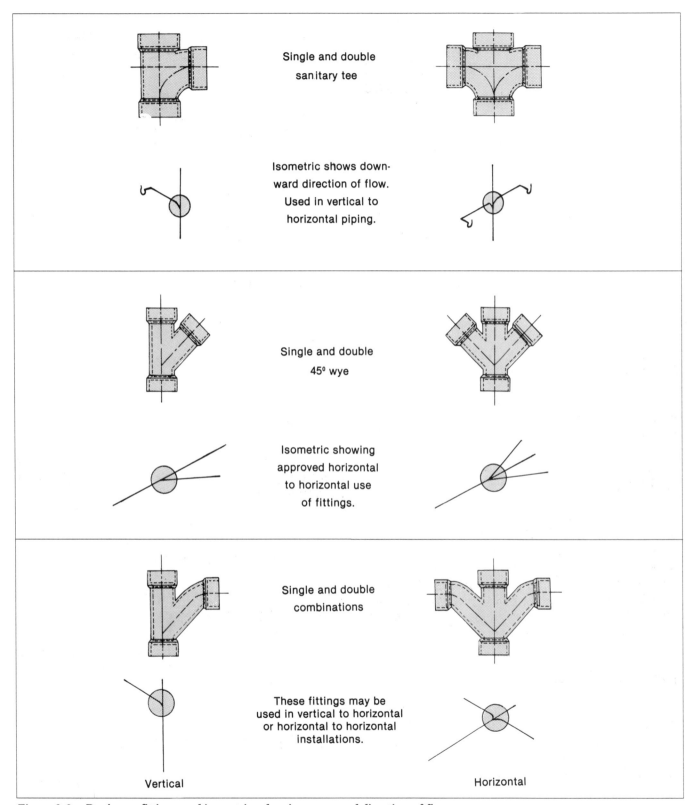

Single and double
sanitary tee

Isometric shows down-
ward direction of flow.
Used in vertical to
horizontal piping.

Single and double
45° wye

Isometric showing
approved horizontal
to horizontal use
of fittings.

Single and double
combinations

These fittings may be
used in vertical to horizontal
or horizontal to horizontal
installations.

Vertical

Horizontal

Figure 2-2   Drainage fittings and isometrics showing approved direction of flow

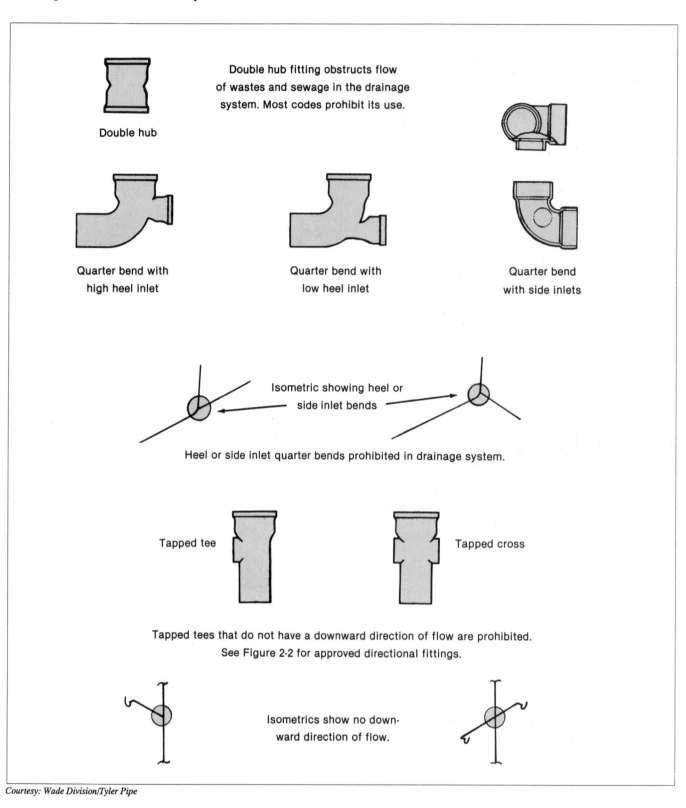

Double hub

Double hub fitting obstructs flow
of wastes and sewage in the drainage
system. Most codes prohibit its use.

Quarter bend with
high heel inlet

Quarter bend with
low heel inlet

Quarter bend
with side inlets

Isometric showing heel or
side inlet bends

Heel or side inlet quarter bends prohibited in drainage system.

Tapped tee

Tapped cross

Tapped tees that do not have a downward direction of flow are prohibited.
See Figure 2-2 for approved directional fittings.

Isometrics show no down-
ward direction of flow.

Courtesy: Wade Division/Tyler Pipe

Figure 2-3 *Drainage fittings and isometrics showing prohibited fittings*

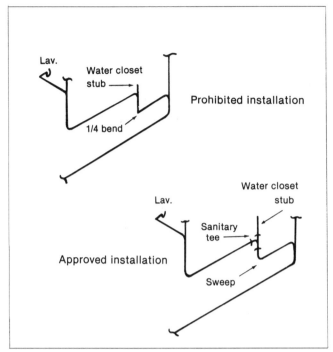

Figure 2-4   Fixture drain waste pipe installations

Prohibited Fittings

These fittings are prohibited in any drainage design: double hub fittings, single or double tee branch, single or double tapped tee branch, or heel or side-inlet quarter bend (Figure 2-3). They should never show up on your drawings.

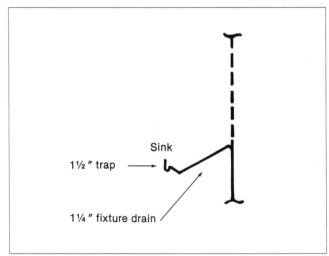

Figure 2-6   Prohibited connection

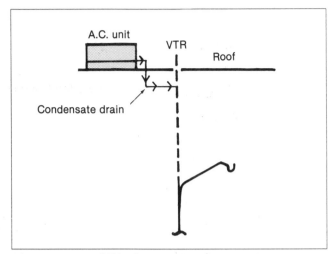

Figure 2-5   Prohibited connection

Selected List of Prohibited Practices

Here are some prohibitions to remember when you design a drainage system:

1) Never connect the waste pipe of any other fixture drain to a water closet bend or stub or similar fixture (Figure 2-4).

2) Never use a vent pipe which serves a fixture as a soil or drain pipe (Figure 2-5).

3) Never use any part that will obstruct the building's drainage or venting system (Figure 2-6). *Exception:* The enlargement of a 3-inch closet bend or stub to 4 inches is permitted (Figure 2-7). It's not considered an obstruction.

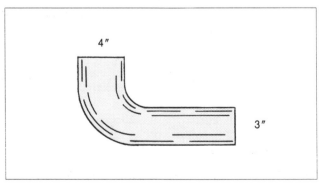

Figure 2-7   2" x 4" closet bend is not considered an obstruction

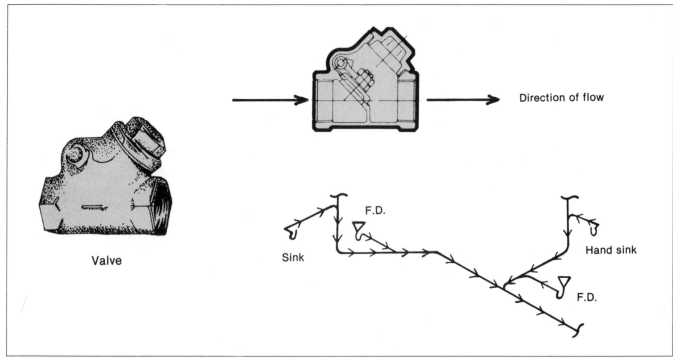

Figure 2-8   Pipe and fittings illustrating direction of flow

4) Don't align valves, pipes and fittings against the direction of flow. They must align *with* the flow (Figure 2-8).

Independent Systems

The plot plan should meet these code requirements:

1) The drainage system of each new building must be separate and independent from any other building (Figure 2-9).

2) You can't connect new plumbing for an existing building or a building addition to the drainage system of any other building. But there is one exception. When a new building is erected behind an existing building, it may connect to the drain or sewer of the building in front if there's no private sewer available, and no space to install one (Figure 2-1).

Alterations and Additions

When a building is torn down or relocated, you can use the existing building sewer or drainage pipes for a new building if they meet code requirements governing new work. But of course you can't use the drainage system for a new building if it's made of materials that aren't approved for use under a building.

When you design a plumbing system that includes piping for future use, your drawings must show that the openings will have permanent plugs or caps approved by the code (Figure 2-10).

When you're renovating the plumbing for an existing building, you can deviate from the code when necessary *if* it's approved by the building department in advance.

Protection of Pipes

Make sure your plans or drawings show that all pipes are protected. It must be clear that

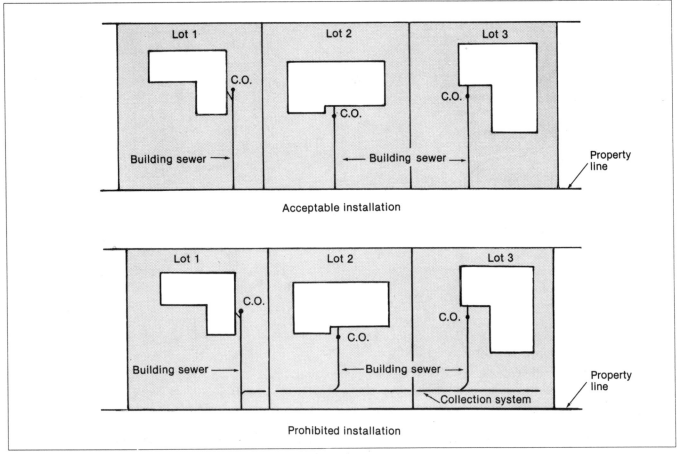

Figure 2-9 *Each building's drainage system must be independent*

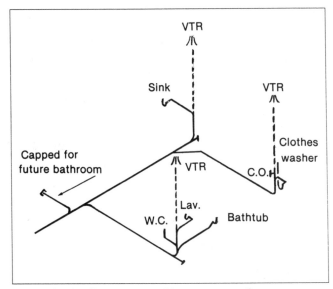

Figure 2-10 *System capped in an approved manner*

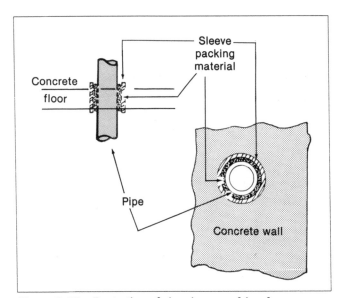

Figure 2-11 *Protection of pipes in poured-in-place concrete*

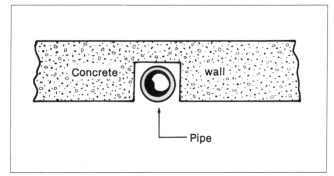

Figure 2-12   One type of approved installation method

no structural strain will be transmitted to the piping system.

Pipes passing through concrete slabs, or through or under concrete or block walls, must be protected from breakage, sags or corrosion by code-approved sleeving (Figure 2-11). The code prohibits piping from being directly embedded in concrete or masonry walls or footings. Figure 2-12 shows one approved installation method.

If a pipe must pass under the building foundation, provide for a 2-inch separation between the top of the pipe and the bottom of the foundation (Figure 2-13). If this isn't possible, design a relieving arch into the building's foundation (Figure 2-14). If you can't do either one, some codes will permit you to use, *with prior approval*, an iron pipe sleeve two pipe sizes larger than the

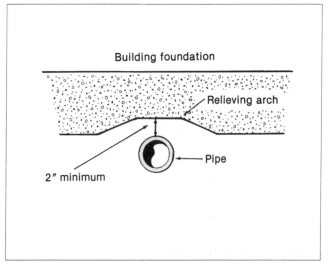

Figure 2-14   Relieving arch

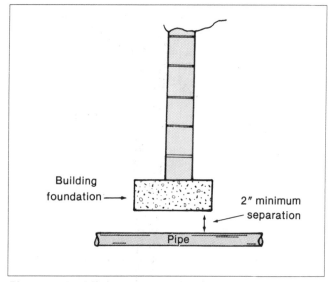

Figure 2-13   Minimum separation between pipe and foundation

pipe you're using. Use this only as a last resort. It usually means you'll need additional steel and concrete to strengthen the building foundation.

If your design calls for installing pipes that may corrode in corrosive fill, you must specify a protective coating or wrapping. If you suspect that corrosive soil is present, have soil samples tested. If it is, specify a non-corrosive material or external protection.

Although certain materials *are* code-approved for sewers (concrete pipe and orangeburg pipe, for example), you can *never* use them under or within 2 feet of a building. It's even further in some codes. For any sewer pipe classified as *fragile* (concrete, orangeburg and PVC), provide for a cover of at least 1 foot over its highest point.

Protecting Pipes from Freezing

When designing plumbing systems in cold-weather areas, you must follow these rules to prevent freezing:

1) Don't locate any soil or waste pipe in an outside wall unless you provide adequate protection from freezing.

2) If you're designing a plumbing system for a vacation home that won't be occupied year-round, make sure all pipes are protected from freezing.

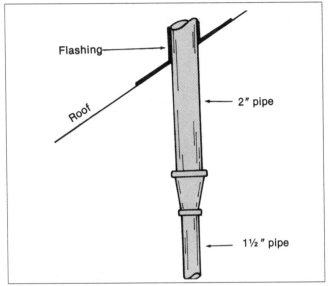

Figure 2-15   Vent terminal protected from frost closure

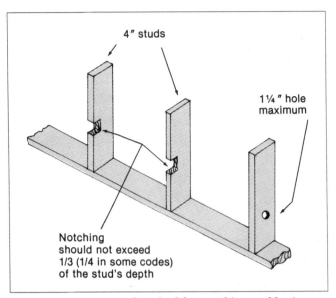

Figure 2-16   Approved method for notching and boring studs

3) Protect the terminal opening of the vent stack from frost closure. The best way is to increase the diameter of the vent terminal at least one pipe size larger than the pipe section below it (Figure 2-15).

Retaining Structural Integrity

Cooperate with the architect to ensure that the structure won't be weakened during the pipe installation. For instance, if partitions must be bored or notched to receive horizontal piping, you'll have to specify studs or joists deep enough to meet minimum building code requirements.

Boring or Notching Studs

When you've decided the size of the horizontal piping, show the required partition depth on your floor plan. Follow these guidelines, and look at Figure 2-16.

1) The largest hole allowed in a 4-inch stud is 1-1/4" in diameter.

2) The largest hole allowed in a 6-inch stud is 2 inches in diameter.

3) Studs may be notched one-third of their depth (one-quarter in some codes).

It's a good idea to specify stud guards in your design. They'll protect the piping from drywall screw or nail damage and reinforce the notched partitions (Figure 2-17).

If you're using 2-inch or larger horizontal piping installed above the floor, design a pipe chase that's deep enough to carry it.

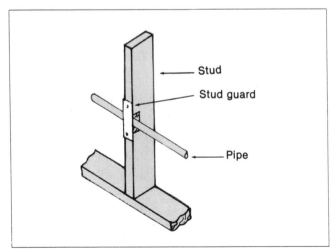

Figure 2-17   Stud guard protects pipe and reinforces notched studs

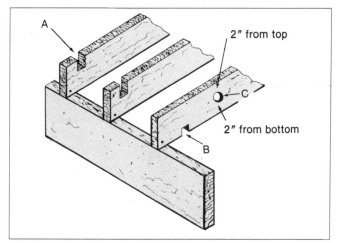

Figure 2-18   *Approved method for notching and boring floor and ceiling joists*

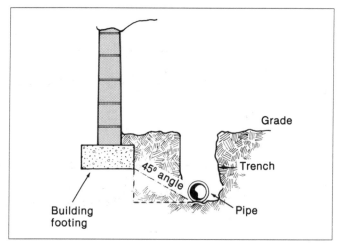

Figure 2-19   *45-degree angle for pipe parallel with building foundation*

Boring or Notching
Floor and Ceiling Joists

If possible, design plumbing systems that don't require the boring or notching of floor and ceiling joists. If that's not possible, make sure that no structural member is weakened. Plumbers should always leave a building as safe as they found it.

The required supports must be included in your plans and approved by the building official. Here are some of the code provisions:

1) Most codes will permit notches in the top or bottom of floor or ceiling joists *not exceeding one-sixth their depth*. Also, never notch the middle one-third of the span (Figure 2-18).

2) You can notch the top of the joists no more than one-third the depth of joist, *if* the notch isn't farther from the support than the depth of the joist. Look at notch A in Figure 2-18.

3) You can drill holes through joists as long as they're not more than 2 inches in diameter *and* they're not closer than 2 inches to the joist edge (hole C in Figure 2-18).

Trenches

If you can, locate the piping so that its trench doesn't run parallel to and deeper than the building footing. If it has to be deeper, the trench

bottom must be at a 45-degree angle below the bottom of the footing. This is called the *45-degree angle of pressure*. Look at Figure 2-19. The pipe can't be located in the triangle marked by a broken line.

Piping Hangers and Supports

Note in your plans or specs the type of hangers and supports required for both vertical and horizontal piping. The hangers and supports must be strong enough to carry the weight of the pipe and contents.

Space the horizontal piping supports at intervals that will maintain pipe alignment and prevent sags. The interval depends on the pipe used. Figure 2-20 shows the intervals for eight kinds of pipe.

Space vertical piping supports close enough together to support the weight of the pipe. You don't want to put stress on horizontal branches. Figure 2-21 shows some of the required intervals.

Base of Stacks

Support the base of all stacks with concrete, bricks, or other material acceptable to the building department.

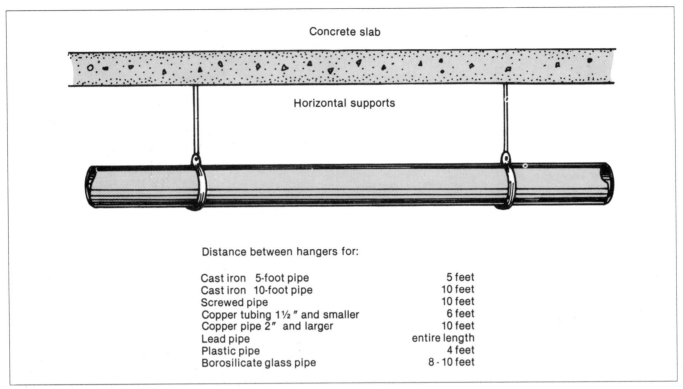

Concrete slab

Horizontal supports

Distance between hangers for:

Cast iron 5-foot pipe	5 feet
Cast iron 10-foot pipe	10 feet
Screwed pipe	10 feet
Copper tubing 1½ ″ and smaller	6 feet
Copper pipe 2″ and larger	10 feet
Lead pipe	entire length
Plastic pipe	4 feet
Borosilicate glass pipe	8 - 10 feet

*Figure 2-20   **Horizontal pipe supports***

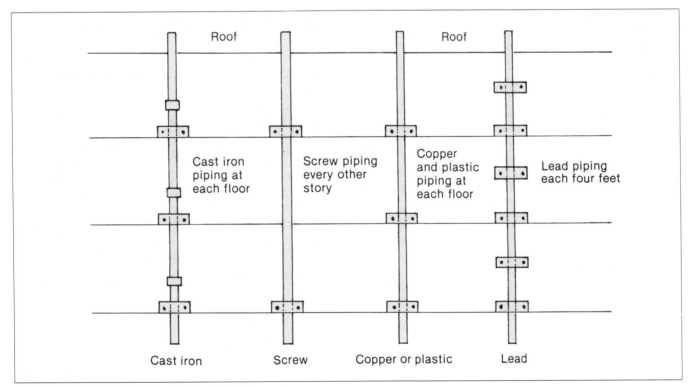

Roof   Roof

Cast iron piping at each floor

Screw piping every other story

Copper and plastic piping at each floor

Lead piping each four feet

Cast iron   Screw   Copper or plastic   Lead

*Figure 2-21   **Vertical pipe supports***

Chapter 3

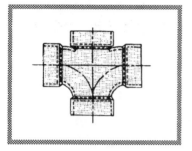

Standards for Plumbing Materials

In the plumbing code, the accent is always on protection. The code protects the health, welfare, and safety of the citizens by regulating plumbing and drainage systems. But even a system with excellent design and admirable workmanship may not do its job — unless the materials provide satisfactory service. That's why the code sets minimum standards for materials in a plumbing system.

In general, the materials must be free from defects and meet the standards of the building department. All pipe, fittings, and fixtures have to be listed or labeled by an approved listing agency, such as ANSI (American National Standards Institute), or ASTM (American Society for Testing and Materials). If listed or labeled materials aren't available, you can substitute material only with the approval of the building department.

Material Standards in the Uniform Plumbing Code

The code serves two functions. First, it describes broad standards of performance. Second, it identifies specific products which are acceptable. When designing a job, you must specify materials that meet the standards listed in Figure 3-1 (Table A of the Uniform Plumbing Code). Include the maker's mark or name, the weight, and the quality of the product.

There's a steady stream of new materials coming on the market. The building department may approve a new product for use until it's tested by a recognized testing agency. But if the test shows that it doesn't meet existing standards, you'll have to replace it with an approved model.

TABLE A - PLUMBING MATERIAL STANDARDS

MATERIALS AND PRODUCTS	ANSI	ASTM	FS	IAPMO	OTHER STANDARDS	FOOTNOTE REMARKS
FERROUS PIPE AND FITTINGS:						
Cast Iron Screwed Fittings (125 & 250 lb) (56.8 & 113.5 Kg)	B16.4-1963	A 126-66				
Cast Iron Soil Pipe and Fittings..........................		A 74-72				Note 4
Cast Iron Soil Pipe and Fittings For Hubless Cast Iron Sanitary Systems					CISPI 301-82	Note 4
Cast Iron Soil Pipe Institute's Patented Joint For Use In Connection With Cast Iron Sanitary Systems					CISPI 310-82	
Cast Iron Threaded Drainage Fittings.....................	B16.12-1871					Note 4
Gray Iron and Ductile Iron Pressure Pipe		A 377-66				
Hubless Cast Iron Sanitary Systems (Installation)...........				IS 6-82		
Malleable Iron Threaded Fittings (150 & 300 lb) (68.1 & 136.2 Kg) .						
Pipe, Steel, Black and Hot-Dipped, Zinc-Coated Welded and Seamless		A 53-83				
Pipe, Steel, Black and Hot-Dipped, Zinc Coated (Galvanized) Welded and Seamless, For Ordinary Uses		A 120-82				
Pipe Threads (Except Dryseal)...........................	B2.1-1968					
Roof Drains	A112.21.2M 1983					
Special Cast Iron Fittings				PS 5-84		
Subdrains For Built-up Shower Pans				PS 16-77		
Threaded Cast Iron Pipe For Drainage, Vent, and Waste Services	A40.5-1943					
Welded and Seamless Carbon Steel and Austenitic Stainless Steel Pipe Nipples		A 733-76				
NONFERROUS PIPE AND FITTINGS:						
Brass-, Copper-, and Chromium-Plated Pipe Nipples........		B 687-81				
Bronze Flanges and Flanged Fittings (150 & 300 lb)........	B16.24-1979					
Cast Brass and Tubing P-Traps				PS 2-83		
Cast Copper Alloy Fittings For Flared Copper Tubes	B16.26-1975					
Cast Bronze Threaded Fittings (Class 120 & 250)	B16.15-1978					
Cast Bronze Solder-Joint Drainage Fittings-DWV	B16.23-1976					Note 4
Cast Copper Alloy Solder-Joint Pressure Fittings	B16.18-1978					

TABLE A - PLUMBING MATERIAL STANDARDS

MATERIALS AND PRODUCTS	ANSI	ASTM	FS	IAPMO	OTHER STANDARDS	FOOTNOTE REMARKS
Copper and Copper Alloy Welded Water Tube (Installation)				IS 21-80		
Copper Drainage Tube (DWV)		B 306-81				
Copper Plumbing Tube and Fittings (Installation)				IS 3-75		
Diversion Tees and Twin Waste Elbow				PS 9-84		
Drains For Prefabricated and Precast Showers				PS 4-83		
Flexible Copper Water Connectors				PS 14-81		
General Requirements For Wrought Seamless Copper and Copper-Alloy Tube		B 251-81				
Seamless Brass Tube		B 135-82				
Seamless Copper Pipe, Standard Sizes		B 42-82				
Seamless Copper Tube		B 75-81a				
Seamless Copper Water Tube		B 88-83				
Seamless Copper-Alloy Water Tube		B 585-80				
Seamless Red Brass Pipe, Standard Sizes		B 43-80				
Seamless and Welded Copper Distribution Tube (Type D).......		B 641-78				
Threadless Copper Pipe		B 302-81				
Tubing Trap Wall Adapters				PS 7-84		
Welded Brass Tube		B 587-80				
Welded Copper-Alloy Water Tube		B 586-80				
Welded Copper-Alloy UNS No. C21000 Water Tube		B 642-78				
Welded Copper Tube		B 447-80				
Wrought Copper and Bronze Solder-Joint Pressure Fittings	B16.22-1980					
Wrought Copper and Wrought Copper Alloy Solder-Joint Drainage Fittings	B16.29-1980					Note 4
NON-METALLIC PIPE:						
Acrylonitrile-Butadiene-Styrene (ABS) Building Drain, Waste and Vent Pipe and Fittings (Installation)				IS 5-83		
Acrylonitrile-Butadiene-Styrene (ABS) Plastic Drain, Waste and Vent Pipe and Fittings		D 2661-82				Note 4
Acrylonitrile-Butadiene-Styrene (ABS) Plastic Drain, Waste and Vent Pipe Having A Foam Core		F 628-81				

Figure 3-1   Table A - Uniform Plumbing Code

TABLE A - PLUMBING MATERIAL STANDARDS

MATERIALS AND PRODUCTS	ANSI	ASTM	FS	IAPMO	OTHER STANDARDS	FOOTNOTE REMARKS
Acrylonitrile-Butadiene-Styrene (ABS) Sewer Pipe and Fittings		D 2751-80				
Asbestos-Cement Nonpressure Sewer Pipe		C 428-74				Notes 1 & 3
Asbestos Cement Pressure Pipe		C 296-73				
Asbestos-Cement Pressure Pipe For Water and other Liquids					AWWA C400-72	
Asbestos Cement Pressure Pressure Pipe For Water Service and Yard Piping (Installation)				IS 15-82		
Bell-End Poly (Vinyl Chloride) (PVC) Pipe		D 2672-80				
Chlorinated Poly (Vinyl Chloride) (CPVC) Plastic Pipe, Schedules 40 and 80		F 441-82				
Chlorinated Poly (Vinyl Chloride) (CPVC) Plastic Hot- and Cold-Water Distribution Systems		D 2846-82				
Chlorinated Poly (Vinyl Chloride) (CPVC) Solvent Cemented Hot and Cold Water Distribution Systems (Installation)				IS 20-84		
Concrete Drain Tile		C 412-80				Note 3
Concrete Sewer, Storm Drain and Culvert Pipe		C 14-80				
Drain, Waste and Vent (DWV) Plastic Fittings Patterns		D 3311-82				Note 4
Fittings For Joining Polyethylene Pipe For Water Service and Yard Piping				PS 25-84		
Non-Metallic Building Sewers (Installation)				IS 1-82		
Plastic Insert Fittings For Polybutylene (PB) Tubing		F 845-84				
Plastic Insert Fittings For Polyethylene (PE) Plastic Pipe		D 2609-74				Note 6
Polybutylene (PB) Cold Water Building Supply and Yard Piping and Tubing (Installation)				IS 17-82		
Polybutylene Hot and Cold Water Distribution Tubing Systems Using Insert Fittings (Installation)				IS 22-84		
Polybutylene Hot and Cold Water Distribution Pipe, Tubing and Fitting Systems Using Heat Fusion (Installation)				IS 23-84		
Polybutylene (PB) Plastic Hot-Water Distribution Systems		D 3309-81				
Polybutylene (PB) Plastic Pipe (SIDR-PR) Based On Controlled Inside Diameter		D 2662-82				
Polybutylene (PB) Plastic Tubing		D 2666-82				
Polybutylene (PE) Cold Water Building Supply and Yard Piping (Installation)				IS 7-83		

TABLE A - PLUMBING MATERIAL STANDARDS

MATERIALS AND PRODUCTS	ANSI	ASTM	FS	IAPMO	OTHER STANDARDS	FOOTNOTE REMARKS
Polyethylene (PE) For Gas Yard Piping (Installation)				IS 12-83		
Polyethylene (PE) Plastic Pipe (SIDR-PR) Based on Controlled Inside Diameter		D 2239-83				
Poly (Vinyl Chloride) (PVC) Building, Waste and Vent Pipe and Fittings (Installation)				IS 9-83		
Poly (Vinyl Chloride) (PVC) Cold Water Building Supply and Yard Piping (Installation)				IS 8-84		
Poly (Vinyl Chloride) (PVC) Natural Gas Yard Piping (Installation)				IS 10-84		
Poly (Vinyl Chloride (PVC) Plastic Drain, Waste and Vent Pipe and Fittings		D 2665-82				Note 4
Poly (Vinyl Chloride) (PVC) Plastic Pipe (SDR-PR)		D 2241-82				
Poly (Vinyl Chloride) (PVC) Plastic Pipe, Schedules 40, 80 and 120		D 1785-82				
Poly (Vinyl Chloride) (PVC) Plastic Pipe Fittings (Schedule 40)		D 2466-78				
Primers For Use In Solvent Cement Joints of Poly (Vinyl Chloride) (PVC) Plastic Pipe and Fittings		F 656-80				
Rubber Rings For Asbestos-Cement Pipe		D 1869-79				
Safe Handling Of Solvent Cements and Primers Used For Joining Thermoplastic Pipe and Fittings		F 402-81				
Socket-Type Chlorinated Poly (Vinyl Chloride) (CPVC) Plastic Pipe Fittings, Schedule 40		F 438-82				
Socket-Type Chlorinated Poly (Vinyl Chloride) (CPVC) Plastic Pipe Fittings, Schedule 80		F 439-82				
Socket-Type Poly (Vinyl Chloride) (PVC) Plastic Pipe Fittings Schedule 80		D 2467-76a				
Solvent Cement For Acrylonitrile-Butadiene-Styrene (ABS) Plastic Pipe and Fittings		D 2235-81				
Solvents Cements For Chlorinated Poly (Vinyl Chloride) (CPVC) Plastic Pipe and Fittings		F 493-80				
Solvent Cements For Poly (Vinyl Chloride) (PVC) Plastic Pipe and Fittings		D 2564-80				
Thermoplastic Accessible and Replaceable Plastic Tube and Tubular Fittings		F 409-81				Note 4

Figure 3-1   Table A - Uniform Plumbing Code (continued)

TABLE A - PLUMBING MATERIAL STANDARDS

MATERIALS AND PRODUCTS	ANSI	ASTM	FS	IAPMO	OTHER STANDARDS	FOOTNOTE REMARKS
Thermoplastic Gas Pressure Pipe, Tubing and Fittings		D 2513-82				
Type PS-46 Poly (Vinyl Choride) (PVC) Plastic Gravity Flow Sewer Pipe and Fittings		F 789-82				
Type PSM Poly (Vinyl Chloride) (PVC) Sewer Pipe and Fittings . . .		D 3034-81				
Type PSP Poly (Vinyl Chloride) (PVC) Sewer Pipe and Fittings		D 3033-81				
Threaded Poly (Vinyl Chloride) (PVC) Plastic Pipe Fittings Schedule 80		D 2464-76				
Vitrified Clay Pipe, Extra Strength, Standard Strength and Perforated		C 700-78				
PLUMBING FIXTURES:						
Enameled Cast Iron Plumbing Fixtures	A112.19.1M-1979					
Jelted Whirlpool Bathtubs	Z124.1-1980				PS 32-84	
Plastic Bathtub Units			WWP-541-71			
Plastic Lavatories	Z124.3-1980		WWP-541-71			
Plastic Shower Receptors and Shower Stalls	Z124.2-1980		WWP-541-71			
Plastic Water Closet Bowls and Tanks	Z124.4-1983		WWP-541-71			
Plumbing Fixtures For Land Use			WWP-541-71			
Porcelain Enameled Formed Steel Plumbing Fixtures	A112.19.4-1977		WWP-541-71			
Stainless Steel Plumbing Fixtures (Designed For Residential Use)	A112.19.3-1976		WWP-541-71	PS 13-79		Note 5
Testing and Rating Procedure For Grease Interceptors				IS 2-82		
Tile Lined Roman Bath Tubs (Installation)				IS 4-82		
Tile Lined Shower Receptors (and Replacements) (Installation) . .			WWP-541-71			
Trim For Water Closet Bowls, Tanks and Urinals	A112.19.5-1979		WWP-541-71			
Vitreous China Plumbing Fixtures	A112.19.2M-1982					
VALVES:						
Backflow Preventers With Intermediate Atmospheric Vent						
Backflow Prevention Devices				PS 31-77	ASSE 1012-78	
Backwater Valves				PS 31-77		
Bronze Gate Valves				PS 8-77		
Cast Iron Gate Valves			WWV-54D-73			
			WWV-58b-71			

TABLE A - PLUMBING MATERIAL STANDARDS

MATERIALS AND PRODUCTS	ANSI	ASTM	FS	IAPMO	OTHER STANDARDS	FOOTNOTE REMARKS
Constant-Level Oil Valves						
Dual Check Type Backflow Preventors					UL 352-1982	
Finished and Rough Brass Plumbing Fixture Fittings	A112.18.1M-1979				ASSE 1024-1979	
Globe-Type Loglighter Valves-Angle or Straight Pattern				PS 10-77		
Hose Connection Vacuum Breakers	ANSI/ASSE 1011-1976				ASSE 1011-1976	
Individual Shower Control Valves Anti-Scald Type	ANSI/ASSE 1016-1979				ASSE 1016-1979	
Manually Operated Gas Valves	Z21.15-1974					
Pipe Applied Atmospheric Type Vacuum Breakers	ANSI/ASSE 1001-1970				ASSE 1001-1970	
Pressure Regulating Valves For LP Gas					UL 144-1978	
Relief Valves and Automatic Gas Shutoff Devices For Hot Water Supply Systems and Addendum	Z21.22-1971				UL 132-1973	
Thermostatic Mixing Valves, Self Actuated For Primary Domestic Use	ANSI/ASSE 1017-1979				ASSE 1017-79	
Valves For Anhydrous Ammonia and LP-Gas (Other Than Safety Relief)					UL 125-1980	
Water Closet Flush Tank Ballcocks	ANSI/ASSE 1002-1979				ASSE 1002-1979	
APPLIANCES AND EQUIPMENT:						
Automatic Storage Type Water Heaters With Inputs Less Than 50,000 Btu Per Hour (Approved Requirements For, Vo. I	Z21.10.1-1971					
Chimneys, Factory-Built Residential Type and Building Heating Appliances					UL 103-1983	
Circulating Tank, Instantaneous and Large Automatic Storage Type Water Heaters (Approval Requirements For Vol. III)	Z21.10.3-1971					
Commercial Electric Dishwashers					UL 921-1978	
Draft Equipment					UL 378-1983	

Figure 3-1   Table A - Uniform Plumbing Code (continued)

TABLE A - PLUMBING MATERIAL STANDARDS

MATERIALS AND PRODUCTS	ANSI	ASTM	FS	IAPMO	OTHER STANDARDS	FOOTNOTE REMARKS
Draft Hoods (Listing Requirements For)	Z21.12-1971					
Drinking Water Coolers					UL 399-1978	
Electric Booster and Commerical Storage Tank Water Heaters					UL 1453-1982	
Gas Fired Steam and Hot Water Boilers and Addenda	Z21.13-1974					
Gas Vents					UL 441-1979	
Heating, Water Supply and Power, Boilers-Electric					UL 834-1980	
Home Laundry Equipment (Plumbing Requirements For)	ANSI/AHAM HLW-2PR-1980					
Household Commercial and Portable Exchange Water Softeners					WQA S-100-81	
Household Dishwashers					UL 749-1978	
Household Dishwashers (Drain Hose)					AHAM DW-1-75	
Household Dishwashers (Plumbing Requirements For)	ANSI/AHAM DW-2PR-1980					
Household Electric Storage Tank Water Heaters					UL 174-1983	
Household Food Waste Disposer Units (Plumbing Requirements For)	ANSI/AHAM FWD-2PR-1980					
Ice Makers					UL 563-1975	
Metal Connectors For Gas Appliances and Addenda	Z21.24-1973					
Motor Operated Water Pumps					UL 778-1980	
Oil-Fired Boiler Assemblies					UL 726-1975	
Oil-Fired Water Heaters					UL 732-1974	
Pigtails and Flexible Hose Connectors For LP-Gas					UL 569-1980	
Pumps For Oil-Burning Appliances					UL 343-1982	
Steel Auxiliary Tanks For Oil-Burner Fuel					UL 443-1979	
Steel Inside Tanks For Oil-Burner Fuel					UL 80-1980	
MISCELLANEOUS:						
Boiler and Pressure Vessel Code					ASME	
Chlorinated Polyethylene (CPE) Sheeting For Containment Membrane		D 4068-81				
Compression Joints For Vitrified Clay Pipe and Fittings		C 425-82				
Copper Alloy Sand Castings For General Applications		B 584-83				Note 2

TABLE A - PLUMBING MATERIAL STANDARDS

MATERIALS AND PRODUCTS	ANSI	ASTM	FS	IAPMO	OTHER STANDARDS	FOOTNOTE REMARKS
Copper Sheet Strip, Plate and Rolled Bar		B 152-71a				
Dishwasher Drain Airgaps (Airbreaks)				PS 23-81		
Joints For Circular Concrete Sewer and Culvert Pipe, Using Rubber Gaskets		C 443-79				
General Requirements For Steel Sheet, Zinc Coated (Galvanized) By The Hot-Dip Process		A 525-70				
Liquified Petroleum Gases, Storage and Handling					NFPA 58-1974	
Low Pressure Air Test For Building Sewers (Installation)				IS 16-84		
Pipe Hangers and Supports-Materials, Design and Manufacture	ANSI/MSS SP-58-1979					
Plant Applied Protective Pipe Coatings				PS 22-84		
Prefabricated Concrete Septic Tanks				PS 1-83		
Protectively Coated Pipe (Installation)				IS 13-84		
Rubber Gaskets For Cast Iron Soil Pipe and Fittings		C 564-82				
Rubber Rings For Asbestos-Cement Pipe		D 1869-79				
Solder; Tin Alloy; Lead-Tin Alloy; & Lead Alloy (and Flux, Type AC Only)		B 32-70	QQ-S-571e(72)			

1 Limited to domestic sewage
2 Alloy C85200 for cleanout plug
3 Type II only

4 Although this Standard is referenced in Table A some of the pipe, tube or fittings shown in the Standard are not acceptable for use under the Uniform Plumbing Code
5 PDI Standard G101 by reference
6 Limited to nylon material only

Figure 3-1   Table A - Uniform Plumbing Code (continued)

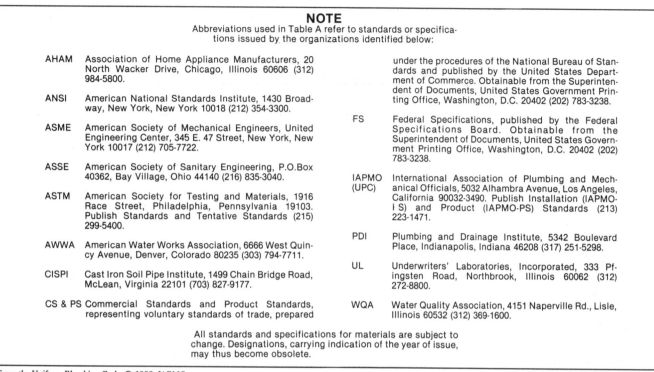

NOTE

Abbreviations used in Table A refer to standards or specifications issued by the organizations identified below:

AHAM   Association of Home Appliance Manufacturers, 20 North Wacker Drive, Chicago, Illinois 60606 (312) 984-5800.

ANSI   American National Standards Institute, 1430 Broadway, New York, New York 10018 (212) 354-3300.

ASME   American Society of Mechanical Engineers, United Engineering Center, 345 E. 47 Street, New York, New York 10017 (212) 705-7722.

ASSE   American Society of Sanitary Engineering, P.O. Box 40362, Bay Village, Ohio 44140 (216) 835-3040.

ASTM   American Society for Testing and Materials, 1916 Race Street, Philadelphia, Pennsylvania 19103. Publish Standards and Tentative Standards (215) 299-5400.

AWWA   American Water Works Association, 6666 West Quincy Avenue, Denver, Colorado 80235 (303) 794-7711.

CISPI   Cast Iron Soil Pipe Institute, 1499 Chain Bridge Road, McLean, Virginia 22101 (703) 827-9177.

CS & PS   Commercial Standards and Product Standards, representing voluntary standards of trade, prepared under the procedures of the National Bureau of Standards and published by the United States Department of Commerce. Obtainable from the Superintendent of Documents, United States Government Printing Office, Washington, D.C. 20402 (202) 783-3238.

FS   Federal Specifications, published by the Federal Specifications Board. Obtainable from the Superintendent of Documents, United States Government Printing Office, Washington, D.C. 20402 (202) 783-3238.

IAPMO (UPC)   International Association of Plumbing and Mechanical Officials, 5032 Alhambra Avenue, Los Angeles, California 90032-3490. Publish Installation (IAPMO-IS) and Product (IAPMO-PS) Standards (213) 223-1471.

PDI   Plumbing and Drainage Institute, 5342 Boulevard Place, Indianapolis, Indiana 46208 (317) 251-5298.

UL   Underwriters' Laboratories, Incorporated, 333 Pfingsten Road, Northbrook, Illinois 60062 (312) 272-8800.

WQA   Water Quality Association, 4151 Naperville Rd., Lisle, Illinois 60532 (312) 369-1600.

All standards and specifications for materials are subject to change. Designations, carrying indication of the year of issue, may thus become obsolete.

Figure 3-1   Table A - Uniform Plumbing Code (continued)

You can use materials that aren't listed in Table A (or other chapters of the code) only with special permission of the building department.

Specifying approved materials on your plans or specs helps the plumbing contractor install just the system you had in mind. Here's an example. List trim for fixtures like this: Traps, tailpiece fittings, and tubular products shall be B & S 17 gauge, chrome-plated brass. No one could misunderstand that. If you don't provide enough detail, the contractor could decide to use 20 gauge materials. That wouldn't meet your quality standards — and in some locations, it wouldn't even meet the code.

Now let's look at some of the specific standards in the Uniform Plumbing Code.

Iron Pipe Size (IPS)

All iron, steel, brass, and copper pipe you use must be *standard iron pipe size*. That means that all pipe, regardless of weight, must have a standard outside diameter (O.D.). The inside diameter (I.D.) depends on the pipe's weight — whether standard (Schedule 40), extra heavy (Schedule 80), or double extra heavy (Schedule 120). Since the outside diameters are always the same, standard threading dies will fit all three weights of pipe. See Figure 3-2.

Pipe weight is an important variable in designing water systems. The water pressure determines the pipe weight you'll use. Unless the water pressure is unusually high, you'll design

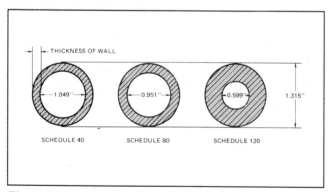

Figure 3-2   Three weights of 1 " nominal size pipe

most plumbing systems in standard weight pipe. But occasionally you'll have to use the next larger pipe size to provide enough volume and pressure to make the fixtures work right.

Copper Tubing (Drainage)

Underground and above ground drainage and vent pipes must be at least the weight of copper drainage tube type DWV. But you can't use copper tubing in a drainage system carrying chemical or industrial wastes.

Copper Tubing (Water)

Copper tubing for carrying water underground and above ground must be at least the weight of Type L. There is one limited exception: Type M copper tubing may be used above ground in a building, or underground outside a building.

Copper tubing must carry additional identification markings, besides the approved standard markings described earlier. That makes it harder to use copper tubing that's the wrong weight or type. It has to be marked by a continuous and indelible colored stripe at least 1/4-inch wide. The color of that stripe identifies the type:

Type	Color	O.D.	I.D.
Type K	green	1.375"	1.245"
Type L	blue	1.375"	1.265"
Type M	red	1.375"	1.291"
Type DWV	yellow	1.375"	1.295"

The tubing with thicker walls, designed to hold greater pressures, costs more than the thin wall pipe.

Special Materials

Lead Products

Here are the code requirements for sheet lead or other lead products used in a plumbing system:

1) Sheet lead for safe pans must weigh at least 4 pounds per square foot.

2) Lead flashings for vent terminals or other uses on a roof should weigh at least 3 pounds per square foot.

3) Lead bends and traps must have a wall thickness of 1/8-inch or more. No particular weight is required.

Copper and Brass Products

Sheet and tubular copper and brass for special uses must meet these weight requirements:

1) Sheet copper for safe pans and general use should weigh at least 12 ounces per square foot.

2) Copper flashings for vent terminals or other roof flashing must weigh at least 8 ounces per square foot.

3) Tubular copper and brass traps and tailpiece fittings for fixtures must usually be at least B & S 17 gauge. But some codes do accept 20 gauge traps, tailpiece fittings, and tubular products.

Water Closet Flanges or Similar Fixtures

Specify flanges of bronze, copper, hard lead, cast iron, galvanized malleable iron, ABS, PVC, or other materials approved by the building department. Water closet flanges must be approximately 7 inches in diameter, with a 1-1/2-inch wide flange to receive a gasket. That makes a tight water and gas connection.

Caulked-on bronze or copper closet flanges must be at least 1/8-inch thick. If they're cast iron or galvanized malleable iron, they must be at least 1/4-inch thick. The overall depth shouldn't exceed

TABLE 2-3
Cleanouts

Size of Pipe (inches)	Size of Cleanout (inches)	Threads per inch
1½	1½	11½
2	1½	11½
2½	2½	8
3	2½	8
4 & larger	3½	8

TABLE 2-3
Cleanouts (metric)

Size of Pipe (mm)	Size of Cleanout (mm)	Threads per 25.4 mm
38.1	38.1	11½
50.8	38.1	11½
63.5	63.5	8
76.2	63.5	8
101.6 & larger	88.9	8

TABLE 2-4
Cleanout Plugs - I.P.S. - Brass

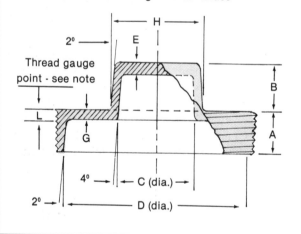

Figure 3-3   Cleanouts and cleanout plugs

2 inches. Hard lead closet flanges must be made of lead alloy with at least 7.75% antimony by weight. They should weigh at least 1 pound 9 ounces.

Bronze, copper or lead closet flanges have to be burned or soldered to lead closet stubs or bends. Cast iron closet flanges must be caulked to cast iron closet stubs or bends.

Secure ABS and PVC closet flanges to plastic closet stubs or bends with a solvent cement. Plastic closet flanges that meet other materials must be screwed or fastened in a manner approved by the building department.

Closet screws, bolts, washers, and similar fasteners must meet two requirements. They have to be corrosion resistant (brass, copper or other approved material) and strong enough to support the fixture.

Cleanout Fittings

The cleanout you'll specify depends on the material used in the system. Cleanouts for cast iron pipe must have brass or cast iron bodies and brass plugs. Galvanized wrought iron, galvanized steel, copper, or brass pipe requires cleanouts with brass plugs or caps. ABS or PVC systems take plastic plugs. Cleanout plugs must have raised square heads unless you have to place them in walking areas. Then countersink them, with rectangular slots for removal. All cleanout plugs must be gastight and watertight.

Materials used for cleanouts must meet the standards in Tables 2-3 and 2-4 of the Uniform Plumbing Code (Figure 3-3).

Drainage Fittings

Drainage system fittings must be of the same type and material as the pipes. They need a smooth interior waterway, and a fall of 1/4-inch per foot. Use recessed drainage fittings on screwed pipe, copper tube, or plastic pipe. Don't use water pipe fittings.

Backwater Valves

Backwater valves must have bodies of cast iron or brass. All bearing and moving parts must be of corrosion-resistant materials. Provide accessibility with an access cover.

TABLE 2-1
Caulking Ferrules

Pipe size (inches)	Inside diameter (inches)	Length (inches)	Minimum weight each Lb.	Oz.
2	2¼	4½	1	0
3	3¼	4½	1	12
4	4¼	4½	2	8

TABLE 2-1
Caulking Ferrules (metric)

Pipe size (mm)	Inside diameter (mm)	Length (mm)	Minimum weight each (kg)
50.8	57.2	114.3	.454
76.2	82.6	114.3	.790
101.6	108	114.3	1.132

Figure 3-4   Caulking ferrules

TABLE 2-2
Soldering Bushings

Pipe size (inches)	Minimum weight each Lb.	Oz.	Pipe size (inches)	Minimum weight each Lb.	Oz.
1¼	0	6	2½	1	6
1½	0	8	3	2	0
2	0	14	4	3	8

TABLE 2-2
Soldering Bushings (metric)

Pipe size (mm)	Minimum weight each (kg)	Pipe size (mm)	Minimum weight each (kg)
31.8	.168	63.5	.622
38.1	.224	76.2	.908
50.8	.392	101.6	1.586

Figure 3-5   Soldering bushings

Valves and Fittings

In a drainage system, use only full-way gate valves (valves with no interior obstructions). Make sure they have working parts of corrosion-resistant metal. Valves 4 inches or larger must have bodies of cast iron. Smaller valves may have cast iron or brass bodies.

Valves in a water pipe of two inches or less must be brass. Fittings must be galvanized cast iron, galvanized wrought iron, copper, brass, or other approved material. There's one exception: Cast iron fittings in a water supply system of more than 2 inches can't be galvanized.

Here's a good rule of thumb for designing water supply systems: Specify valves and fittings of the same material as the pipe. For example, for copper pipe, specify copper fittings; for galvanized wrought iron pipe, specify galvanized wrought iron fittings.

Caulking Ferrules

Ferrules must be made of bronze or copper and meet the standards in Table 2-1 of the Uniform Plumbing Code (Figure 3-4).

Soldering Bushings

Bushings must be made of bronze or copper and meet the standards in Table 2-2 of the UPC (Figure 3-5).

Chapter 4

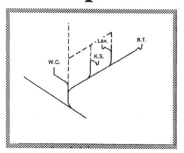

An Introduction to Sanitary Drainage Systems

Drainage piping is the heart of the plumbing system — and it's so complex that understanding the code is especially important. But the plumbing code books aren't much help. Because their language is so legalistic and arbitrary, they're not effective guides for designing a plumbing system.

Until the plumbing codes are simplified and standardized, you need help understanding the regulations for drainage systems. This chapter, and the next two, will guide you through the "gray areas" of the code. They'll help you design plumbing systems that meet the code requirements.

Throughout this book, I'm quoting code regulations from the Uniform Plumbing Code (with permission, of course). In spite of code variations throughout the country, the basic principles of sanitation and safety are the same.

Parts of a Drainage, Waste & Vent System

The private DWV system is the largest part of any designer's work. Figure 4-1 shows the three major classes of piping and fittings in a simple drainage system.

1) *Drainage pipes:* They receive and convey the used water to a public or private disposal system.

2) *Fixture traps:* They provide a liquid seal protection without restricting the flow of sewage or other waste.

3) *Vent pipes:* They admit air to and exhaust air from all parts of the drainage system. That protects fixture traps against siphonage and back pressure.

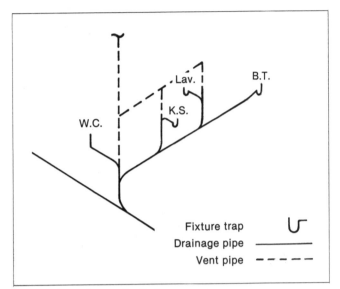

Figure 4-1   Parts of a drainage system

Because these three major parts are so important and so complex, I'll treat each in a separate chapter. In this chapter, I'll focus on the drainage system.

The Drainage System

Pipes that carry waste must not be hazardous to health under normal conditions. Build safeguards into your design that protect against ignition, radiation hazard or excessive noise. Also make sure your design prevents any fouling or clogging.

Don't forget to allow for normal atmospheric pressure in your design. Make sure that the liquid waste will flow easily from a higher to a lower elevation. Design only *vertical* vent, waste and soil stacks. Avoid offsets when possible. And slope the horizontal pipes just enough to carry the waste water away from the fixtures quickly. Remember that using minimum pipe sizes promotes a scouring action in the pipe that helps avoid blockages.

Sewage Disposal

Plumbing fixtures mark the end of the potable water supply system and the beginning of the sewage system. Every building that has plumbing fixtures must also have a sanitary drainage system to carry waste to an approved sewage disposal system.

The best way to dispose of sewage is in a public sewer system, if one is available. If a public sewer isn't available, use an *approved private sewage disposal system* — usually an adequately-sized septic tank and drainfield.

There's a great demand for plumbing system designers who can plan safe and reliable sanitary drainage systems. An important ingredient in that planning — and a good starting point for our discussion — is the issue of adequate sewage disposal.

Public Sewage Disposal Systems

Before starting work on a project, make sure someone — the designer, architect or developer —has evaluated its feasibility. This is especially true if they're not from the local area. There may be restrictions that make it impossible, or at least impractical, to put a proposed building on a particular site. Let's look at a couple of the potential problem areas.

Availability— This common word occurs often in some codes — and it can be an expensive word. Many sewer district directors consider their sewer system available, even though it ends some 100 to 500 feet from your site. The Uniform Plumbing Code, for example, calls a public sewer available if the proposed connecting drainage pipe is within 200 feet.

It just takes a visit or phone call to the district director's office to find out if a sewer abuts the property or if an extension is planned. If the builder has to extend the sewer, he should know that before he commits to the project.

Moratoriums— Rapid growth in some areas of the country has placed a heavy burden on existing sewage systems and treatment plants. That's why some systems have placed a moratorium on new sewer connections. Check it out. There's no point in drawing up a plan for a drainage system if you can't get a building permit.

Private Sewage Disposal Systems

There's an expensive word in private sewage systems, too. That word is *approved*. It translates into "if a permit is issuable." Unless engineering data and test results show that your site will support a private sewer system, you won't get a building permit.

Here are the two relevant code sections:

"No property shall be improved in excess of its capacity to properly absorb sewage effluent by the means provided in the code."

"When there is insufficient lot area or improper soil conditions for adequate sewage disposal for the building or land use proposed, and administrative authority so finds, no building permit shall be issued and no private sewage disposal shall be permitted. Where space or conditions are critical, no building permit shall be issued until engineering data and test reports satisfactory to the administrative authority have been submitted and approved."

That's typical building code language. Although it uses broad terms, it places many limitations on private sewer systems. Don't take a chance. If you need an approved private sewage system to get a building permit, read the specific requirements in Chapter 9 of this manual before you begin your design work.

Objectionable Waste

The code prohibits the discharge of objectionable waste into any public or private sewage system. Here's the code section:

"It shall be unlawful for any person to deposit, by any means whatsoever, into any plumbing fixture, floor drain, interceptor, sump, receptacle or device which is connected to any drainage system, public sewer, private sewer, septic tank or cesspool, any ashes, cinders, solids, rags, inflammable, poisonous or explosive liquids or gases, oils, grease or any other thing whatsoever which would, or could, cause damage to the drainage system or public sewer."

Most objectionable wastes come from commercial buildings. They must empty into a separate system and be treated in an approved manner. (We'll cover this in more detail in Chapter 7.)

Building Sewers

Your design for the building sewer has to meet code requirements, of course. But there's more to your job than that. It's not enough that a plumbing system is well-designed. It's also your responsibility to make sure that your specified equipment and materials are properly installed. That includes making sure the components are carefully protected during the installation. You can only verify this by periodic, on-the-job inspections.

The building sewer begins 2 feet from the exterior wall (more in some codes) and continues to an on-site collection system, a public sewer, or a private sewage disposal system.

Existing Building Sewers

Most codes let you use existing building sewers for new buildings *if* they meet the requirements governing new work. How do you know if they do? You probably have to uncover them to see if the sewer material is in good condition, watertight, in proper alignment, and large enough to handle the anticipated fixture loads for the new building. That's an expensive process. In most cases, it's more cost effective to install a new building sewer for new buildings or expansion projects.

There's one more requirement for existing building sewers you need to be aware of. You can't put any part of a building over or within 2 feet of a drainage system unless it's made of materials approved for use under a building.

Independent Systems

The drainage system of each new accessory building or addition must be separate. It must also connect independently with the sewer, public or private, if possible. If there's a public sewer connection on the lot, it has to connect directly to it. If there isn't a separate sewer connection, the code makes an exception. You may connect the addition sewer to the primary building sewer when they're both located on the same lot.

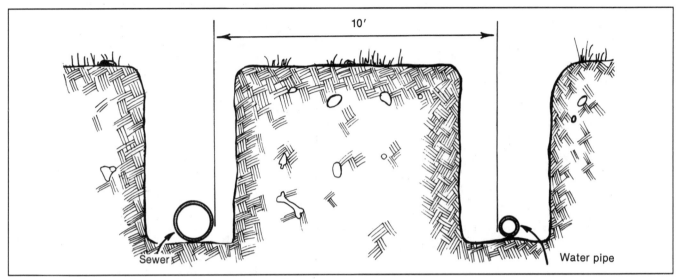

Figure 4-2   Sewer and water pipe in separate trenches

For an example, look back to Figure 2-1 in Chapter 2. It shows a guest house sewage line connecting with the building sewer for the main house.

Location of Building Sewers

The plumbing code imposes seven restrictions on the location of building sewers.

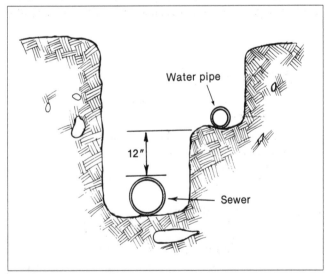

Figure 4-3   Water supply pipe and sewer pipe in common trench

1) Every building sewer must be on the lot with the building it serves. (See Chapter 2, Figure 2-9).

2) The building sewer must be at least 2 feet horizontally from porches, steps, breezeways, carports, and covered walks, driveways and patios. Some codes require more than 2 feet.

3) Sewer pipes must not encroach on private property lines.

4) Keep sewer pipes at least 50 feet away from clear domestic water wells. There's one exception, however. If the pipe material is approved for use within a building, you can reduce this distance by as much as 25 feet. This code section usually applies to a building sewer which connects to a private sewage disposal system. Most areas with a public sewer system don't have domestic water wells.

5) Sewers can't run within 50 feet of streams or other bodies of water on private property.

6) Unless the sewer pipes are approved for use in a building, they can't share a trench with the water service pipe. Most codes require separate trenches separated by at least 10 feet. See Figure 4-2.

If both pipes *must* share the same trench, the bottom of the water pipe must be at least 12 inches above the top of the sewer pipe. Place the water supply pipe on a solid shelf excavated at one

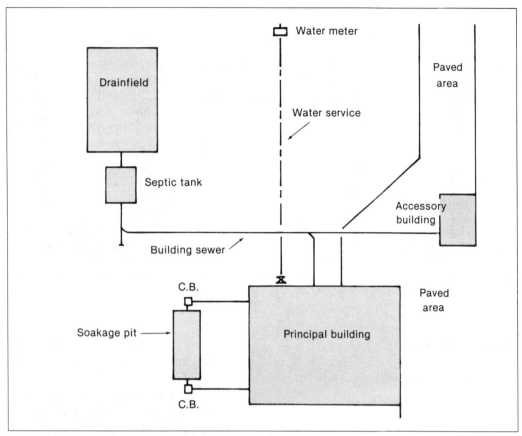

Figure 4-4   Building sewer crossing water service pipe

side of the common trench. See Figure 4-3. If you can't maintain the 12-inch elevation, you'll have to change the direction of the water pipe to provide the 10-foot separation.

7) You may find situations where the water service pipe must cross the sewer line. Figure 4-4 shows an example. The bottom of the water pipe must be at least 12 inches above the top of the sewer pipe within 10 feet of the point where they cross. Figure 4-5 is an elevation view of the crossing.

If you can't maintain those minimum distances between pipes, you need approval from the building officials for an alternate system.

Protection of Sewer and Drainage Piping

Every plumbing system must meet all the code requirements designed to protect the building drainage pipes. We covered this in Chapter 2.

Some codes also require that you specify cast iron building sewer or drainage pipes in *filled* or *unstable* ground. Again, there's an exception. You may use nonmetallic drainage pipes if they're installed on an *approved* continuous trench supporting

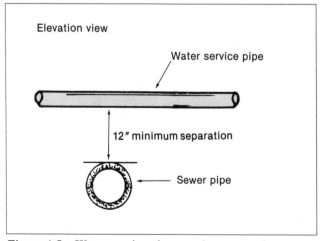

Figure 4-5   Water service pipe crossing sewer pipe

system. An acceptable trench supporting system can be expensive, however. It may cost more than you save by using nonmetallic pipe.

Sub-Building Drains

The best and easiest way for drainage pipes to drain to the sewage disposal system is by gravity. But that's not possible when any part of the drainage system is below the crown of the building drain. Then it must empty into a sump or receiving tank that's large enough to handle the volume and suitable for the liquids it will hold. Finally, pumps must lift and discharge the wastes into the building gravity drainage system.

Design and size the sub-building drainage and vent system as you would a gravity system. Figure 4-6 is the table you use to find maximum fixture unit loads and the maximum length of drainage and vent piping.

Here's how to use it. Assume you've got a *horizontal* branch drain with 250 fixture units at 1/8-inch slope per foot. What size pipe do you need? The column for 5-inch diameter pipe shows a maximum load of 428 F.U. — but that's for a slope of 1/4-inch per foot. According to footnote 5, you have to adjust the figure for a 1/8-inch

Diameter of pipe (inches)	1¼	1½	2	2½	3	4	5	6	8	10	12
Max. units drainage piping[1] Vertical	1	2[2]	16[3]	32[3]	48[4]	256	600	1380	3600	5600	8400
Horizontal[5]	1	2[2]	8[3]	14[3]	35[4]	216	428	720	2640	4680	8200
Max. length drainage piping Vertical (feet)	45	65	85	148	212	300	390	510	750		
Horizontal (unlimited)	---	---	---	---	---	---	---	---	---	---	---
Vent piping horizontal & vertical Max. units	1	8[3]	24	48	84	256	600	1380	3600		
Max. lengths (feet)	45	60	120	180	212	300	390	510	750		

[1] Excluding fixture drain

[2] Except sinks, urinals or dishwashers

[3] Except six-unit traps or water closets

[4] Maximum of four water closets or six-unit traps permitted on any vertical stack. Maximum of three water closets or six-unit traps allowed on any horizontal branch drain or drain pipe.

[5] For pipe sloped ⅛ inch per foot, multiply horizontal fixture units by factor 0.8 and add to allowed fixture units.

From the Uniform Plumbing Code, © 1988, IAPMO

Figure 4-6   Maximum fixture unit loading and maximum length of drainage and vent piping (based on 1/4" slope/ft)[5]

slope. Multiply the fixture units by a factor of 0.8, and add that to the original number. (250 x 0.8 = 200. 250 + 200 = 450 F.U.) That's too much for a 5-inch pipe. You'd have to specify a 6-inch pipe instead.

Here are some other requirements:

♦ You can't use individual vent pipes smaller than 1-1/4 inches. A vent pipe must be at least one-half the diameter of the waste pipe

Type of fixture	Minimum traps and fixture drain size	Fixture units
Bathtubs	1½	2
Bidets	1½	2
Dental units or cuspidors	1¼	1
Drinking fountains	1¼	1
Floor drains	2	2
* Interceptors for grease, oil, solids, etc.	2	3
* Interceptors for sand, auto wash, etc.	3	6
Laundry tubs	1½	2
Clothes washers	2	2
* Receptors (floor sinks), indirect waste receptors for refrigerators, coffee urns, water stations, etc.	1½	1
* Receptors, indirect waste receptors for commercial sinks, dishwashers, airwashers, etc.	2	3
Showers, single stall	2	2
* Showers, gang (one F.U. per head)	2	
Sinks, bar, private (1½" minimum waste)	1½	1
Sinks, bar, commercial (2" minimum waste)	1½	2
Sinks, commercial or industrial, schools, etc., including dishwashers, wash up sinks and wash fountains (2" minimum waste)	1½	3
Sinks, flushing rim, clinic	3	6
Sinks, and/or dishwashers, (residential) 2" minimum waste	1½	2
Sinks, service	2	3
Mobile home park traps (one for each trailer)	3	6
Urinals, pedestal, trap arm only	3	6
Urinal, stall	2	2
Urinals, wall (2" minimum waste)	1½	2
Wash basins (lavatories), single	1¼	1
Wash basins, in sets	1½	2
* Water closet, private installation, trap arm only	3	4
Water closet, public installation, trap arm only	3	6

* The size and discharge rating of each indirect waste receptor and each interceptor should be based on the total drainage fixture unit values discharging into it, as listed on Table 5-3, (Figure 4-9).

From the Uniform Plumbing Code, © 1988, IAPMO

Figure 4-7   Sanitary drainage fixture units and trap sizes

Drainage fixture unit equivalents	
Trap size (in inches)	Fixture units
1¼	1
1½	3
2	4
3	6
4	8
Note: The unit equivalent of plumbing fixtures listed in Figure 4-7 should be based on the required trap size.	

From the Uniform Plumbing Code, © 1988, IAPMO

Figure 4-8   Sanitary drainage fixture unit equivalents and trap sizes

it serves. For instance, a 4-inch waste pipe needs at least a 2-inch vent pipe.

♦ The horizontal portion of a vent can't exceed one-third the permitted length. A 60-foot vent pipe can't have a horizontal section more than 20 feet long, for example.

Compute the fixture load values for drainage and vent piping from Figures 4-7, 4-8 and 4-9.

The length limits in Figure 4-7 don't apply if you increase the vent pipe by one pipe size. For instance, if a 3-inch vent pipe is required but you use a 4-inch pipe instead, there's no length limit.

In *public use* occupancy, all sumps and receiving tanks must be automatically discharged. That means they can be set by the installer to automatically discharge their contents when the liquid reaches a certain level. They also need dual pumps or ejectors that function independently in case of overload or mechanical failure.

Figure 4-10 shows a sewage ejector *public use* sump that requires dual pumps. It also has to meet these requirements:

♦ Any sump receiving body wastes must have a minimum discharge capacity of 20 gallons per minute (GPM) and a discharge of at least 2 inches.

♦ A sump vent can't be smaller than 1-1/2 inches or longer than 60 feet. A 1-1/2-inch vent can serve a maximum of eight fixture units.

♦ The vent pipe in Figure 4-10 must be 2 inches. It serves 13 fixture units (public water closet, 6 F.U.; lavatory, 1 F.U.; 3-inch floor drain, 6 F.U.). According to Figure 4-6, a 2-inch vent can serve up to 24 fixture units and may be up to 120 feet long.

♦ Sumps for single dwelling units may have a single ejector.

There are a couple of additional requirements for sumps or receiving tanks that receive body wastes. First, the discharge pipe must be at least 2 inches. And some codes require you to size the discharge pipe according to the number of fixture units for building drains and sewers. Second, they must have a local vent large enough to maintain atmospheric pressure in the sump under normal operating conditions.

GPM	Fixture units
up to 7½	equals 1
8 to 15	equals 2
16 to 30	equals 4
31 to 50	equals 6
Note: Any flow that exceeds 50 GPM must be approved by the administrative authority	

From the Uniform Plumbing Code, © 1988, IAPMO

Figure 4-9   Discharge capacity (in GPM) for intermittent flow only

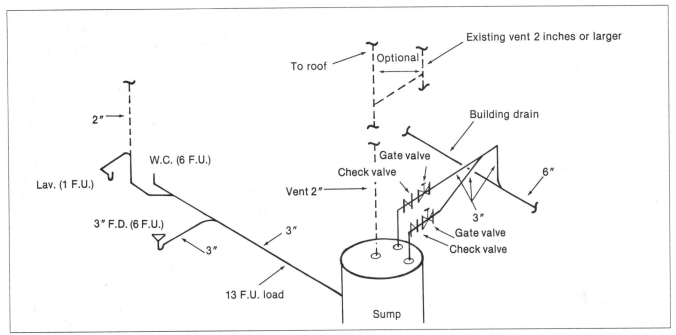

Figure 4-10   Sewage ejector "public use" sump

Size the vent for the number of fixtures discharging into the sump (Figure 4-6), but never less than 1-1/2 inches in diameter. It may vent independently through the roof, or connect to an adequate existing vent. But the code prohibits a local sump vent from connecting to other vents if the sewage ejector is an *air-operated type*.

A sub-building drainage system must empty into a building drain or sewer that's large enough to avoid overloading. The code allows two fixture units for each gallon per minute of continuous flow.

The discharge pipe must connect to the gravity drainage line from the top through a wye fitting. And it must have an accessible swing check valve and a gate valve on the discharge side of the check valve. See Figure 4-10.

Sumps or receiving tanks must be made of approved materials and have watertight access covers — unless they receive only clear water waste. If their only waste is from floor drains or air conditioning condensate drains, they don't have to be covered or vented. Figure 4-11 is a detail drawing of a clear water sump pump.

Here's a note of caution: When designing sub-building drainage systems, always review the code sections in force for that area. Model codes differ in their system design and pipe size requirements. Don't take any chances. Specify only code-approved materials and construction methods. Choose manufactured tanks, pumps and ejectors already approved by the local authorities.

Special Wastes

Commercial sites generate what the code refers to as *special wastes*, which usually have their own separate disposal systems. They're not connected to the building drainage system. Some codes do a good job of defining that separate disposal system, while others give you very little direction. But every code states that special waste systems must be acceptable to the local building officials. I'll cover this subject more fully in Chapter 8.

Materials for Drainage Systems

For all drainage systems, specify durable materials that are approved for your specific use and location. You can usually choose from several materials. I'll list the materials for each use that are accepted by most codes. If any material requires special installation methods or restrictions, I've noted it in a qualifying comment. Check with local authorities before specifying a restricted material.

Building Sewer

Sewer pipes may be made of either ABS or PVC plastic sewer pipe, asbestos cement pipe, bituminized fiber pipe, concrete pipe, extra strength vitrified clay or cast iron pipe.

Note: Most codes define all these materials, except cast iron, as fragile material which requires a minimum earth cover of 12 inches.

Underground Building Drains

All underground building drains must be made of ABS or PVC DWV Schedule 40 plastic pipe, cast iron pipe, lead pipe, copper tube, or extra strength vitrified clay pipe.

Note: Some codes won't let you use vitrified clay pipe in a building drainage system. Where you are allowed to use it, there are two requirements: It must not be subjected to pressure from a pump or ejector, and an earth cover of at least 12 inches must be provided. Copper tube used for underground drainage must have a weight equal to copper tube DWV or heavier. But never specify copper tubing to carry chemical or industrial wastes.

Above-Ground Building Drains

All above-ground building drains must be made of either copper pipe DWV weight, brass pipe, galvanized wrought iron pipe, galvanized steel pipe, cast iron pipe, ABS or PVC DWV Schedule 40 plastic pipe.

Note: Galvanized wrought or galvanized steel pipe must begin at least 6 inches above ground. Use ABS and PVC DWV piping systems only in structures where combustible construction is allowed.

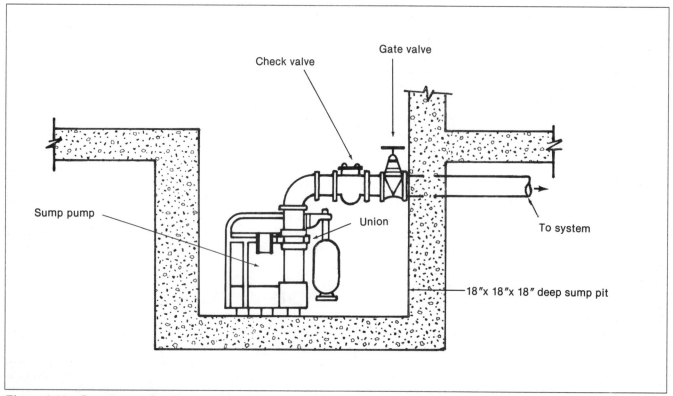

Figure 4-11   Sump pump detail

Fittings

Choose fittings of materials that are compatible with the pipe material. All fittings must have a smooth interior waterway that's the same diameter as the pipes. They must also be free of ledges, shoulders or reductions which can slow or obstruct flow in the pipes.

You must specify recessed drainage-type fittings on screwed pipe. Some codes require that threads of drainage fittings are tapped to allow a 1/4-inch fall (grade) per foot.

Isometric Drawings

Any professional plumbing system designer has the basic draftsman tools, equipment and training needed to draw acceptable isometrics — and a pretty good grasp of the plumbing code. Even so, most designers have had plans rejected by the plans examiner. It's probably happened to you. But if you understand the regulations, it won't happen often. It shouldn't happen at all.

The code usually requires plumbing isometrics for all commercial work, and sometimes for residential work as well. The purpose of isometric drawings is simply to communicate your design for a particular plumbing system. Only a professional or a tradesman with considerable experience can accurately interpret an isometric drawing, even one that's well done.

You don't need to draw your isometrics to scale, or to include the developed length of fixture drains. But they must show that you've met the intent of the code. If a fixture location noticeably exceeds the code limitations, the examiner can reject the plan and require a relief vent.

Many isometrics are rejected because the designers were just plain careless. If you produce your drawings too fast, you may omit a basic code requirement, like the direction of flow for fittings. The plans examiner's experienced eye will likely catch such omissions. Work slowly and carefully to produce acceptable drawings the first time.

Sizing the Drainage Systems

Use these factors to determine the minimum vertical and horizontal sizes for drainage pipes:

♦ Total fixture unit load

♦ Types of fixtures used

♦ Slope of drain pipe in inches per foot

♦ The vertical length of drain pipes

First, consider the *maximum fixture unit loads*. Of course, you know that the fixture unit load is the total gallons discharged by the fixture per minute. Residential lavatories are rated as one fixture unit. That's equal to 7.5 gallons per minute, or about one cubic foot per minute. This is the nationally-accepted standard flow rate for different types of plumbing fixtures.

When calculating fixture unit loads for other fixtures, check your local code fixture unit table carefully. (In this book, it's Figure 4-7.) And consider these requirements:

♦ Size drainage pipes that serve a group of appliances capable of producing continuous flows to handle *peak loads*.

♦ Rate clothes washers in groups of three or more at six fixture units each to determine the common waste pipe size.

♦ Rate water closets as six fixture units each to determine septic tank size. See Chapter 9.

Don't use trap sizes larger than those listed here or they won't be self-scouring.

The residential or commercial fixture units may vary between codes. That affects the pipe sizes. Let's consider just one variation. The Uniform Plumbing Code counts two fixture units for a clothes washer with a 2-inch trap. The Standard Plumbing Code and the National Plumbing Code count three fixture units for this particular fixture.

Whatever code book you're using, there will almost certainly be three tables listing the various fixture unit loads. Using these tables, you can find the total fixture load for the building. Figure 4-7 lists the most common plumbing fixtures, along with their fixture unit load and trap size. Use this table to calculate the fixture unit loads and find the fixture drain size.

Figure 4-8 (fixture unit equivalents) lists fixtures not shown in Figure 4-7. It's based on the size *trap* required. This table provides maximum trap loadings for sizes up to 4 inches and the fixture unit loads you need to size the building drain. (For example, a 4-inch floor drain equals eight fixture units.)

Figure 4-9 (discharge capacity) also lists fixtures not shown in Figure 4-7. These are fixtures, equipment or appliances with an *intermittent flow* and an indirect connection to the drainage system. Some of these special fixtures are water stations, coffee urns, bottle coolers, milk or soft drink dispensers, and ice making machines. (See Chapter 8 for more information.)

To understand how to use Figure 4-9, let's consider one illustration. A coffee urn is a special fixture with intermittent flow. It comes from the manufacturer equipped with a 1/2- or 3/4-inch drain from the drip pan. Its flow rate is less than 7-1/2 gallons per minute so it's rated as one fixture unit.

Some fixtures, including pumps, sump ejectors, and air conditioning equipment, have *continuous flow*. Allow two fixture units for each gallon per minute of continuous flow. The manufacturer usually provides the flow rate information.

The Uniform Plumbing Code gives special attention to building sewers. Figure 4-12 gives the maximum and minimum fixture unit loads according to pipe diameter and slope. For example, for an 8-inch pipe sloped at 1/8 inch per foot, the maximum fixture unit load is 2,800. The minimum fixture unit load for the same pipe is 625.

The basic code information I've included in this chapter is enough to help you begin sizing drainage pipes. Although I've used text and illustrations from the Uniform Plumbing Code, the other codes have similar requirements and fixture unit load tables. If you understand this chapter and follow your local code book, you can size drainage piping that passes the scrutiny of your local building officials — the *first* time.

Sizing the Sample Drainage System

Compute the load on our sample drainage system (Figure 4-13) by using the drainage fixture units (D.F.U.) in the tables in this chapter (Figures 4-7, 4-8 and 4-9). Use the similar tables in your local code book for actual projects. There are two steps to follow:

1) Do an isometric drawing from your floor plan. Then mark the fixture types on the layout — water closet (W.C.), lavatory (L. or LAV.), bathtub (B.T.), and so on.

2) Assign drainage fixture units (D.F.U.) to each fixture using the fixture unit tables. For example: public water closets have six, urinals two, and 3-inch floor drains have six.

Drainage system size— To size the drainage system in a multi-story building, start with the *top floor* fixtures and work down to the building drain.

(MM) Diameter of pipe in inches	Slope (grade) in inches per foot (MM/M)		
	1/16	1/8	1/4
6 and smaller	as required in Figure 4-6		No minimum loading
8	1,950/1,500	2,800/625	3,900/275
10	3,400/1,600	4,900/675	6,800/300
12	5,600/1,700	8,000/725	11,200/325

From the Uniform Plumbing Code, © 1988, IAPMO

Figure 4-12   *Maximum/minimum fixture unit loading on building sewer piping*

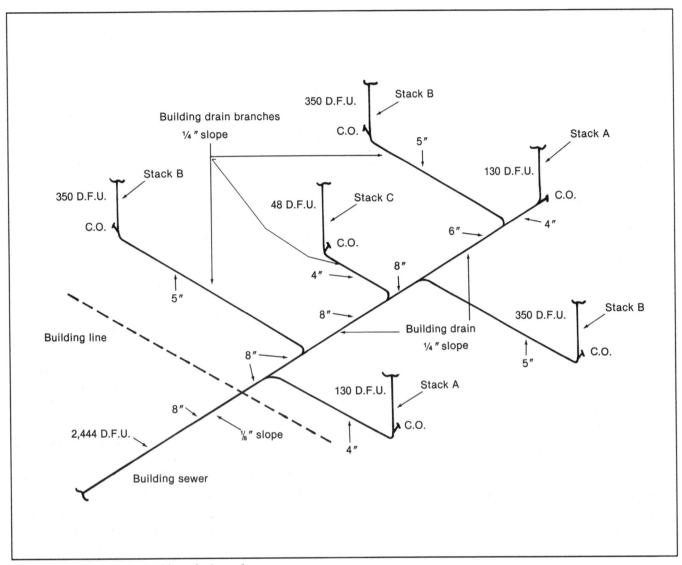

Figure 4-13   Sizing the building drain and sewer

Accumulate the total fixture loads at the base of the stack. That total determines the size and length of the entire vertical stack and the horizontal drain pipe it empties into. The vertical waste or soil stack must be the same size throughout its length. And remember that a larger horizontal branch can't empty into a smaller vertical waste or soil stack.

Look at Figure 4-13. For building sewers sloped at 1/8-inch fall per foot, multiply the total building D.F.U. times 0.8. (1,358 x 0.8 = 1,086) Then add that answer to the original D.F.U. (1,358 + 1,086 = 2,444 D.F.U.) Now, using Figure 4-6, size the horizontal branch drains, fixture drains and stacks based on their fixture unit loads.

Figure 4-14 shows my calculations. Remember that the stack can't be smaller than any horizontal branch. So even though stack B has fewer than 600 D.F.U., it has to be a 5-inch stack because a 5-inch horizontal drain empties into it.

Building drain size— If there's a 1/4-inch slope, the building drain size depends on the accumulated drainage fixture units. Some codes accept a grade of more or less than 1/4 inch without special approval. But most codes require prior approval if you have to use a slope of less

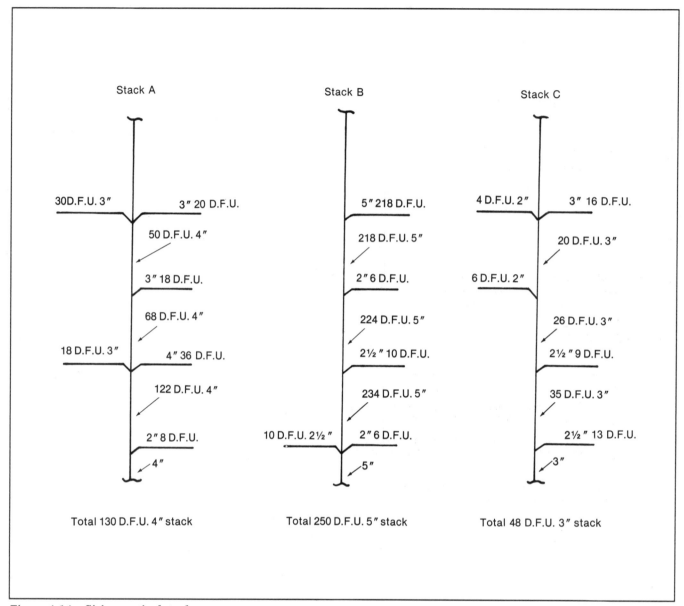

Figure 4-14 **Sizing vertical stacks**

than 1/4 inch because of the street sewer depth or structural features.

Building sewer size— The slope and total fixture units determine the size of the building sewer. The three acceptable slopes for the building sewer are 1/16 inch, 1/8 inch and 1/4 inch. Some codes will accept a 1/2-inch slope in special cases. You can choose any approved slope for your job, but specify the slope for building sewers and horizontal drains on your plan. Notice that the

drawing in Figure 4-13 shows a building sewer slope of 1/8 inch.

More Sample Isometrics

I'll end the chapter with several partial isometrics that meet code requirements. Figures 4-15 through 4-21 show some of the code sections that are open to interpretation. For more complete isometrics, look at Chapter 11.

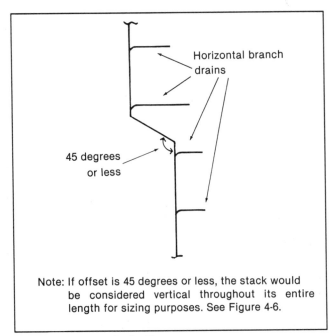

Note: If offset is 45 degrees or less, the stack would be considered vertical throughout its entire length for sizing purposes. See Figure 4-6.

Figure 4-15   **Vertical offset**

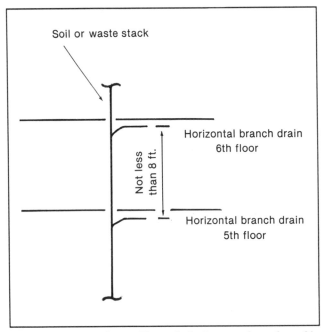

Figure 4-16   **Horizontal branch drain must be at least 8' center to center**

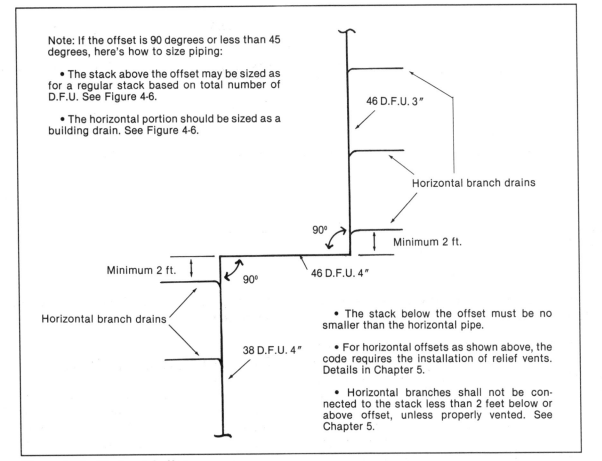

Note: If the offset is 90 degrees or less than 45 degrees, here's how to size piping:

• The stack above the offset may be sized as for a regular stack based on total number of D.F.U. See Figure 4-6.

• The horizontal portion should be sized as a building drain. See Figure 4-6.

• The stack below the offset must be no smaller than the horizontal pipe.

• For horizontal offsets as shown above, the code requires the installation of relief vents. Details in Chapter 5.

• Horizontal branches shall not be connected to the stack less than 2 feet below or above offset, unless properly vented. See Chapter 5.

Figure 4-17   **Horizontal offset**

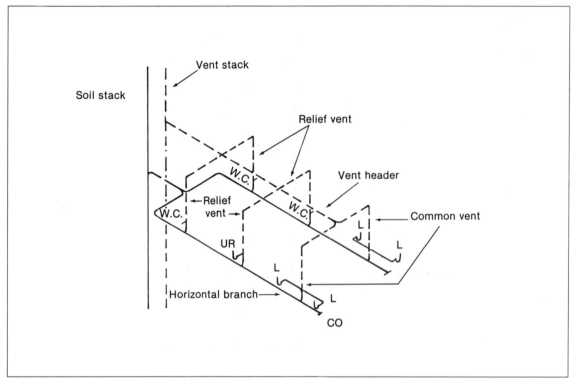

Figure 4-18 **Battery of fixtures properly vented**

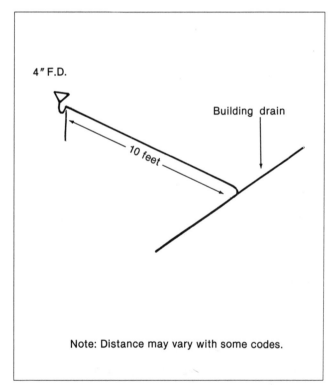

Figure 4-19 **Maximum distance of floor drain from vented building drain**

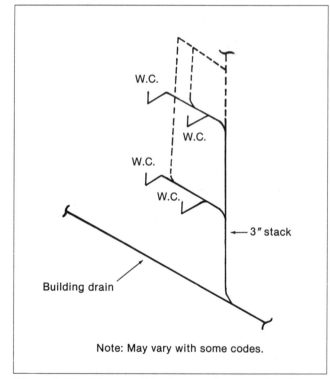

Figure 4-20 **No more than 4 water closets or 6-unit fixtures are allowed on a 3" stack**

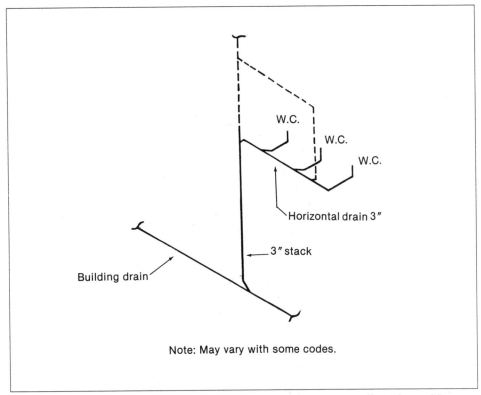

W.C.

W.C.

W.C.

Horizontal drain 3″

3″ stack

Building drain

Note: May vary with some codes.

*Figure 4-21   No more than 3 water closets or 6 unit fixtures are allowed on a 3″
horizontal drain*

Chapter 5

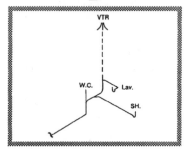

Vents and Venting

No matter where you're located, your plumbing code makes at least these two demands: First, every fixture trap must be protected from back pressure and siphonage. Second, vent pipes must allow air to circulate throughout the entire drainage system. In this chapter, we'll take a close look at the vent system.

Every sanitary drainage system needs a vent system that lets all gases, pressures and odors escape into the atmosphere above the roof. And it has to let air into the system. To achieve this, the air pressure in the system has to be within 1 inch of the water column of the atmosphere. For example, consider a fixture trap with a 2-inch minimum water seal. It has to allow enough air circulation to limit air pressure variations in the fixture drains to no more than 1 inch of water column above or below atmospheric pressure. The code tables for size, location and length are based on this rule.

Preventing Back Pressure and Siphonage

This is so important that I want to repeat it: There must be a free flow of air in all vent piping. But keep in mind that air is perfectly elastic. That means it compresses under pressure and returns to its original volume when the pressure is removed. Since fixture trap seals aren't very deep, they can only tolerate a small pressure rise in the sanitary drainage system. If the pressure is too great, the fixture traps are vulnerable to back pressure or siphonage.

Conditions for Back Pressure

When fixtures are used, water comes in contact with air in the partially-filled vertical or

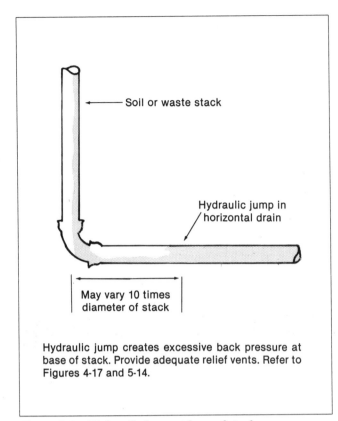

Hydraulic jump creates excessive back pressure at base of stack. Provide adequate relief vents. Refer to Figures 4-17 and 5-14.

Figure 5-1   Hydraulic jump at base of stack

horizontal drain. That creates friction between the water and air. What does that do? It creates *hydraulic jump*. Look at Figure 5-1. Let's consider a multi-story building as an example. At the base of the waste stack, the cross section of the water-filled drain increases sharply, constricting the area available for air flow. That temporarily blocks the flow of air.

The effect is obvious. When fixtures on upper floors empty into a drainage system with an air blockage, the air that's blocked becomes pressurized. It may reach a level considerably above atmospheric pressure. And if it's not properly vented, the back pressure may be strong enough to break the trap seal.

Conditions for Siphon Action

The upper section of a vent system must bring in air as fast as downward-flowing air removes it. If it doesn't, it can cause negative pressure considerable *below* atmospheric pressure. If

it's strong enough, the negative pressure can siphon the water seals of the fixture traps. There are two conditions that make fixture traps vulnerable to siphon action. The vent pipes may be undersized, or the vents extending above the roof could be partially blocked. See Figure 5-2.

The vent section of the plumbing code is extensive — and complex. It places many restrictions and limitations on drainage system vents. That makes interpreting it a real challenge. I'll try to make it as clear and simple as possible. Let's start with a look at the materials you can use for vent piping.

Materials for Vent Piping

Underground

Underground, you can use vent pipes made of cast iron, hard tempered copper tube (type DWV or heavier), brass, ABS or PVC plastic or lead. The building department may also approve other

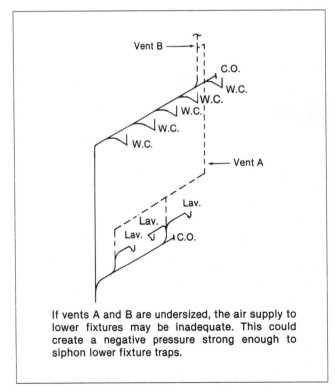

If vents A and B are undersized, the air supply to lower fixtures may be inadequate. This could create a negative pressure strong enough to siphon lower fixture traps.

Figure 5-2 Negative pressure

materials. But you can never use galvanized wrought iron or galvanized steel for underground venting.

Above Ground

Vent pipes for use above ground can be made of cast iron, galvanized steel, galvanized wrought iron, lead, hard tempered copper tube (type DWV or heavier), brass, ABS or PVC plastic, or any other material approved by the building department. But there's one limitation: If you want to use steel pipe in an above-ground vent system, put it at least 6 inches above ground level.

Fittings

Use vent fittings made of cast iron, galvanized malleable iron or galvanized steel, lead, copper, brass, or ABS or PVC plastic. The building authorities may also approve others. The fittings must *always* be compatible with the pipe. You can't randomly mix materials. If the installation requires dissimilar materials, you can use only approved couplings.

Protecting Vent Pipes

When you design a building vent system, make sure the code-required protection shows on the plans or in the drawings. Here are the requirements:

♦ Provide approved sleeving for vent pipes passing through concrete slabs or through block walls to protect them from breakage, sags or corrosion. (Refer back to Figure 2-11 in Chapter 2.)

♦ You can't embed vent pipes directly in concrete or masonry walls, or in corrosive soils, unless they're protected against corrosion.

♦ In areas subject to freezing, don't locate vent pipes in any outside building wall. Even in areas where freezing temperatures aren't likely, the local code may frown on placing vent pipes on the outside of any new building.

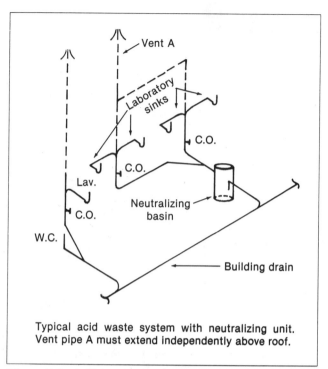

Typical acid waste system with neutralizing unit. Vent pipe A must extend independently above roof.

Figure 5-3 Acid waste system

♦ Design the vent piping so it doesn't weaken the building's structural integrity. (Look back to Figures 2-16 and 2-18.)

♦ Use enough supports on horizontal vent pipes to maintain the pipe alignment and prevent sags. (See Figure 2-20.)

♦ The supports for vertical vent pipes must carry the weight of the pipe (Figure 2-21).

♦ If vent pipes serve a drainage system carrying corrosive liquids or fumes that might injure them, specify materials resistant to corrosion. Chemically-resistant glass, high-silicon content iron and plastic are corrosion-resistant. You can't connect vent pipes serving an acid waste system into the regular venting system of a building. They must vent independently to the building roof. Figure 5-3 shows a separate vent system for an acid waste system.

♦ You can't allow any waste substance to drain into a vent pipe. That could restrict air flow into the drainage system, possibly leading to siphonage of fixture traps. Refer back to Figure 2-5.

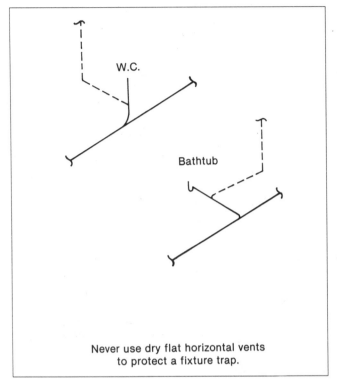

Figure 5-4 Prohibited installations

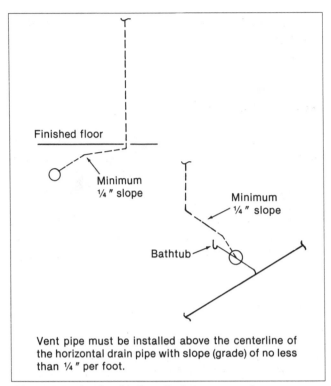

Figure 5-5 Acceptable installations

To protect the vent system, you *can't* install vent pipes in certain places. Here's a list of prohibited installations.

◆ Never locate vent pipes in stairways or hoistways.

◆ Don't put vent pipes where they might interfere with doors or windows.

◆ Don't install vent pipes that an owner might be tempted to use as a flag pole, TV antenna, or clothesline.

◆ Don't connect a horizontal inlet to a heel one-quarter bend, or to a side-inlet one-quarter bend. Look back to Figure 2-3.

◆ Don't vent any fixture with a flat dry horizontal vent. It's subject to fouling that can reduce the air flow needed to protect the fixture trap. Figure 5-4 shows two of these prohibited installations. The base of all vent pipes should be washed by waste water from a fixture.

◆ Never place vent pipes in rooms subject to freezing temperatures, such as food freezer or cold storage rooms.

Code-Required Vent Slopes and Connections

Vent slope— Design horizontal dry vent pipes to slope upward. That way gravity brings in air to ventilate the drainage system. And make sure any horizontal vent pipes are supported to prevent drops or sags. If condensation collects in the low spots, it restricts air circulation and accelerates corrosion of the pipe.

Vertical vent rise— When you have to connect a vent to horizontal drain pipe, take it off *above* the centerline of the drainage pipe. That reduces the possibility of a blockage caused by sewage or other matter. Also locate it downstream from the trap being served. Figure 5-5 shows two acceptable installations.

Vent height above fixtures— If horizontal vent pipes used as branch, relief, individual, circuit or loop vents connect to a vent stack or stack vent, place the horizontal section at least 6 inches above the flood level rim of the fixture it serves. That prevents waste from overflowing into the horizontal vent if the drain is stopped. See Figure 5-6.

The Uniform Plumbing Code makes one exception here. If you can't maintain the 6-inch separation because of structural limitations, you can install the horizontal vent pipe with approved drainage fittings and materials. But *always* check with the building officials before you design an alternate substandard venting system.

Although offsets don't affect vent pipe sizes, a 90-degree offset must slope upward at least 1/4 inch per foot.

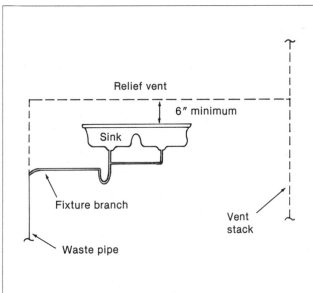

Figure 5-6   Minimum separation of overflow rim and horizontal relief vent

Vent Stacks and Stack Vents

All vent pipes must be full size when they extend above the roof unless they connect below the roof to an approved vent stack or stack vent.

Main Vent Stack

Every building must have at least one main vent that's 3 inches or larger. Then calculate the other vent pipe sizes from the length of the main

vent and the number of fixture units served. If there are two or more buildings on a single lot that share a common sewer, use the length of the main vent and the number of fixture units to figure the vent pipe size. Look at Figure 4-6 in Chapter 4.

The combined cross section of the vent pipes of any building must be as large as the largest building sewer. It doesn't matter if the building is connected to a public sewer or a private sewer or sewage disposal system.

Here's an example. The cross section of the stack vent for a single-family house with one bathroom, a kitchen sink, clothes washer and one vent pipe must be 4 inches in diameter if it connects to a 4-inch building sewer.

Because codes vary widely, always check the local code requirements for vent sizes.

Main Vent Connections

All main vents in multi-story buildings must connect full size at their base either to the horizontal building drain (Figure 5-7) or to the main soil or waste stack, at or below the lowest fixture branch (Figure 5-11).

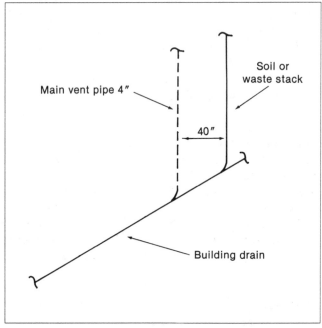

Figure 5-7   Maximum 40" separation of the two pipes, according to the Standard Plumbing Code

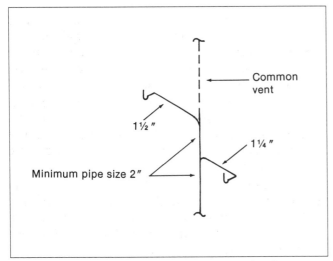

Figure 5-8   Wet venting fixtures at different levels

There are some situations where you can't connect the main vent to the base of a main soil or waste stack. In that case, it must connect to the horizontal building drain. Under those circumstances, some codes have placed limits on the distance the two can be separated. For example, the Standard Plumbing Code states: "All main vents or vent stacks shall connect full size at their base to the building drain within 10 pipe diameters of the main soil or waste stack . . . ."

Let's see how that works. If a 4-inch main vent pipe connects directly to the horizontal building drain, it must be within 40 inches of the base of the main soil or waste stack. See Figure 5-7.

Venting Adjacent Fixtures

You can use one continuous vertical drain and common vent to serve two back-to-back or adjacent fixtures. But you have to stay within the distance set by code. We'll cover that in the next chapter. And make sure that each fixture drains separately into an approved double fitting with inlet openings located at the same level. Look in the Glossary in the back of this book. The common vent on page 171 in the Glossary shows this.

Venting Fixtures at Different Levels

You can use a common vent to serve two fixtures on the same floor level if they connect into

the stack at different levels. The vertical drain must be one pipe size larger than the upper fixture drain, but it can't be smaller than the lower fixture drain. See Figure 5-8.

Venting a Fixture Drain

The vent pipe opening from a soil or waste stack or drain pipe can't be below the weir of the trap. Putting it below the weir would create a partial S-trap, which could break the trap seal by creating a siphon action in the fixture drain. Figure 5-9 shows this prohibited drain connection. Water closets and other fixtures with integral traps are an exception to the rule.

Side-Inlet Closet Bends

There are many ways to wet vent a fixture or group of fixtures. Some codes let you use a side-inlet closet bend when it connects to a vent pipe that's washed by a fixture. There's an illustration later in the chapter under Wet Venting.

Check with your local building department before designing a side-inlet closet bend. Some won't permit them if the fixture isn't properly vented and its trap might be vulnerable to siphonage. Figure 5-10 shows a shower drain that isn't vented. Not all codes would accept this design.

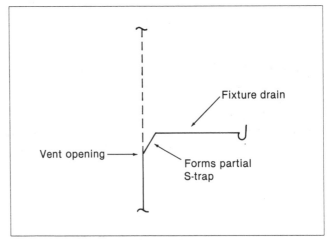

Figure 5-9   Prohibited fixture drain connection: vent opening should not be lower than trap weir

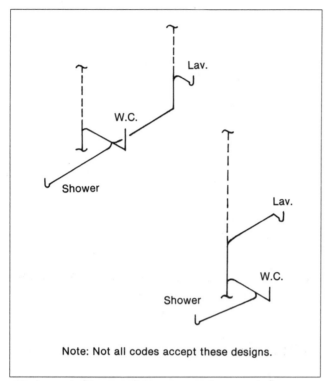

Figure 5-10   Shower drain not vented

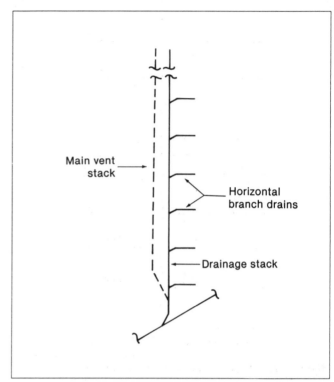

Figure 5-11   Main vent stack properly connected

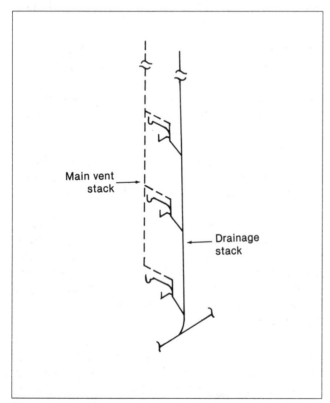

Figure 5-12   Alternate design for main vent stack

Vent Stacks and Relief Vents

Yoke Vents

Provide a parallel main vent stack for any drainage stack that's ten or more stories long. The stack must remain full size from its upper terminal. And it has to connect to the drainage stack at or just below the lowest horizontal branch drain (Figure 5-11) or vertical fixture drain (Figure 5-12). Use a yoke vent to connect the main vent stack to the drainage stack at each fifth floor below the top fixture branch. (Some codes make it every tenth floor.) The yoke vent can't be smaller than the main vent stack it connects to.

Connect the yoke vent to the main vent stack at least 42 inches above floor level. (It's 36 inches in some codes.) Use a wye branch fitting placed below the horizontal branch drain or the vertical fixture drain serving that floor. Figure 5-13 shows the yoke vent connection to the main vent.

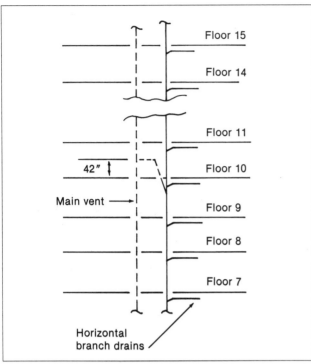

Figure 5-13 Yoke vent connection to main vent

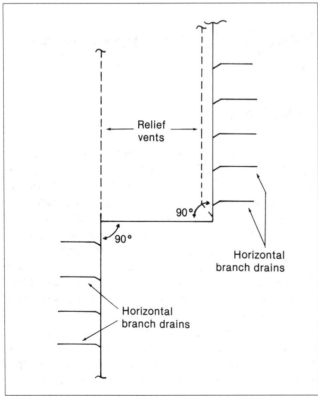

Figure 5-14 Horizontal drainage piping protected by relief vents

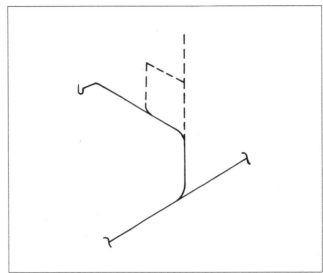

Figure 5-15 Reventing fixture drain, when fixture drain exceeds distance limitation

Relief Vents

When you can't avoid a horizontal offset between the vertical portions of the building drain, provide relief vents. Figure 5-14 shows relief vents protecting the horizontal branch drains. Here's where you have to provide relief vents:

♦ Vent the vertical lower section below the offset as a separate soil or waste stack.

♦ Also vent the vertical upper section above the offset as a separate soil or waste stack.

♦ Provide a relief vent at the top of the lower section and a yoke vent at the base of the upper section, above the offset. Use Figure 4-6 in Chapter 4 to size the relief vent.

***Reventing fixture drains*—** In some cases, you'll have to put fixtures where the fixture drain exceeds the distance allowed between fixture trap and vent. You can do that if you revent the fixture drain. Provide a relief vent that's the right size and in the right place to satisfy code requirements. Figure 5-15 shows how.

The code allows fixtures with a lower D.F.U. than water closets to empty into a horizontal branch drain downstream from a water closet or similar fixture. These fixtures usually need a relief vent. In Figure 5-16, a shower trap has a relief vent

55

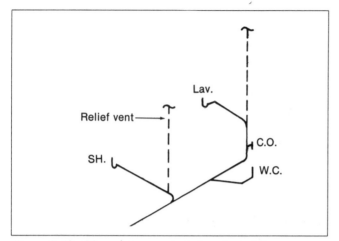

Figure 5-16 Shower trap protected against siphonage

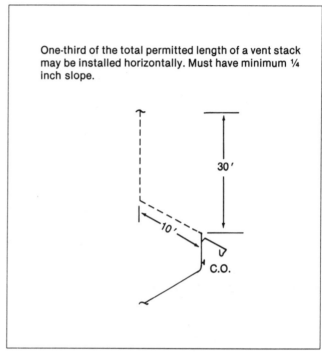

One-third of the total permitted length of a vent stack may be installed horizontally. Must have minimum ¼ inch slope.

Figure 5-17 Maximum distance of horizontal vent pipe

to protect against siphonage. Some codes permit an installation like this without a relief vent in single-family homes only. But don't do it without checking it out with local building officials first.

Relief vent size— Most codes have a vent table like Figure 4-6 in the previous chapter. You'll have to size your vents according to the table in the local code. The general rule is that a relief vent can't be smaller than one-half the diameter of the drainage pipe it serves — and never smaller than 1-1/4 inches.

Horizontal length of vent pipes— Only one-third of the total length of a vent pipe can be horizontal. If you're using a 30-foot vent pipe, install not more than 10 feet of it horizontally. And make sure the horizontal portion has at least a 1/4-inch slope. See Figure 5-17.

Once again, the code makes an exception to the rule. If you increase the vent pipe by one pipe size for its entire length, you can ignore the limitation on horizontal installation.

Vent Terminals

The codes place many restrictions on vent terminations. Here are some of them:

♦ Don't locate vent terminals within 10 horizontal feet of any door, window or air intake. If you can't avoid it, extend the vent at least 3 feet (2 feet in some codes) above the opening. Look at Figure 5-18.

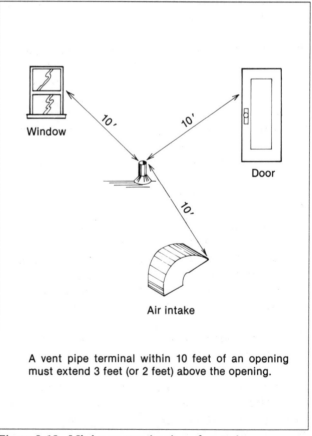

A vent pipe terminal within 10 feet of an opening must extend 3 feet (or 2 feet) above the opening.

Figure 8-18 Minimum termination of vent pipes

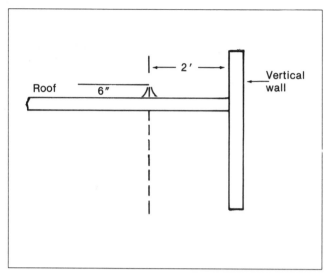

Figure 5-19   Separation of vent pipe terminal from vertical wall

♦ When vent pipes extend through the roof, they must terminate at least 6 inches above the roof and at least 2 feet from any vertical surface (Figure 5-19).

♦ A vent pipe that runs through an exterior wall must be at least 3 feet from the property line, alley or street. It also must terminate downward in most codes. But some codes mandate a 10-foot separation. Others call for an upward terminal. Always screen the vent opening and keep the vent terminal at least 10 feet from any doors or windows.

♦ In cold-weather areas, protect the vent terminal from frost closure. Each vent extension must be at least 3 inches in diameter and terminate 10 inches or more above the roof. Make the diameter change inside the building, at least 1 foot below the roof. Refer back to Figure 2-15.

♦ An outdoor vent pipe has to be at least 10 feet from property lines and 10 feet above ground level. This rule might apply if you're venting a trailer park sewage collection system. We'll cover this in Chapter 10.

♦ What if you have a vent pipe extending through a roof that's used for other

purposes? Say there's a sun deck or solarium on the roof. Any vent terminal within 10 feet must be at least 7 feet above the roof.

♦ Any vent that extends through the roof must be made weathertight with code-approved materials.

Types of Vents and Venting Systems

Protecting fixture drains is an issue that is treated differently in different codes. Some are vague, while some are very specific. Let's just concentrate on designing workable vent systems. Avoid difficulties with the plans examiner by clearly showing an approved layout for fixtures on your floor plan.

Provide each individual fixture drain with a vent pipe. And the arrangement of the vent pipes must protect the water seal of each fixture trap. There are many approved vent arrangements. Here are some of them.

Circuit Vent

Circuit vents protect the trap seals of batteries of floor-outlet and above-floor-mounted fixtures. It's a good system for multi-story buildings with batteries of fixtures on each floor. Design a vent stack with each soil or waste stack. There's an example in the Glossary, on page 170.

Loop Vent

A loop vent, like a circuit vent, protects the trap seals of fixtures in batteries. But there's a restriction. You can only use a loop vent in a one-story building or on the top floor of a multi-story building. It doesn't have a vent stack. Instead, it loops back and connects to the stack vent. The loop vent in the Glossary (page 177) shows the system.

Vertical Combination Waste and Vent Stacks

Vertical combination stacks receive waste and vent plumbing fixtures for buildings of two or more stories. The single vertical pipe riser makes it economical and practical — but not all codes allow it. Where it's permitted, it's a good system for any building where the plumbing fixtures on each floor are located directly above each other.

Use Figure 5-20 to compute the size and length of vertical combination waste and vent stacks. The code limits the stack size, number of fixture units, type of plumbing fixtures, and the total length of the stack itself.

Now look at Figure 5-21. Section A shows a four-story building with eight kitchen sinks, back-to-back, for a total of 16 fixture units. Section B is a six-story building with six kitchen sinks, one on each floor, for a total of 12 fixture units. The number of fixture units and the length of the stack determine its diameter.

Diameter stack in inches	Fixture units on stack	Maximum length in feet
2 (no kitchen sink.)	4	30
2½	10	40
3	16	50
4	32	100
5	50	200

Note: Water closets or fixtures requiring a flushometer valve and fixtures with a waste opening 2 inches or larger can't be installed on a vertical combined waste and vent stack.

From the Uniform Plumbing Code, © 1988, IAPMO

Figure 5-20 **Vertical combination waste and vent stack**

Check Figure 5-20. You'll find that a 3-inch combination stack can accommodate 16 fixture units with a maximum length of 50 feet. Since a four-story building is about 40 feet high, the fixture units and total length in Section A are within the limits.

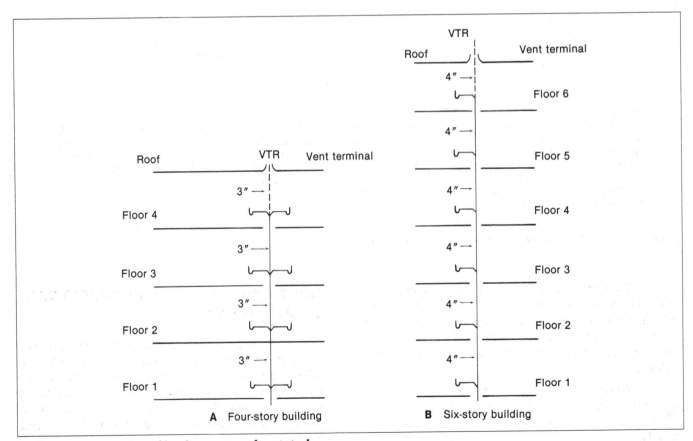

Figure 5-21 **Vertical combination waste and vent stack**

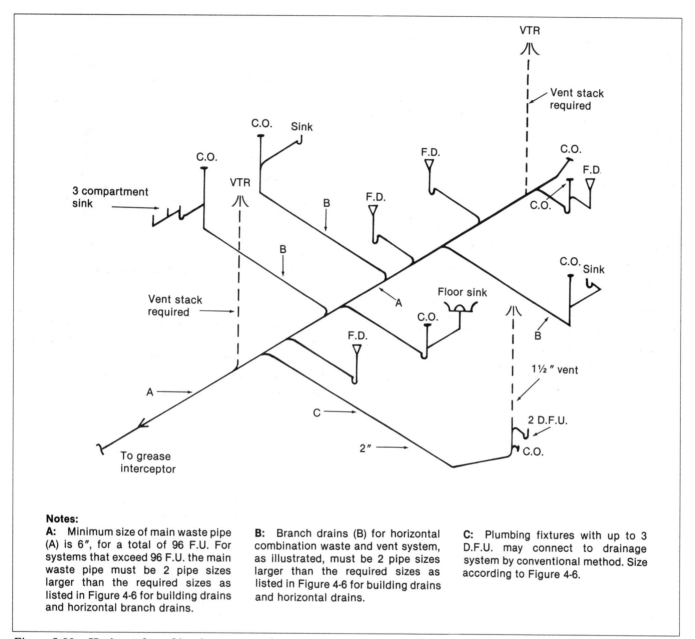

Notes:

A: Minimum size of main waste pipe (A) is 6″, for a total of 96 F.U. For systems that exceed 96 F.U. the main waste pipe must be 2 pipe sizes larger than the required sizes as listed in Figure 4-6 for building drains and horizontal branch drains.

B: Branch drains (B) for horizontal combination waste and vent system, as illustrated, must be 2 pipe sizes larger than the required sizes as listed in Figure 4-6 for building drains and horizontal drains.

C: Plumbing fixtures with up to 3 D.F.U. may connect to drainage system by conventional method. Size according to Figure 4-6.

Figure 5-22   Horizontal combination waste and vent system

Section B has only 12 fixture units — but it's over the 50-foot height limit for a 3-inch stack. You'll have to use the next larger size. Note that Section B shows a 4-inch combination stack. Remember, the length of the stack is the final determiner.

Before designing a vertical combination system, check your local code. The Standard Plumbing Code accepts it, but some local codes don't.

Horizontal Combination Waste and Vent Systems

A horizontal waste and vent system is a one-pipe system that's useful where special fixtures aren't adjacent to walls or partitions. But it's only allowed where you can't use a conventional system because of structural conditions. Consider it for plumbing fixtures usually found in restaurants.

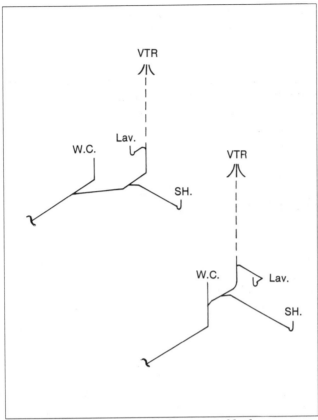

*Figure 5-23   Flat and stacked wet vented bathroom
groups*

You can connect other plumbing fixtures (up to a maximum of three fixture units) to the combination waste and vent system by using regular-size waste and vent pipes. Look at Figure 5-22 and Figure 4-6 in Chapter 4. There's also more information on the restrictions in Chapter 7.

Wet Venting

Wet venting, which connects fixtures to a horizontal drain, is common in residential bathroom and kitchen groups. There are some limitations, however. The vertical portion can only receive waste from one or two fixture units. You can only vent four fixture units this way. But most codes don't include the water closet in the total fixture units if it's wet vented as shown in Figure 5-23. All wet vented fixtures must be on the same floor.

The vertical piping between any two fixture inlets at different levels is a wet vented section. Here are the requirements for wet vented sections.

They have to be at least one pipe size larger than the minimum waste pipe size of the upper fixture *or* the sum of the fixture units, whichever is larger. They can never be less than 2 inches. See Figure 5-8.

The size of the common vents in a wet vent system depends on the total fixture units served. Make sure they're not smaller than 1-1/4 inches. That's the minimum vent pipe size for any fixture served. Look back to Figure 4-6 in Chapter 4.

Single Bathroom Groups

In high-rise buildings, you can usually use an individually vented lavatory as a wet vent for a bathtub, shower, or water closet. Here are the restrictions:

- The fixture unit load can't exceed one fixture unit.

- The dry vent portion must be at least 1-1/2 inches.

- The vertical wet vent section must be at least 1-1/2 inches and drain into a 2-inch horizontal drain pipe.

- This arrangement is limited to the top story of a building only. See Figure 5-24.

For a single bathroom and kitchen group on the top floor, a common-vented lavatory and kitchen sink can vent a bathtub or shower as well as the water closet. But only if there are not more

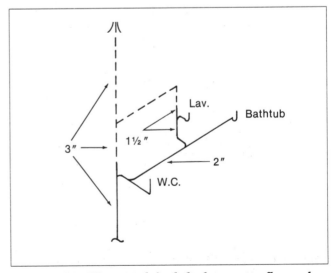

Figure 5-24   Wet vented single bathroom, top floor only

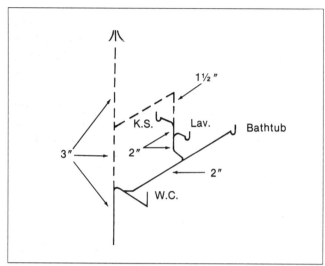

Figure 5-25 Wet vented single bathroom and kitchen sink, top floor only

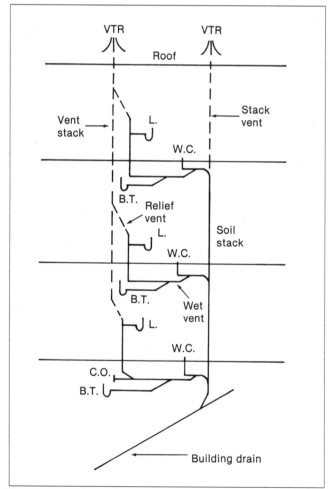

Figure 5-26 Alternate method of wet venting single bathrooms in multi-story building

than four fixture units and the pipe is 2 inches in diameter. Figure 5-25 shows the arrangement.

Here's the usual note of caution: Check the local code before including the kitchen sink in this design. While the arrangement in Figure 5-25 is accepted by the Standard Plumbing Code, the design in Figure 5-26 is more common for venting single bathroom groups in a multi-story building. You can use it on any floor, not just the top floor.

Double Bathroom Groups

On the top floor of multi-story buildings, most codes allow a common vent to wet vent two back-to-back lavatories, bathtubs, or showers, and the water closets. Make the vertical wet vent section 2 inches in diameter. The vent extension to the stack vent or vent stack must be 1-1/2 inches.

Figure 5-27 shows how you can wet vent a double bath on the top floor. Figures 5-28 and 5-29 show two ways to wet vent double bathroom groups on lower floors. Most codes accept the economical design in Figure 5-28.

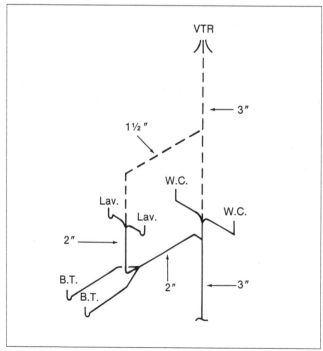

Figure 5-27 Wet vented double bath, top floor only

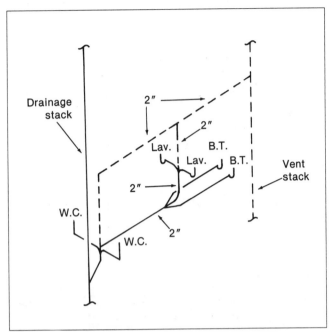

Figure 5-28 Wet vented double bath, lower floors

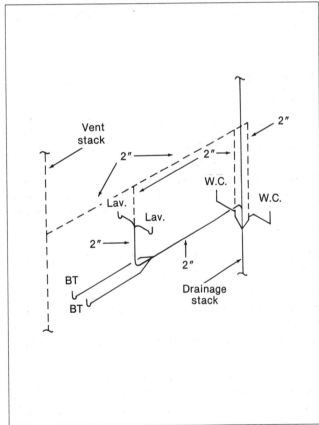

Figure 5-29 Alternate method of wet venting double bath, lower floors

The alternate method in Figure 5-29 is also acceptable, but it's more complex. You can use an individually-vented lavatory — or a common vent for back-to-back lavatories — as a wet vent for two bathtubs or showers. Both the wet vent and its extension to the vent stack must be at least 2 inches in diameter. And each water closet must be separately vented.

Stack Venting Fixture Groups

There's an economical way to stack vent the fixtures in one bathroom, and a kitchen sink, without individual fixture vents. It's illustrated in Figure 5-30. But you can only use it in a one-story building or on the top floor of a multi-story building. Each fixture drain must connect independently to the stack. The water closet and bathtub or shower drain must enter the stack at the same level. You can do it with a 3-inch by 2-inch side-inlet sanitary tee.

Reventing Not Required

A 2-inch horizontal waste branch— This branch, within a developed length of 8 feet from a main-vented line, can serve three lavatories, one sink and one lavatory, or one bathtub or shower. See Figure 5-31. The grade of the branch drain can't exceed 1/4 inch per foot. Sink traps are

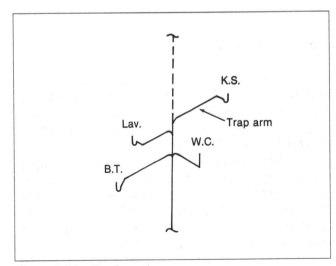

Figure 5-30 Stack venting

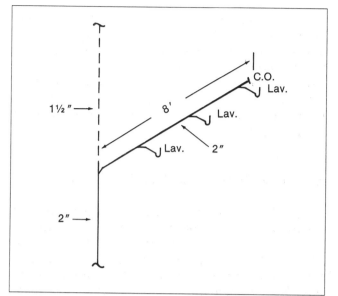

Figure 5-31   Reventing not required in 2-inch horizontal waste branch as illustrated

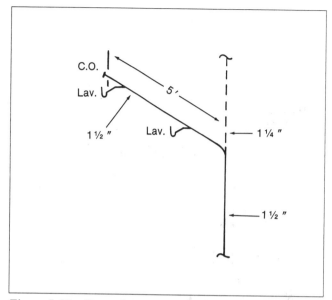

Figure 5-32   Reventing not required in 1-1/2" horizontal waste branch as illustrated

limited to 1-1/2 inches. Bathtub or shower traps must be a minimum of 2 inches.

A 1-1/2 inch horizontal waste branch— Within a developed length of 5 feet from a main-vented line, this branch can serve one or two lavatories without reventing. Figure 5-32 shows the arrangement. Keep the branch drain grade at 1/4 inch or less and the lavatory trap sizes at not more than 1-1/4 inches.

Check your local code before using either of these designs.

Battery Venting

Battery venting is a battery of fixtures connected to a horizontal soil or waste branch that's a uniform diameter throughout its length. They may be vented by a circuit or loop vent. Check pages 170 and 177 in the Glossary.

The size of the circuit or loop vent pipes varies from code to code. Some require the circuit or loop vent to be at least one pipe size smaller than the horizontal soil or waste branch. Others specify a diameter of at least 1-1/2 inches, but not less than one-half the pipe size of the horizontal waste line. Still others call for the same diameter as the vent stack, or half the size of the horizontal soil or waste branch, whichever is smaller.

Figure 4-6 in Chapter 4 offers guidance, but also check your local code. Find out the required circuit or loop vent sizes before you begin your design.

Vents for Sumps and Receiving Tanks

Most sumps and receiving tanks which receive sewage operate at atmospheric pressure from gravity-flow drains. They need enough air flow to replace the sewage as it's pumped out. Using Figure 4-6, you can find the vent size based on the required air flow and the developed length.

Special Venting for Island Fixtures

You may occasionally want to locate residential sinks away from any wall or partition. That takes a special venting arrangement. Some codes ignore island fixtures. But most codes will accept one of these arrangements:

1) Extend the vent pipe at least as high as the underside of the drainboard. Then it can fall and connect to the horizontal drain line immediately downstream from the vertical fixture drain. Code may require 3-inch cleanouts above floor level on the vertical fixture drain and on the vent

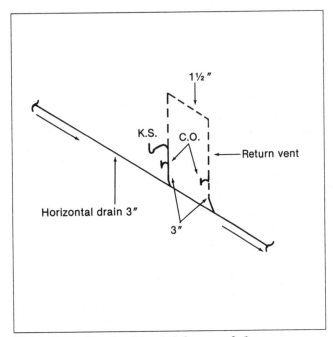

Figure 5-33   Venting island sink, example 1

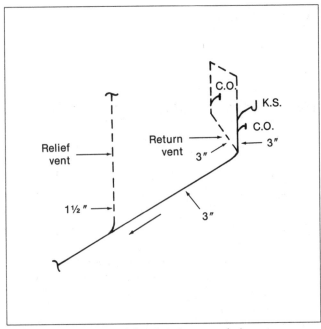

Figure 5-34   Venting island sink, example 2

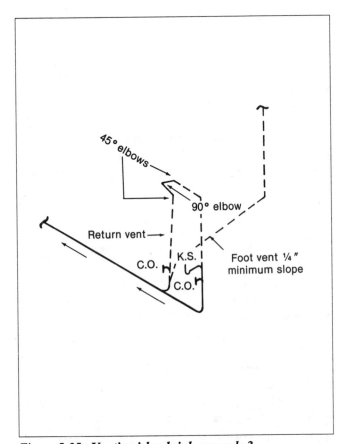

Figure 5-35   Venting island sink, example 3

as it returns downward. The pipe sizes shown in Figure 5-33 are usually acceptable.

2) If you can't connect the vent turning downward to the horizontal fixture drain, connect it directly at the base of the vertical fixture drain. Then install a relief vent downstream as near to the fixture as possible. Look at Figure 5-34.

3) Here's a third possibility. It's specified in the Uniform Plumbing Code. Connect the returned vent to the horizontal drain through a wye branch fitting. You'll have to provide a foot vent off the vertical fixture vent with a wye branch immediately below the floor. Run that second wye branch to the nearest partition and then through the roof, or connect it to other vents at least 6 inches above the flood level rim of the fixtures. Use drainage fittings on all parts of the vent below floor level. And maintain a minimum slope of 1/4 inch per foot back to the drain. Use a one-piece fitting or an assembly of a 45-degree, a 90-degree, and a 45-degree elbow for the return bend under the drainboard.

The Uniform Plumbing Code doesn't address cleanouts. You'll have to assume that cleanouts are required, and illustrate them in your isometric drawings. Note the cleanouts shown in Figure 5-35.

Chapter 6

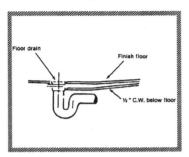

Fixture Traps and Cleanouts

Fixture traps create a liquid seal that prevents drainage system odors, gases and even vermin from entering the building through the fixtures. That's easy to accomplish. But the trap must provide this protection without restricting the flow of sewage or other liquid wastes through it. That's a little trickier.

Fixture Trap Requirements

Because of the trap's unique importance in protecting the public health, the code includes some strict controls. For instance, a single trap may serve a maximum of three single-compartment sinks or three laundry tubs of the same depth, or three lavatories — if they're adjacent to each other in the same room. But that's not the only requirement. Their waste outlets can't be more than 30 inches center to center. You must put the trap in a central location. Figure 6-1 shows the acceptable arrangement.

Every plumbing fixture connected directly to the sanitary drainage system must have a separate water seal trap. The only exceptions are water closets and other fixtures with integral traps built into the fixture body.

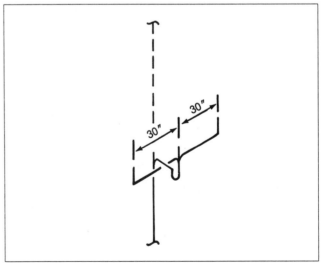

Figure 6-1   Permitted use of single trap serving three approved fixtures

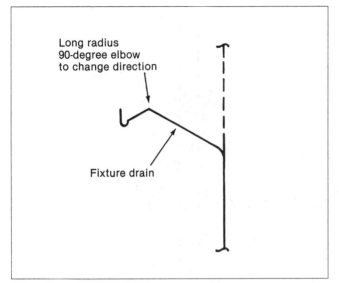

Figure 6-2 *Fixture drain change of direction - no cleanout needed*

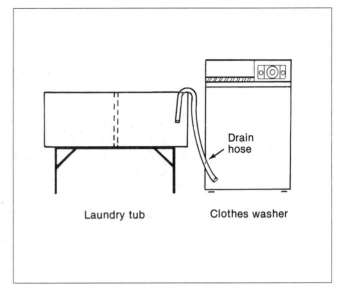

Figure 6-3 *Laundry tub used as indirect waste receptor may be acceptable*

Restrictions on Fixture Traps

Here are some of the code restrictions on the design of fixture traps.

♦ When a fixture drain (trap arm) changes direction, include a cleanout if the offset is more than two 45-degree fittings or one long radius 90-degree elbow. See Figure 6-2.

♦ You can't have a garbage disposal unit sharing a trap with any set of restaurant, commercial or industrial sinks. Each unit must have a separate trap. They have to connect independently to the sanitary drainage system, not to the greasy waste system. See Chapter 7.

♦ Don't connect domestic clothes washers and laundry tubs to the drainage system through a single trap. Give each a separate and independent trap. There's one exception, however. When a laundry tub is next to a clothes washer, the washer can discharge into the tub. Look at Figure 6-3.

♦ The code restricts the vertical distance between a fixture outlet and the trap weir to 24 inches. See Figure 6-4. But closer is better. Vertical lengths that exceed the maximum can lead to self-siphonage of the trap.

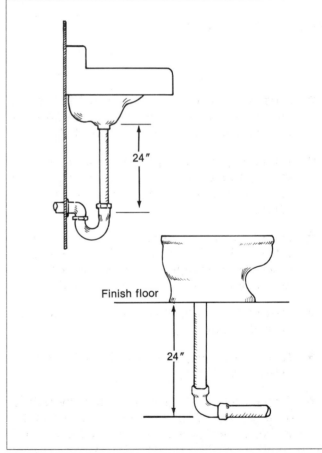

Figure 6-4 *Maximum vertical drop for plumbing fixtures permitted by code*

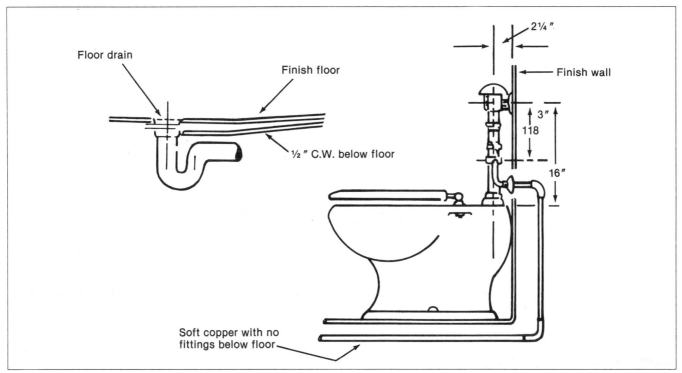

Figure 6-5 Trap primer detail

♦ Because floor drains are included in the fixture family, they're covered by the 24-inch vertical distance shown in Figure 6-4.

♦ You can't place the vent pipe opening from a soil or waste stack (except water closets) below the weir of a fixture trap. Look back to Figure 5-9.

♦ Each fixture trap must have a water seal of between 2 inches and 4 inches. The exceptions are interceptors and separators that need deeper seals to function properly.

♦ Fixture traps installed below the floor can't have cleanouts.

♦ To prevent stoppages, specify self-cleaning fixture traps.

♦ Trap outlets can't be larger than the fixture drain to which they connect. For example, you can't design a 1-1/4 inch drain pipe for a sink with a 1-1/2 inch trap. Make the trap and the fixture drain the same size. Refer to Figure 3-1

♦ Supply automatic trap primers for infrequently-used floor drains that connect directly to the sanitary drainage system. Most floor drains are in public toilet rooms. See Figure 6-5.

♦ Traps for floor drains must be easy to clean and large enough to be efficient. Locate the drain inlet so it's in full view, not hidden under cabinets or equipment. If it might be subject to reverse flow, protect the drain with an approved backwater valve. Look at page 166 in the Glossary.

Prohibited Fixture Traps

The code doesn't allow fixture traps which depend on movable parts or concealed interior partitions for their seal. It also prohibits full "S" traps, bell traps and crown-vented traps. And fixtures equipped with integral traps can't have a second (exposed) trap.

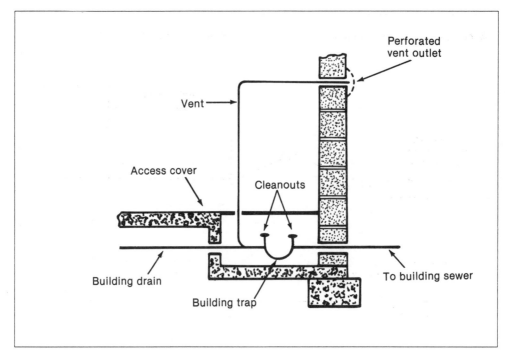

Figure 6-6   Building trap detail

You can use drum traps in special situations with prior approval, as long as they're designed with a vent.

Trap Materials

Most concealed fixture traps are made of cast iron, cast brass, lead or plastic.

You can choose exposed traps of cast iron, cast brass, copper, lead, 17 gauge chrome brass, copper or plastic. Some codes accept 20 gauge chrome brass. All traps, regardless of material, must have a smooth, uniform interior waterway. And the manufacturer's name and the gauge of the tubing must be stamped legibly into the metal of each trap.

The Uniform Plumbing Code allows you to use only one approved slip joint fitting on the outlet side of the trap. Some codes, however, approve solid connections, slip joints or couplings on the trap inlet, trap outlet, or within the trap seal.

Building Traps

In the days before modern drainage and vent systems, a building trap was essential to keep rats, vermin, sewer gases and odors out of a building. Today most codes don't require a building trap in a building drainage line. In fact, they may actually prohibit it. Don't design a building trap in a drainage line unless your building department requires it.

If you do need a building trap, connect a relieving vent or fresh air intake to the building drain directly upstream from the building trap. Carry the relieving vent above grade and terminate it in a screened outlet outside the building. The vent pipe's minimum size is usually one-half the diameter of the building drain to which it connects. Provide cleanouts for each building trap. For full design details see Figure 6-6.

Fixture Traps Protected by Vents

Siphonage causes most fixture trap seal failures. It happens when a fixture drain (trap arm) is too far from its vent. The sloped fixture drain

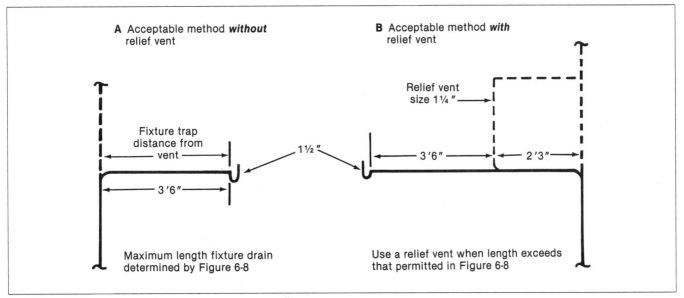

Figure 6-7   Protect the fixture traps

can act as the long outlet leg of a gravity siphon, siphoning out the last water flowing from the fixture into the trap. Don't let that happen in your designs. Protect each plumbing fixture trap by including a vent to prevent siphonage in the fixture drain. Look at Figure 6-7.

Each code contains strict guidelines that specify the maximum horizontal distance between fixtures and their vents. And as always, the codes vary considerably. For example, the Uniform Plumbing Code says a 1-1/4-inch fixture drain must be within 2-1/2 feet of its vent, measured horizontally. The UPC table is shown in Figure 6-8. The Standard Plumbing Code allows a horizontal distance of 3-1/2 feet for the same fixture.

Why the difference? Only the code writers know. If a fixture trap 2-1/2 feet from its vent works in California, wouldn't it work just as well in Tennessee? There has been some progress in the movement toward uniformity, but there are still regional variations. Always rely on your local code for the specifics on your jobs.

Drainage Pipe Cleanouts

Over the years, cleanouts have become an integral part of the drainage system. Even well-de-signed drainage pipes are subject to stoppages. Always provide accessible cleanouts.

Today's model codes specify the location, size and type of cleanouts, and the distance between them. There are two basic types of code-approved cleanouts; conventional cleanouts, and manholes.

Trap arm	Distance of trap to vent	
Inches	**Feet**	**Inches**
1-1/4	2	6
1-1/2	3	6
2	5	0
3	6	0
4 and larger	10	0

Notes: Slope 1/4 inch per foot. The developed length between the trap of a water closet or similar fixture (measured from top of closet ring closet flange to inner edge of vent) and its vent must not exceed 6 feet.

Figure 6-8   Horizontal distance of trap arms

Conventional cleanouts with removable plugs are required on drainage pipes within a building or on a private sewer. Some codes also approve cleanouts, rather than manholes, on building sewers more than 10 inches in diameter.

Manholes serve as junctions to join one or more sewer lines. They allow access to inspect and clear the lines of solids that accumulate there. Manholes are common in private sewage collection systems that serve several large buildings. Refer to Figure 6-9.

Cleanout Locations

Provide a cleanout on the upper terminal of each horizontal drainage pipe. It's usually at the base of a stack. If the total developed length exceeds 100 feet, include a cleanout for each 100 feet of the run. Look at Figure 6-10. But be aware that some codes require cleanouts every 75 feet.

You may want to locate a full size two-way cleanout fitting where the building drain and the building sewer meet. Some codes insist that you put it within 2 feet of the outside building wall. Extend the cleanout to grade. If the building drain is less than 100 feet long (75 feet, in some codes) and any change in direction is within code allowances, you may be able to substitute the two-way cleanout for an upper terminal cleanout. Figure 6-11 shows the arrangement.

Most codes require a cleanout at the base of all stacks. The Uniform Plumbing Code makes an exception. If the base of a stack can be rodded by a downstream cleanout, you may omit the cleanout there.

Extend outside cleanouts to above grade, unless they're installed under an approved cover plate. They must be readily accessible for easy cleaning.

All cleanouts are classified as drainage piping. Each 90-degree cleanout extension must extend from a wye fitting or sweep. Design the cleanout so it opens in a direction opposite to the flow in the line it serves. Take it off vertically above the flow line of the pipe. Figure 6-12 shows a 90-degree cleanout installation.

Many codes require a cleanout in the building sewer at the property line. Bring it to grade so it's readily accessible. See Figure 6-13.

Virtually every code requires that cleanouts in areas of pedestrian traffic (hallways, rooms, sidewalks) have countersunk heads or approved cover plates. That's to prevent people from tripping over them, of course.

When a horizontal drainage line changes direction more than 135 degrees, furnish additional cleanouts. The details of the number and location of cleanouts varies in the model codes. Most codes require cleanouts at each change of direction larger than 45 degrees. Check your local code. Figure 6-14 shows typical requirements for cleanout locations.

The Uniform Plumbing Code doesn't require cleanouts on the following:

♦ Horizontal drains less than 5 feet in length which don't serve sinks or urinals.

♦ Drainage pipes installed on a slope of 72 degrees or less from the vertical.

♦ Any pipe or piping above the first floor of the building (except horizontal branch lines).

Concealed Drainage Piping

Where cleanouts are required on concealed vertical piping, extend them through or flush with the finish wall or floor. If you can't do either, provide an access plate.

Cleanout Sizes, Clearances and Equivalents

Some codes require cleanouts the same size as the pipes they serve, up to 4 inches. They can't be smaller than 4 inches for larger pipes. Check your local code for the approved cleanout sizes for pipes 1-1/2 inches and larger.

The codes generally agree about the acceptable clearances in front of cleanouts. You have to provide a 12-inch clearance for rodding cleanouts in pipes 2 inches and smaller. For pipes

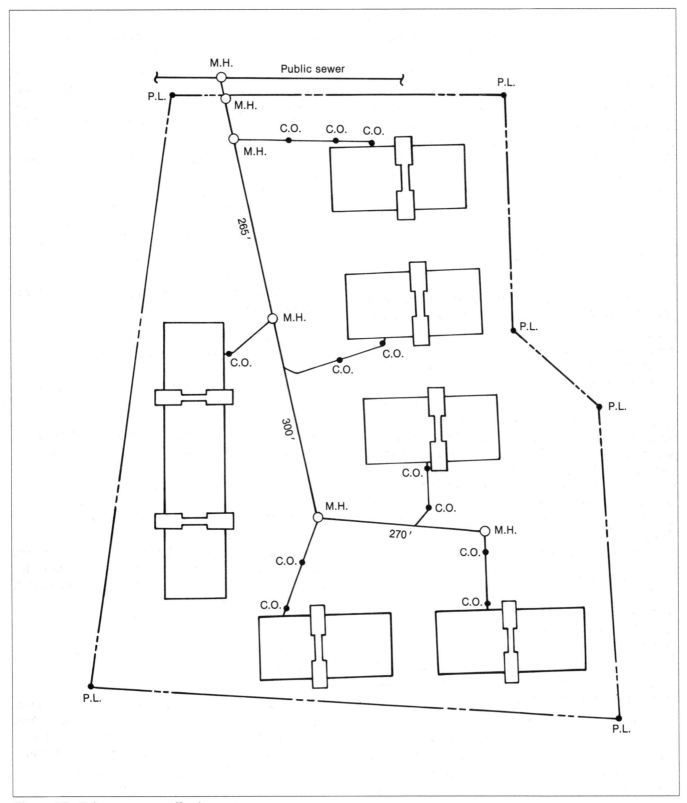

Figure 6-9 Private sewage collection system

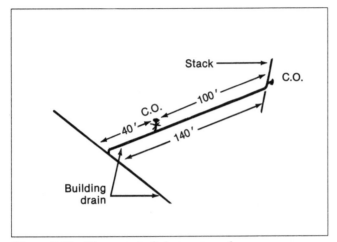

Figure 6-10   Placement of cleanouts on long run

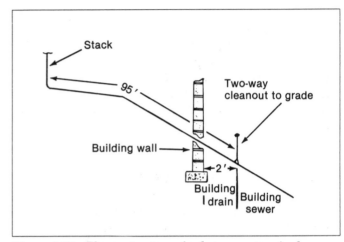

Figure 6-11   Cleanout not required at upper terminal

larger than 2 inches, allow an 18-inch clearance for cleanouts.

For underfloor pipe cleanouts with less than 18 inches vertical and 30 inches horizontal clearance, extend the cleanout to or above the finish floor, or outside the building.

There are three requirements for cleanouts located in building sewers under concrete or paving. First, choose cleanouts made of approved material. Second, protect them adequately. Finally, extend them flush with paving or put them in accessible yard boxes.

Instead of a cleanout, some codes accept a fixture trap or a water closet that can be removed without disturbing concealed piping.

Manholes

With prior approval, you can use manholes instead of cleanouts on private sewage systems or building sewers larger than 10 inches in diameter. Locate the manholes where they're best suited to receive the building sewers. In Figure 6-9, each building sewer joins the sewage collection system directly or through a manhole, then continues directly to the street sewer.

Install manholes at every change in grade, change in direction, and junction of two or more sewers. And don't exceed 300 feet between manholes.

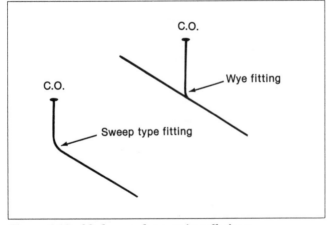

Figure 6-12   90-degree cleanout installations

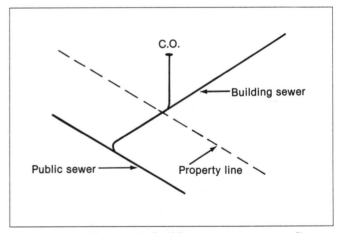

Figure 6-13   Cleanout in building sewer at property line

Under the Uniform Plumbing Code, you have to connect the inlet and outlet to the manhole with a flexible compression joint. It has to be between 12 inches and 36 inches from the manhole. And it can't be embedded in the manhole base. That makes it more resistant to earthquake damage.

Manhole Construction

You can be sure that the manholes you design will be built right if you include the necessary detail in your drawings and specifications. This detailed information will guide the plumbing contractor in building precisely the manholes you designed. If you're specific enough, any defect in the manhole is the responsibility of the contractor.

Begin any manhole design with the *base*, either poured in place or precast. There are two factors that influence the width and thickness of the base. First, consider the height and weight of the manhole the base will support. Second, evaluate the quality of the ground it will be placed on.

The *walls* of most of the manholes you design will be of brick, poured concrete or precast concrete. The code in some areas may approve concrete block.

There's no place in modern construction for a poorly-built manhole. Faulty design or construction can cause the manhole to settle or crack,

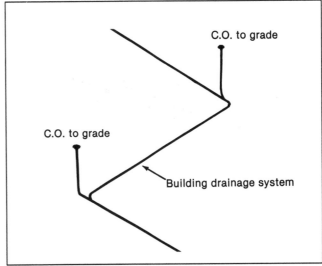

Figure 6-14   Provide cleanouts at any change of direction greater than 45 degrees

permitting raw sewage to seep into the ground. That's a real health hazard.

The local authorities must approve your manhole designs before construction begins. In many areas it's the responsibility of the public works department. Figures 6-15 through 6-21 show standard manhole designs that most departments will approve. But before you begin, get details on acceptable designs from your local authorities.

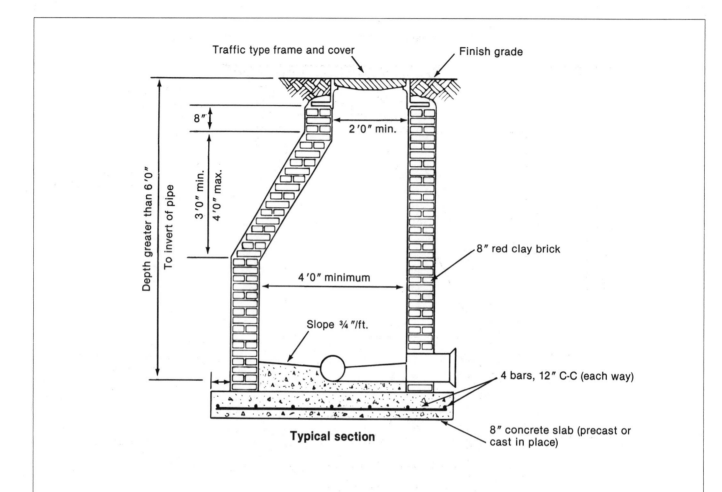

Figure 6-15 Standard manhole (brick)

Notes:

1. Brick masonry construction stuccoed with ¾" mortar inside and outside.
2. The first three sections of pipe at both influent and effluent of each manhole are a maximum 2'0" in length.
3. A flow channel inside the manhole will direct influent into flow stream.

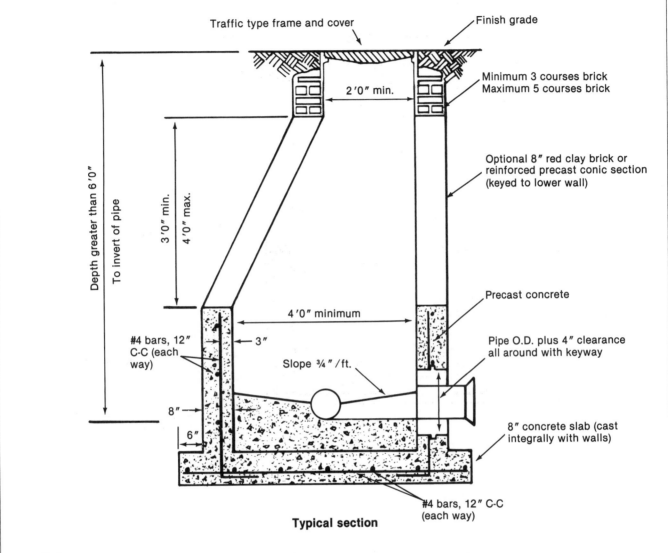

Typical section

Notes:
1. Brick masonry construction stuccoed with ¾" mortar inside and outside.
2. The first three sections of pipe at both influent and effluent of each manhole will be a maximum of 2'0" in length.
3. Lift holes through precast structure are not permitted.
4. See technical specifications for placement of construction joints.
5. All openings shall be sealed with a waterproof, expanding grout.
6. A flow channel inside the manhole will direct influent into flow stream.

Figure 6-16   Standard manhole (precast)

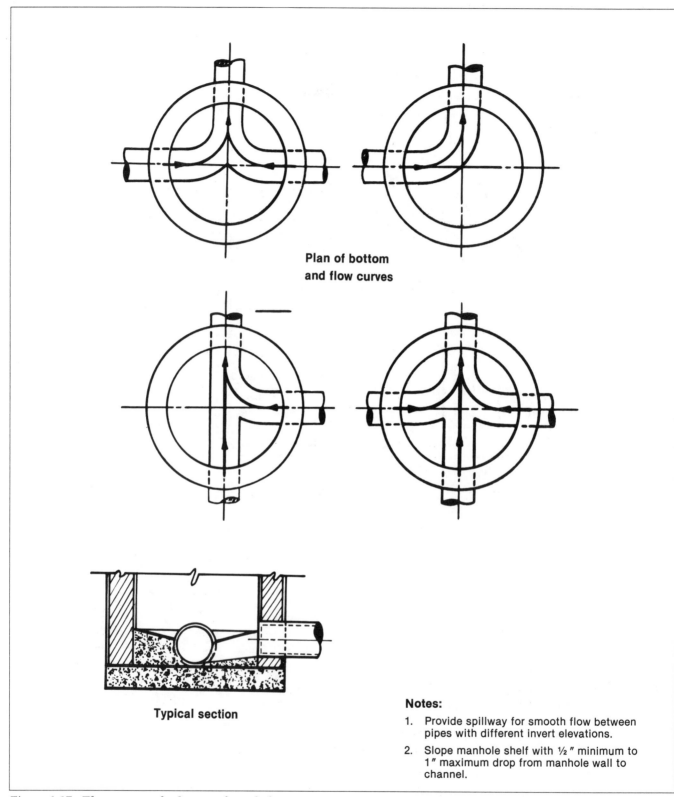

Plan of bottom and flow curves

Typical section

Notes:

1. Provide spillway for smooth flow between pipes with different invert elevations.
2. Slope manhole shelf with ½" minimum to 1" maximum drop from manhole wall to channel.

Figure 6-17 Flow patterns for bottom of manhole

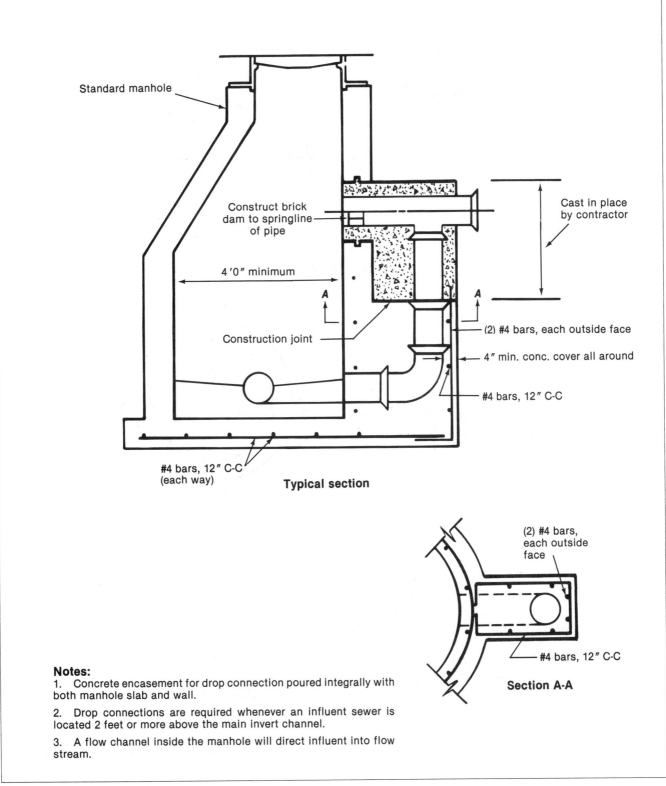

Typical section

Standard manhole

Construct brick dam to springline of pipe

4'0" minimum

Construction joint

#4 bars, 12" C-C (each way)

Cast in place by contractor

(2) #4 bars, each outside face

4" min. conc. cover all around

#4 bars, 12" C-C

(2) #4 bars, each outside face

#4 bars, 12" C-C

Section A-A

Notes:
1. Concrete encasement for drop connection poured integrally with both manhole slab and wall.

2. Drop connections are required whenever an influent sewer is located 2 feet or more above the main invert channel.

3. A flow channel inside the manhole will direct influent into flow stream.

Figure 6-18 Drop connection (new precast manhole)

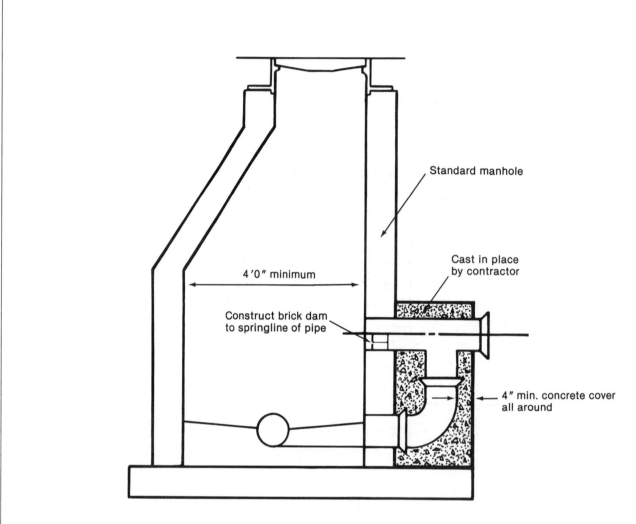

Typical section

Notes:

1. Drop connections are required whenever an influent sewer is located 2 feet or more above the main invert channel.

2. A flow channel inside the manhole will direct influent into flow stream.

3. Construction of brick manholes will provide an oversized slab to extend under the drop connection.

Figure 6-19 ***Drop connection (new brick manhole)***

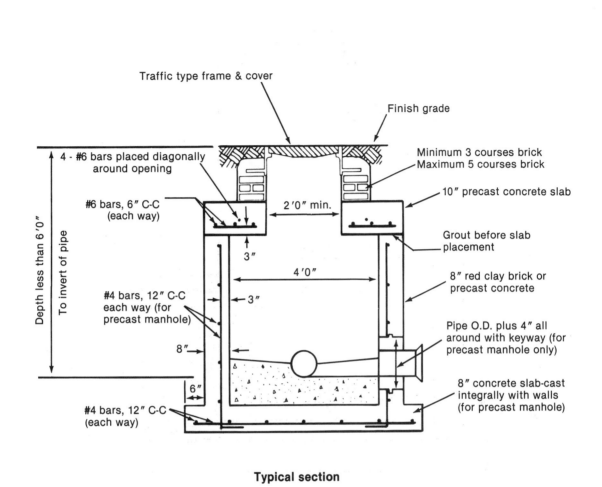

Typical section

Notes:

1. Brick masonry stuccoed with ¾″ mortar inside and outside.

2. The first three sections of pipe at both influent and effluent of each manhole will be a maximum of 2′0″ in length.

3. Lift holes through precast sections not permitted.

4. All openings shall be sealed with a waterproof, expanding grout.

5. A flow channel inside the manhole will direct influent into flow stream.

Figure 6-20   Shallow manhole (brick or precast)

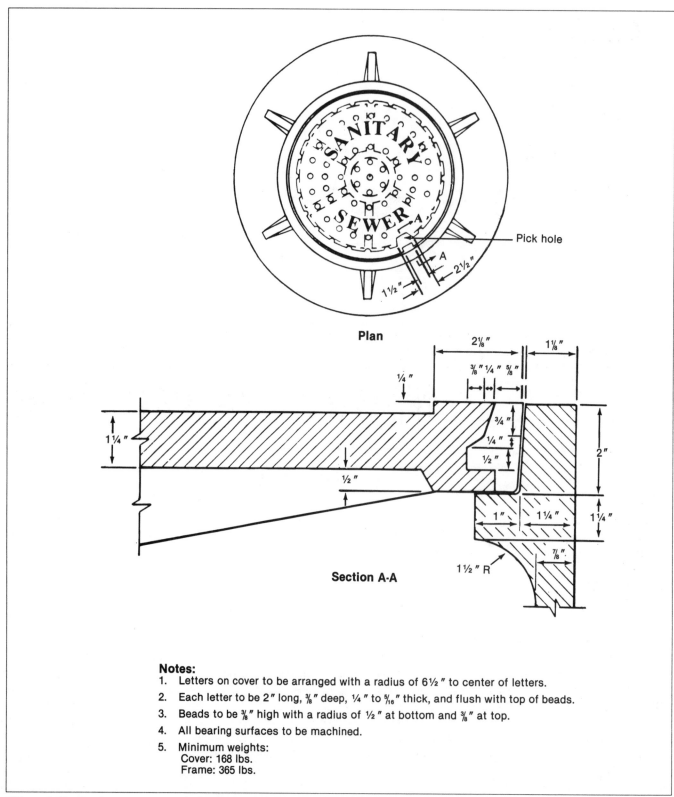

Plan

Section A-A

Notes:
1. Letters on cover to be arranged with a radius of 6½″ to center of letters.
2. Each letter to be 2″ long, ⅜″ deep, ¼″ to 5/16″ thick, and flush with top of beads.
3. Beads to be ⅜″ high with a radius of ½″ at bottom and ⅜″ at top.
4. All bearing surfaces to be machined.
5. Minimum weights:
   Cover: 168 lbs.
   Frame: 365 lbs.

Figure 6-21   Sanitary sewer manhole (frame and cover)

Chapter 7

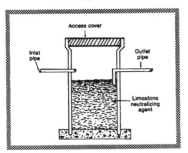

Interceptors, Separators and Neutralizing Devices

You're probably familiar with the term *objectionable waste*. You might know that every code requires special handling of anything harmful to the building drainage system, the public sewer, or the sewage treatment plant. But do you know the appropriate method for every situation? That's what this chapter's about.

Some businesses discharge waste containing an unacceptable level of grease, oil, flammable waste, sand, plaster, lint, hair, glass or acids. These materials can't discharge into the regular drainage system until they're intercepted, separated or neutralized.

Interceptors and *separators* accumulate and recover objectionable substances from liquid waste. *Dilution* or *neutralizing* tanks treat corrosive liquids to make them safe before discharge into the drainage system.

Code requirements for the size and type of interceptors, separators or neutralizing tanks vary widely. You have to submit detailed drawings and specifications for advance approval from the building department.

Grease Interceptors

In commercial buildings where food is processed, prepared or served, you *must* install grease interceptors in the waste line. If you don't, the accumulated grease will clog the drainage pipes. Cafes, restaurants, lunch counters, bars and clubs, cafeterias and hotels must all have grease interceptors. So must hospitals, sanitariums, factory or school kitchens, supermarkets, meat processing plants, soap factories, slaughterhouses and tallow rendering plants.

If you're designing the plumbing for a business which discharges waste with an unaccept-

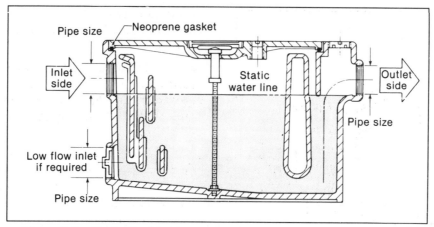

Figure 7-1   Typical inside grease receptor

able amount of grease, you're going to have to drain it into the sanitary drainage lines through an approved interceptor. But take note of this: No waste that *doesn't* require separation can pass through grease interceptors.

Grease interceptors *aren't* usually required in single-family homes, apartment buildings, or restaurants that prepare or sell only take-out food.

There are two types of grease interceptors — inside and outside installations. Let's look at the inside type first.

Inside installations— Most codes don't dictate the sizing method to use. They just recommend design criteria or leave it to the discretion of the local health department or plumbing officials.

Depending on code approval, you'd probably use an inside interceptor for small restaurants or other businesses generating minor amounts of grease. Figure 7-1 shows a factory-built unit of cast iron. It's available in sizes with a grease capacity ranging from 14 pounds to the maximum 100 pounds allowed by code. It may be floor-mounted or installed below the floor as shown on Figure 7-2. You need advance approval to install an interceptor of less than 20-pound capacity.

On a small grease interceptor like this, you have to install an approved flow control device in an accessible, visible location. Look at Figure 7-3. The flow can't exceed the rated capacity of the interceptor. And any flow control device with adjustable or removable parts is *prohibited*.

You can omit fixture traps for discharge into an approved grease interceptor located less than 4 feet from the single fixture it serves. Vent each inside grease interceptor in an approved manner to prevent it from becoming air locked. The interceptors in Figure 7-2 are properly vented.

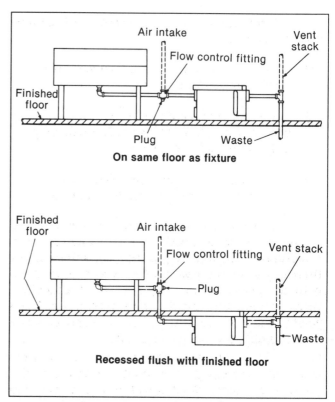

Figure 7-2   Typical installations of grease interceptors

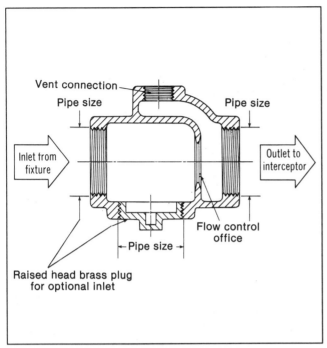

Figure 7-3 Flow control fitting detail

There are three requirements for the interceptor location.

♦ It has to be in an area that's accessible for service and maintenance.

♦ You can never locate an interceptor where people would have to use ladders or move bulky objects to service it.

♦ And finally, don't put the interceptor in a part of the building where food is handled.

In some areas, you can buy water-cooled interceptors which accelerate the coagulation of the grease. But that's a paradoxical situation, for there's always the potential for cross-connection with the potable water supply. Codes almost always prohibit the use of such interceptors. Don't waste time drawing up a design for a greasy waste system using a water-cooled unit.

When grease interceptors are required, they must have a grease retention capacity of 2 pounds for each GPM of flow. Figure 7-4 gives you the most common code sizing criteria for small

establishments. Grease interceptors for small restaurants require a retention time of at least 1.5 hours.

Outside installations— Larger restaurants or other businesses generating sizable grease accumulations require interceptors located outside of the building. They need a retention time of 2.4 hours.

Most large interceptors are made of precast or poured-in-place concrete, as shown in Figure 7-5. Some codes approve the use of other materials, including steel or glass fiber.

You'll usually size commercial grease interceptors according to the number of fixed seats or meals served at peak hours. But each code has a different formula. Identical restaurants in different areas will require interceptors of different sizes.

Let's compare two major codes for a restaurant with a seating capacity of 150 which provides 16 hours of customer service each day.

Code A of the South Florida Plumbing Code has a simple formula: Multiply the number of seats by a waste flow rate of 15 gallons. That means you need to design a liquid capacity of 2,250 gallons. The hours open per day isn't a factor.

The *Uniform Plumbing Code* has a more complicated formula — and it requires a much larger grease interceptor. Figure 7-6 shows the UPC formula. Let's say our sample restaurant

Total number of fixtures connected	Required rate of flow per minute (gallons)	Grease retention capacity (pounds)
1	20	40
2	25	50
3	35	70
4	50	100

Figure 7-4   Sizing criteria for inside grease interceptor

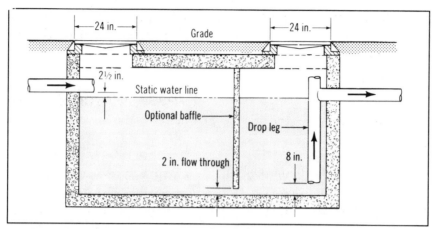

Figure 7-5 Outside grease interceptor detail

serves 150 meals per peak hour, with two peak hours each day. Here's the calculation: 150 meals x 6 gallons x 2.4 x 2 = 4,320 gallons liquid capacity. That's almost twice as large as the first example.

Why this great difference? The Uniform Plumbing Code's formula *does* consider the number of hours the restaurant is open. Each 8-hour period includes one peak hour. Let's review each

Number of meals per peak hour[1]	x	Waste flow rate[2]	x	Retention time[3]	x	Storage factor[4]	=	Interceptor size (liquid capacity)
[1]Meals served at peak hour								
[2]Waste flow rate								
A. With dishwashing machine						6 gallon flow		
B. Without dishwashing machine						5 gallon flow		
C. Single service kitchen						2 gallon flow		
D. Food waste disposer						1 gallon flow		
[3]Retention time								
A. Commercial kitchen waste, dishwasher						2.4 hours		
B. Single service kitchen, single serving						1.5 hours		
[4]Storage factors								
Fully equipped commercial kitchen						8-hour operation:	1 hour	
						16-hour operation:	2 hours	
						24-hour operation:	3 hours	

Figure 7-6 Sizing criteria for outside grease interceptor

8-hour period according to the UPC, for our 150-seat restaurant.

One 8-hour operation:

150 x 6 x 2.4 x 1 peak hour period = 2,160 gal.

One 16-hour operation:

150 x 6 x 2.4 x 2 peak hour periods = 4,320 gal.

One 24-hour operation:

150 x 6 x 2.4 x 3 peak hour periods = 6,480 gal.

If you're designing an outside interceptor for a restaurant, save some time by calling the plumbing official or plans examiner in your area. They can probably tell you which interceptor size will meet local code standards.

Grease Interceptor Design

Grease interceptors must be designed to retain congealed grease on the surface of any liquid. Although the codes vary widely across the country, the structural design criteria for outside installations are quite uniform. Read the relevant section in your particular code to see whether special interior designs are required. Here's how one major code puts it: *Grease interceptor fittings shall be designed for grease retention.* Period. Clearly, that leaves the rest up to you!

Figure 7-5 shows the principal requirements for outside structural designs in many parts of the country. Here are the common specifications:

♦ The inlet invert must discharge at least 2-1/2 inches above the liquid level line. The outlet tee has to be within 8 inches of the bottom of the tank.

♦ To make maintenance easy, provide 24-inch diameter gastight manhole covers over the inlet and over the outlet pipe. (Some codes allow 20 inches.) The cover must be at grade level.

♦ Some codes require that interceptors have at least two components. See the optional baffle illustrated in Figure 7-5.

♦ In areas with vehicular traffic, grease interceptor lids must be reinforced to support the additional weight.

Grease Interceptor Locations

When locating a grease interceptor on a site plan, consider these common restrictions:

♦ Place each grease interceptor where there's easy access for inspection, cleaning and removal of intercepted grease.

♦ Each grease interceptor can serve only one business. There is one notable exception, however. In a large shopping center, one or more centrally located grease interceptors can serve several businesses *if* the shopping center management assumes full maintenance responsibility — in writing.

♦ You can't place an interceptor within 5 feet of a building foundation or private property line.

Greasy Waste Systems

You must design greasy waste lines as a separate drainage system. Wastes containing greasy deposits can drain into the building drain line after passing through an interceptor. This includes kitchen sinks, dishwashers, garbage can washers and floor drains that might receive kitchen spills. Floor drains and floor sinks that receive wastes from fixtures or appliances in or near the kitchen (except commercial food grinders) can also connect there.

Conventional Greasy Waste Systems

The conventional system meets perhaps 90 to 95 percent of all construction needs. You've probably designed at least one if you've ever done work for a restaurant.

Even for a large restaurant, designing a greasy waste system is no different from designing

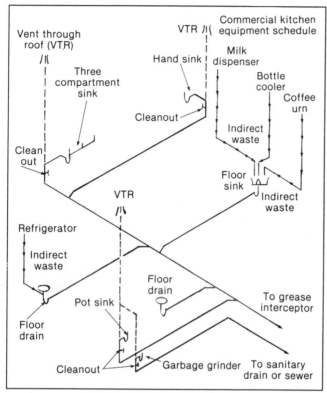

Figure 7-7 **Conventional greasy waste collection system**

a building's sanitary drainage system. To size the pipes and locate the vents, floor drains and fixtures, just follow the conventional method described in your local code. An acceptable conventional greasy waste system is shown in Figure 7-7. Notice that the garbage grinder isn't connected to the greasy waste line.

Combination Waste and Vent System

The combination waste and vent system is much less common. And it requires advance approval. That's because it's acceptable only where a conventional system is impossible — or at least impractical. The combination system provides the horizontal wet venting of a series of traps with a common waste and vent pipe. At best, it's a custom-designed system for locations where you can't provide venting in the usual manner.

You'll usually use a combination waste and vent system for extensive floor drain installa-

tions, like floor drains or floor sinks in supermarkets and for demonstration or work tables in schools. This system also solves the problem of venting fixtures that aren't adjacent to walls or partitions.

Codes require you to oversize a combination system, so it's not self-scouring. Consider this when you're deciding what types of fixtures to connect to it.

To prevent the loss of trap seals or the possibility of an air-lock condition, design the system to balance the air pressure in the pipes with the outside atmospheric pressure. We covered that in Chapter 5.

Some codes require that the grease interceptor be installed *inside* the building for the disposal of grease from kitchen fixtures and other grease-generating equipment. Figure 7-8 shows an inside grease interceptor. Other codes may require the entire system to pass through a grease interceptor located *outside* the building.

Look at Figure 7-8. Here are the requirements for this greasy combination waste and vent system.

♦ Each waste pipe and trap in this system must be two pipe sizes larger than the sizes required by conventional methods. As an example, let's assume that waste line A would normally be 4 inches, and B would be 3 inches. So in this combination system, A would be 6 inches and B, 5 inches.

♦ Don't attach anything that delivers large water surges, such as pumps or sand interceptors, so adequate venting can be maintained.

♦ The vertical distance from the fixture or drain outlet to the top of the trap (weir) can't exceed 24 inches.

♦ The vertical waste pipe must be two pipe sizes larger than the fixture outlet. (The required waste pipe size is 2-1/2 inches for any fixture outlet which is 1-1/2 inches.)

♦ You must provide separate venting if branch line C exceeds 15 feet in length.

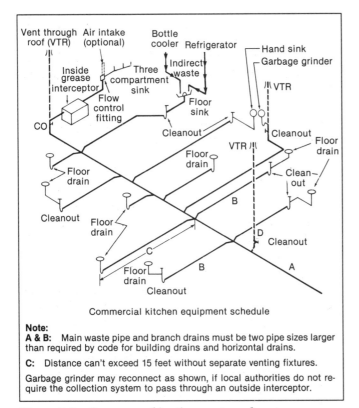

Figure 7-8   Greasy combination waste and vent system

Note:

A & B: Main waste pipe and branch drains must be two pipe sizes larger than required by code for building drains and horizontal drains.

C: Distance can't exceed 15 feet without separate venting fixtures.

Garbage grinder may reconnect as shown, if local authorities do not require the collection system to pass through an outside interceptor.

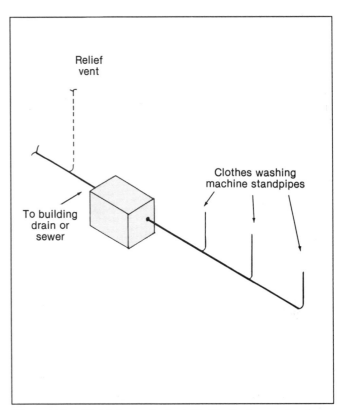

Figure 7-9   Lint interceptor installed in drainage pipe from laundry

♦ Branch line B (and each trap for floor drains or floor sinks) must be two pipe sizes larger than normally required by code, and at least two pipe sizes larger than the fixture tailpiece.

♦ The vent pipes must be at least one half the size of the waste pipe served. If waste pipe A is 6 inches, then vent pipe D must be 3 inches.

♦ Provide one vent upstream and one vent downstream in the system.

♦ Each vent must have an accessible cleanout. However, on a wet vented branch serving a single trap, with a 2-inch tailpiece that provides access for cleaning through the trap, some codes don't require cleanouts.

Lint Interceptors

The discharge of solids from commercial laundries can clog the building drainage pipe or public sewer. That's why codes require an interceptor in laundry drainage pipes to trap string, rags and buttons before they reach the drainage system. Look at Figure 7-9.

Lint interceptors are *not* a code requirement in single-family houses or apartment buildings when the washers are in each unit, rather than in a central laundry room.

Sizing Lint Interceptors

Size lint interceptors for a commercial laundry based on the number of washers it has. Provide for a retention period of at least 1.5 hours (2 hours in some codes). In general, codes don't provide established sizing methods. Instead, they recommend design criteria or leave it to the discretion of the local authorities.

The Uniform Plumbing Code provides the guidelines shown in Figure 7-10 for sizing lint interceptors for commercial laundries. Verify the sizes with your local building authorities. The codes assign a wide variety of fixture units for commercial washers. The required sizes of lint interceptors may vary as much as one-half from the sizes recommended by the Uniform Plumbing Code.

Number of ma-chines	x	2 cycles per hour	x	Waste flow rate	x	Reten-tion time	x	Storage factor	=	Intercep-tor size (liquid capacity)

Figure 7-10   Clothes washing machine formula

Let's look at a sample interceptor sizing problem based on the Uniform Plumbing Code. Assume a commercial laundry with ten washers, open 16 hours a day. The UPC rates commercial washers in groups of three or more at 6 fixture units per washer. (Some codes use 3 fixture units.) Each fixture unit equals 7.5 gallons per minute flow rate. To establish the flow rate for each clothes washer, multiply 6 fixture units by 7.5 gallons per fixture unit, which equals 45 GPM per washer.

Here's the calculation for our sample laundry, using the formula in Figure 7-10:

10 washers x 2 cycles per hour x 45 GPM waste flow rate x 1.5 hours retention time x 2 peak hours operation = 2,700 gallons liquid capacity. (This laundry is open 16 hours. Peak hours are calculated at the rate of one for each eight hours of operation.)

Lint Interceptor Construction

Lint interceptors may be made of precast concrete, poured-in-place concrete, steel or other approved materials. The lint interceptor must be equipped with removable screens or baskets to trap materials that would harm the building drain pipes. (The screens must be nonremovable in some codes.) The screens or basket must be easy to clean.

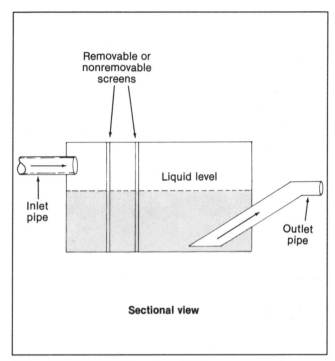

Figure 7-11   Lint interceptor detail

In most cases, you'll locate the inlet pipe one pipe size above the liquid level. Design the outlet of the discharge pipe to extend downward on a 45-degree angle to approximately 2 inches from the bottom of the lint interceptor. This achieves two purposes. First, light objects that pass through the screen and float in the water won't sink into the outlet pipe and on into the sanitary drainage system. Second, it creates a liquid seal that serves as a trap to prevent sewer gases from entering the building through the washer standpipes. Figure 7-11 shows the construction.

Indirect Waste Pipe

The horizontal drainage pipes serving commercial washers are considered to be indirect waste pipes. This indirect waste system is an economical and practical method of piping in this application. It doesn't have to be trapped or vented like most conventional plumbing systems. The washing machine standpipes are open-ended, extending to about 26 inches above the finished floor. They receive the discharge from the washers through a flexible hose. A 3-inch standpipe can usually accommodate two machines. A 4-inch standpipe can serve four machines.

The outlet pipe from the lint interceptor connects to the regular sanitary drainage system. Install a vent pipe as close as possible to the lint interceptor on the discharge pipe. The vent pipe serves the drainage pipes between the lint interceptor and the building drainage system or sewer. It supplies and removes air to prevent the interceptor from becoming air locked. That ensures a free flow of waste water.

Gasoline, Oil and Sand Interceptors

You have to provide interceptors to keep gasoline, grease, oil and sand out of the sanitary drainage system. Here's where they're required:

♦ Anyplace where motor vehicles are repaired and floor drainage is provided.

♦ Anyplace where motor vehicles are commercially washed.

♦ Any public storage garage where floor drainage is provided.

♦ Anyplace where oil, gasoline or other volatile liquids can be discharged into the sanitary drainage.

♦ Any factory which has oily or flammable wastes from storage, maintenance, repair or testing processes.

Although the codes agree that you need interceptors or separators, they don't provide much direction about the size or type of interceptor to install. The code wording usually goes something like this: *The size, type and location of each interceptor or separator shall be approved by the local administrative authority, in accordance with its standards.*

There are two widely-accepted sizing and design methods for handling volatile liquids. The first is for systems with small concentrations of such liquids. The second is designed to handle larger concentrations. We'll look at the guidelines for both types.

Small Concentrations of Volatile Liquid

Commercial garages that service or store ten vehicles or less generate small amounts of volatile liquids. Service stations and repair shops that service but don't store vehicles are also included here.

Figure 7-12 shows a typical poured-in-place or precast interceptor. This oil interceptor with a bucket-type floor drain may be approved for small installations without a separate sand interceptor. Here are some typical design criteria that would meet the requirements of most codes:

♦ The interceptor capacity should equal 18 cubic feet per 20 gallons of design flow per minute.

♦ The discharge pipe should enter the interceptor on a 45-degree angle and terminate near the bottom of interceptor. The liquid depth should be at least 2 feet below the invert of the discharge pipe.

♦ The discharge pipe should be 4 inches in diameter (3 inches, in some codes) with a full-size cleanout at grade. A minimum 2-inch vent is required on the discharge side of interceptor.

♦ There must be a minimum 3 inch (2 inch, in some codes) vapor vent in the evaporation space of interceptor, venting into the open air. It must terminate in an approved location (most often the outside wall of a building) at least 12 feet above grade.

♦ The inlet drain pipe should enter the interceptor above the liquid level line. Some codes require the drainage pipe to be vented. Others consider that the evaporation space provides adequate venting.

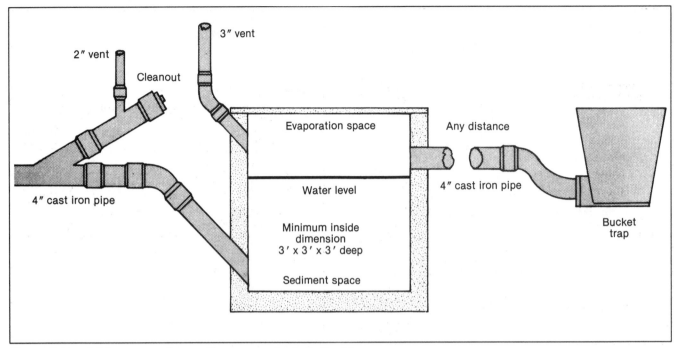

Figure 7-12   Oil interceptor for small amounts of volatile liquids

♦ Interceptors must be located outside the building and shown on the approved building plan.

♦ Each interceptor cover must be accessible for servicing.

♦ Use bucket-type floor drains connected to a trap, with a 4-inch diameter outlet. The bucket must be made of the same material as the floor drain, and be removable for cleaning. The solid portion of the bucket retains sand. Drainage holes or slots near the top of the bucket let liquid pass out of the bucket and into the drain pipes leading to the interceptor. Figure 7-13 shows a typical bucket floor drain.

Large Concentrations of Volatile Liquid

Codes often require a storage tank to receive and store liquids for businesses which generate large amounts of volatile liquids.

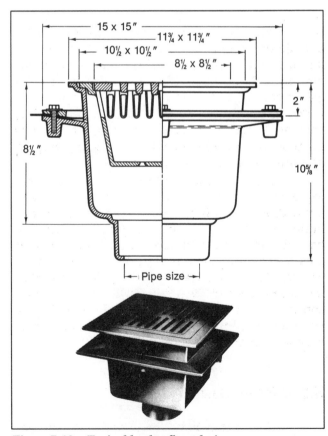

Figure 7-13   Typical bucket floor drain

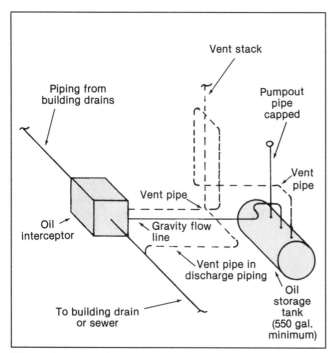

Figure 7-14   Oil interceptor and oil storage

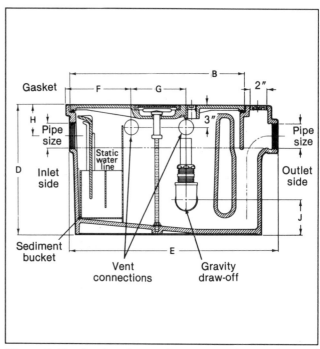

Figure 7-15   Sectional view of typical oil interceptor

The waste oil storage tank must be located outside the building. The designer will determine its size and capacity, with building department approval. Some codes require a minimum 550 gallon capacity. The tank must be U.L. approved. It needs at least a 1-1/2 inch vent ending in the open air 12 feet above grade or through the building roof. Include a 2-inch minimum pumpout pipe at grade for oil removal. Look at Figure 7-14.

A gravity draw-off line from the oil interceptor (or separator) is connected to the oil storage tank. Provide a 2-inch vent to remove any accumulation of explosive vapors. Figure 7-15 shows a typical cast iron manufactured unit, accepted by most codes. It has two vent openings in the interceptor, which are required by some local codes to increase the air circulation. If you use two vents, connect one vent to the vent stack at a higher elevation than the other. The unbalanced air pressure will generate the needed circulation.

Sand Interceptors

Most codes mandate a floor drainage system for all garage buildings. Most codes say some-thing like this: *Where a floor drain discharges through an oil interceptor, it must first discharge through a sand interceptor. Multiple floor drains may discharge into one sand interceptor.* Floor drains might also be required for other areas, including stairwells or planter drains.

Floor drains are needed in commercial garage buildings for a number of reasons. Automobiles drip debris onto the floor, especially on wet or snowy days. And the garage floors are regularly washed down.

Large parking garages, where many automobiles are parked daily, may produce a lot of sand, grit, grease and oil drippings. They would allow unacceptable amounts of sand and volatile liquids to enter the drainage system. Most codes insist that parking garage drains first pass through an approved sand interceptor before discharging into the sanitary or storm drainage system.

The sand interceptor holds sand and grit in the sediment section, as shown in Figure 7-16. The waste water containing volatile substances passes on into the oil interceptor. At this point the volatile liquids are separated from the waste water

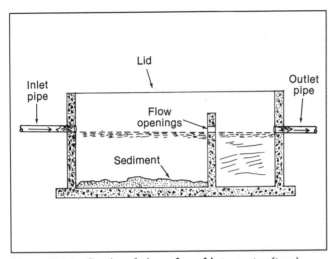

Figure 7-16   Sectional view of sand interceptor (trap)

Single-story garages— When floor drainage is required for a single-story parking garage, you can usually use a system like the one in Figure 7-15. The interceptor is small enough to intercept and retain small amounts of volatile liquids, yet large enough to trap sand and grit before it reaches the building's drainage system.

Multi-story parking garages— The critical parking problems in many of our congested cities have created a need for multi-story garages. Figure 7-17 presents a more complex design for floor drainage in a multi-story parking garage using a separate sand interceptor.

Footing drainage systems— Occasionally a building is approved for a site where surface water accumulation during heavy rains could weaken the foundation wall and the footing supports. The structural engineer may request a sub-soil drainage system. That's the responsibility of the plumbing designer.

and retained in the oil interceptor or waste oil storage tank. The waste water, now free of sand, grit and volatile liquids, may discharge safely into the building's drainage system.

Your local building department will decide if the system you're designing constitutes a *small* or *large* volatile liquid concentration. Use Figure 7-12 as a guide for a small concentration, Figure 7-14 for a large concentration.

A footing drain is shown in Figure 7-18. It's designed to intercept the surface water before it reaches the building's foundation wall or footings. The drainage line in the illustration is shown near, but slightly above, the bottom of the footing. The pipe is laid on a firm bed of crushed rock for

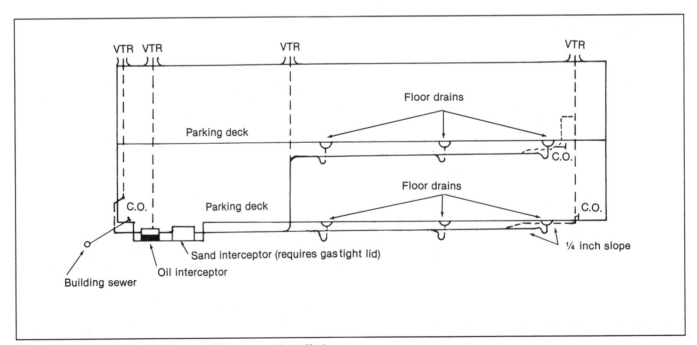

Figure 7-17   Typical multi-story parking garage installation

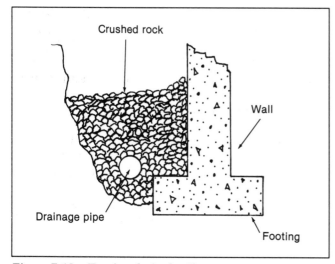

Figure 7-18 Footing drain detail

perforated for seepage. Such piping is generally available in 4-inch diameter and in lengths of 2 or 3 feet. Use bituminous saturated paper or other approved materials at the openings to prevent sand from entering. Since water always follows the least restricted path, it will flow through the sub-soil drainage system to the point of discharge. Most codes will require the drainage pipe to have a slope (grade) of no less than 1/4 inch per foot.

The accumulated rainwater must pass through an adequately-sized sand interceptor before discharging, preferably into the building storm water drainage system. Even then, small amounts of sand will probably get through. So most codes require adequate cleanouts for rodding in a system like this. Figure 7-19 shows footing drains and a sand interceptor with the required cleanouts.

support. Crushed rock around and above the pipe facilitates easy drainage.

The piping itself is usually of clay or concrete. It may be open-jointed, horizontally split or

Drainage wells— Many of our growing cities have such a space problem that new buildings cover their entire lot. If there are no storm sewers and a combined building sewer isn't ac-

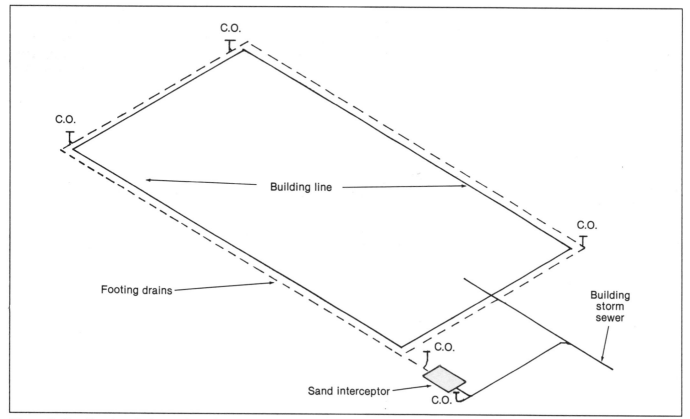

Figure 7-19 Footing drains and sand interceptor

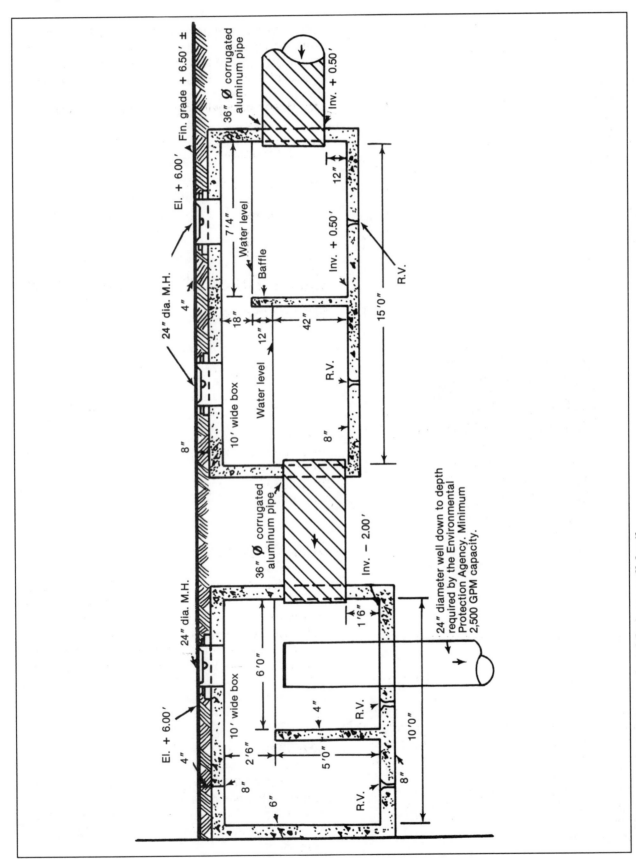

Figure 7-20   Settling tank and drainage well detail

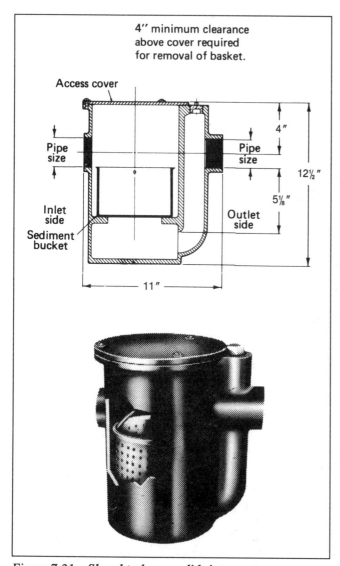

Figure 7-21   Slaughterhouse solids interceptor

Other sand interceptor requirements— Sand interceptors are usually required in any drainage line leading from an area subject to unacceptable levels of sand. Some of these are:

♦ Beach bars with plumbing area drains.

♦ Beach cabanas with showers connected to the plumbing system.

♦ Swimming pools located on or near beaches with showers and area drains connected to a plumbing system.

Other Types of Interceptors or Separators

Bottling Plants

Bottling plants have a unique need for interceptors. Before liquid wastes can discharge into the drainage system, they must filter through an interceptor to separate out broken glass or other solids. You can use a properly-sized sand interceptor to do it. The interceptor shown in Figure 7-16 would do the job.

Slaughterhouses

The code requires interceptors or separators for all drains in slaughtering rooms and dressing rooms. Obviously, all feathers, scales, entrails and other unacceptable materials must be excluded from the building drainage system. One acceptable solids interceptor is shown in Figure 7-21. Note the removable perforated sediment bucket for easy cleaning.

Hair Interceptors

Figure 7-22 shows a hair interceptor with a removable screen basket. The code may require an interceptor like this for barber shop sinks, beauty salon sinks and fixtures used for bathing animals.

ceptable, then rainwater disposal becomes a serious problem.

The solution to the problem is a storm drainage system that collects rainwater from the roof, parking decks and any other floor drains in the system. Your building department might allow the disposal of the storm water through a drainage well. The system would have to discharge into a settling tank to filter out objectionable wastes (sand, leaves, oil and grease drippings) before the waste water could enter the drainage well. Figure 7-20 shows a design that's usually acceptable when you can't design a conventional system.

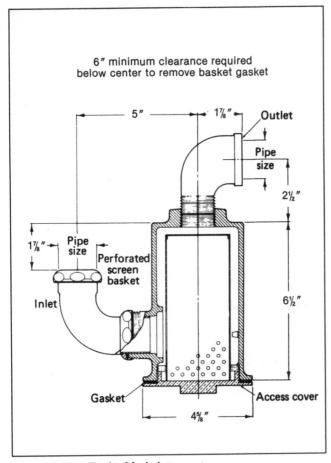

Figure 7-22 **Typical hair interceptor**

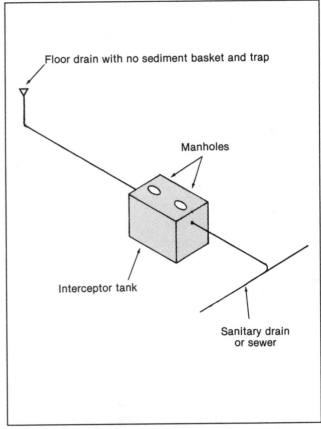

Figure 7-23 **Interceptor tank and component piping arrangements for animal boarding establishments**

Animal Boarding Businesses

Where animals are confined (dog kennels and zoos), most codes mandate the special handling of waste before discharging to a legal point of disposal, whether private or public.

The wash-down drain for such a system has a perforated or slotted grate but no sediment basket. The floor drain isn't equipped with a trap. The drainage pipe empties into an interceptor tank. The design may be similar to a septic tank.

This tank separates the solids, retains them, and allows the liquid wastes to pass on to a legal point of disposal. The bacterial process that is so effective in digesting human waste isn't very effective with animal waste. That means animal solids have to be removed more frequently. Provide adequate manholes at grade when designing such a tank. See Figure 7-23.

As always, your local authority can give you the criteria for an acceptable system.

Transformer Oil Spill Holding Tank

Transformer vault rooms within a building must have floor drainage. As a rule, a 3-inch floor drain is installed at floor level. There's no sediment basket or trap. The drain pipe which connects to an oil spill holding tank is accepted as an indirect waste pipe not requiring a vent. The oil spill holding tank must have a pumpout connection at grade. The local power company is your authority on sizing the tank, which must be able to hold the amount of oil contained in the transformers if a rupture occurs. Figure 7-24 gives a detailed design for a typical transformer oil spill holding tank and piping.

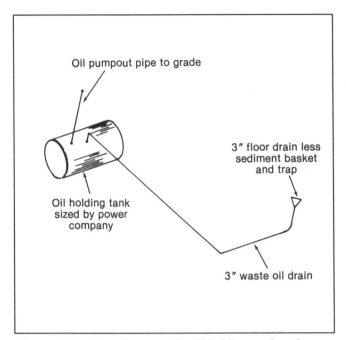

Figure 7-24   Transformer oil spill holding tank and piping detail

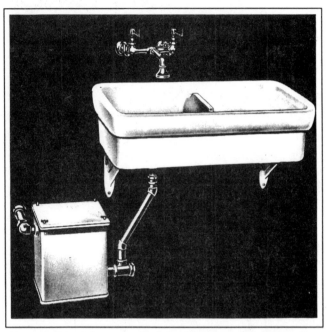

Figure 7-25   Plaster work sink with integral right hand tray

Plaster Work Sink

Installation of an interceptor trap is mandatory for dental and orthopedic sinks where plaster, wax or other objectionable substances may be discharged into the building drainage system. Figure 7-25 illustrates a typical installation.

Neutralizing Tanks

Corrosive Wastes

Corrosive liquids, spent acids and other chemicals might damage or destroy a DWV drainage system or create noxious or toxic fumes. They can't discharge into a building drainage system until they've been diluted, neutralized or treated. That means the waste must be discharged through a separate and independent system. It must pass through a properly-designed dilution or neutralizing tank. The tank must automatically provide enough water to dilute the corrosive liquids until they're not damaging to the drainage system.

Before you complete your design, get approval from the building department. They'll want to know the type of corrosive waste generated and your method for treating it. Figure 7-26 illustrates one type of special treatment neutralizing tank.

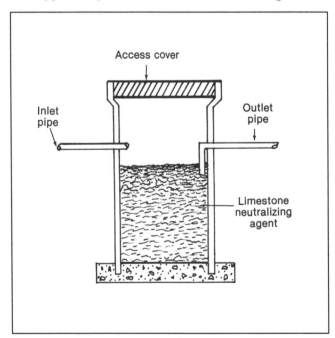

Figure 7-26   Typical neutralizing tank

Also, see Figures 5-3 and page 163 in the Glossary for installation details.

Excessively Hot Wastes

The code prohibits the direct discharge of excessively hot wastes into the sanitary drainage system. High pressure steam exhaust, boiler blow-off or similar drip pipes should be cooled to a reasonable temperature before discharging into the drainage piping.

High temperature wastes can promote expansion and contraction of drainage piping. This could disturb or even destroy the pipe joints. When designing a system with a boiler blowoff tank for cooling purposes (Glossary, page 167), try to connect the floor drain branch drain to the drainage piping that carries a good flow of waste water. The mixing of the two could prevent drainage system damage if the cooling process fails.

Chapter 8

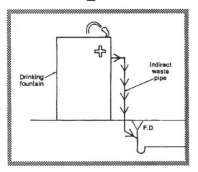

Indirect Waste Piping and Special Wastes

Every commercial building generates what the code defines as *special wastes* — including oil, sand, grease, glass and storm water. These wastes must connect indirectly, rather than directly, to the drainage system. Some of them, like dental units, cuspidors, drinking fountains and clothes washers, may connect to the drainage system by indirect means. But some special wastes, like rainwater, can't discharge into the drainage system at all. You'll have to dispose of them through other approved methods, like dry wells or soakage pits.

Indirect Waste Pipes

In this chapter we'll look at the requirements for indirect waste pipes, including their materials, sizing, venting, location and cleanouts. Then we'll cover the appliances and equipment that require indirect drainage. Many of them have drips or drainage outlets.

Indirect Waste Piping Materials

You can only use indirect waste piping made of approved, durable materials. Specify materials approved for drainage and vent pipes installed underground or above ground. Chapter 3 lists approved materials. And the fittings you use must be compatible with and have the same diameter as the pipes. On screw pipe, specify fittings that are recessed and tapped to allow a fall of 1/4 inch per foot.

Sizing Indirect Waste Piping

Businesses that store, prepare, sell or serve food need indirect waste pipes. The fixture unit equivalents back in Chapter 4, Figure 4-7, are based on the required trap size. But most of your work with indirect waste pipes will involve *unit equivalent of fixtures and devices*, which don't appear in Figure 4-7. For anything that's not included in Figure 4-7, use the rated discharge capacity in GPM. That's in Figure 4-8, based on the size of the drips or drainage outlets.

Refrigerator coils, walk-in freezers, ice boxes, ice-making machines and bar sinks need indirect waste pipes. So do extractors, steam tables, egg boilers, coffee urns, water stations and any enclosed equipment or sinks used for soaking or washing ready-to-serve food.

Use Figure 4-9 in Chapter 4 to find the waste discharge from evaporative coolers, air washers and air handling equipment. These are classified as *continuous flow* wastes. For sizing purposes, allow two fixture units for each GPM of flow. You can get the flow rates from the equipment manufacturers, then size the drainage pipe by using Figure 4-6.

The drainage inlet and the waste of certain hospital equipment must connect indirectly to the sanitary drainage system. That includes stills, sterilizers and similar equipment. Use Figure 4-6 to size this waste piping.

Any arrangement that results in clear water overflow and relief pipes on the water supply system must connect indirectly to the building drainage system. Water lifts, expansion tanks, cooling jackets, sprinkler systems and drip or overflow pans fall into this category. Size the waste pipe per outlet, using Figure 4-6.

Above-floor indirect waste pipe must be at least 3/4 inch in diameter but not smaller than the outlet drains of the fixtures or appliances it serves. The diameter of below-the-floor indirect waste piping must be at least 1-1/4 inches.

When you design indirect waste piping for *special fixtures* rated at more than one fixture unit, size it according to Figure 4-6.

Venting Indirect Waste Pipe

You'll usually have to directly trap indirect waste pipe that's between 5 and 15 feet long, but you don't need to vent the traps. Some codes don't require trapping or venting on indirect waste pipes of any length, as long as they're properly graded to drain dry.

Cleanout Requirements

Indirect waste pipes usually carry waste materials that don't have offensive odors to the receiving fixture (floor sink or floor drain). Because the liquid moves slowly in the pipe, slime deposits can build up in low places and eventually cause stoppages. It's important to support indirect waste pipes to eliminate sags or low spots. That lets gravity do its job. Placing all receiving fixtures in well-ventilated areas also reduces the likelihood of slime buildup. Provide accessible cleanouts for cleaning and flushing the pipe.

Indirect Waste Receptor Location and Designs

Place receiving fixtures in accessible locations for inspection and cleaning. Make sure workers can get to them without moving or disconnecting equipment or heavy objects. Don't put them in a bathroom, closet, cupboard or storeroom.

Indirect waste pipes must discharge into receptors that are shaped and sized to prevent splashing and flooding. And you'll have to get approval for the particular use you propose.

Indirect Waste Connections

Design all indirect waste connections so they won't contaminate the special fixtures or appliances in case there's a stoppage in the building drainage system.

The code requires all indirect waste piping to discharge into the building sanitary or storm drainage system, soakage pits or dry wells. You

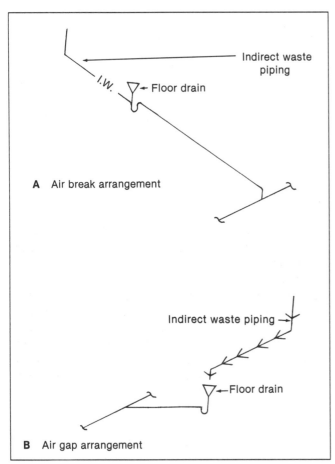

Figure 8-1   Two methods of showing indirect waste piping

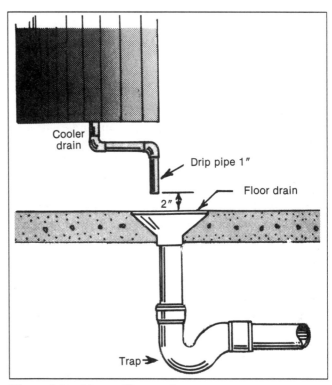

Figure 8-2   Air gap illustrated

can use either an air gap or air break as the indirect waste connection. Each type is appropriate for certain conditions.

Whichever one you use, show it clearly on your drawings. Then identify the indirect waste pipes by one of the methods shown in Figure 8-1. That will help the plans examiner and the installer pick out the indirect waste pipes quickly.

Air Gap Drainage

The air gap is the unobstructed vertical distance between the waste pipe outlet and the flood level rim of the receptacle. Figures 8-2 through 8-8 show air gaps for several installations, including air conditioners, dishwashers and sinks.

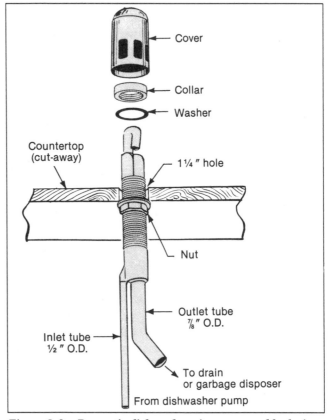

Figure 8-3   Domestic dishwasher air gap assembly device

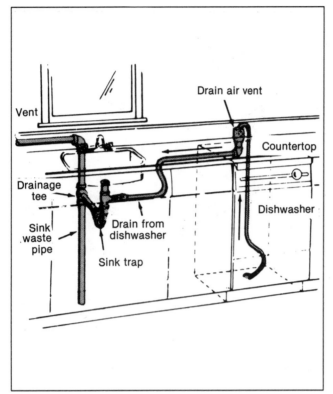

Figure 8-4 **Domestic dishwasher illustrated with air gap device properly illustrated**

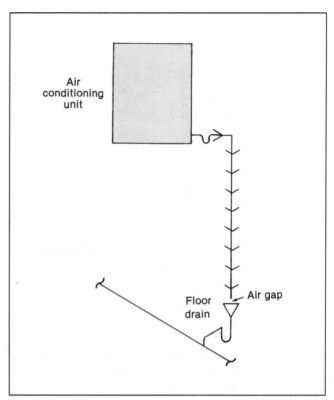

Figure 8-5 **Air gap illustrated**

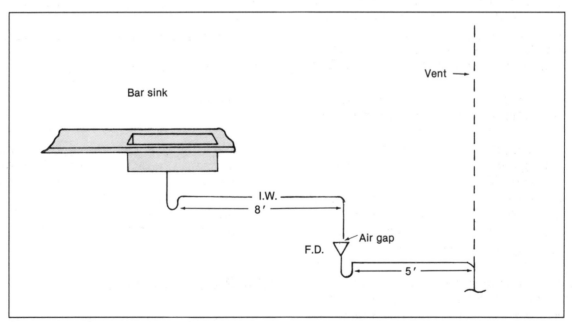

Figure 8-6 **Air gap arrangement for bar or hand sinks and soda fountains**

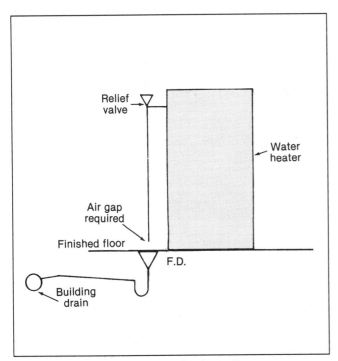

Figure 8-7 Water heater relief valve indirect waste discharge through air gap

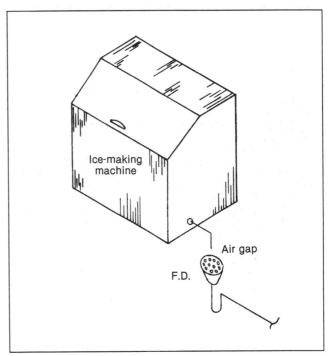

Figure 8-8 Air gap for ice-making machine

Figure 8-6 shows an air gap arrangement for bar or hand sinks and soda fountains. When you can't vent their traps because of their location, make sure their drains discharge through an air gap or air break to a vented floor drain or floor sink.

In Figure 8-7, a water heater has an indirect waste discharge through an air gap. That protects against backflow contamination of the potable water supply. The ice maker in Figure 8-8 is protected against contamination if there's a stoppage in the building drainage system.

As a rule, you'll have to design the indirect waste piping with an air gap above the finished floor. Here are the code restrictions on the above-floor installed pipes and receptacles:

♦ Indirect waste pipe doesn't have to be larger in diameter than the drain outlet or tailpiece it serves, but it can't be smaller than 1/2 inch.

♦ Each change of direction in indirect waste pipe must have a cleanout.

♦ Codes usually require you to locate indirect waste pipe at least 3 inches above the finished floor to allow for floor cleaning.

♦ Locate the receptor as near as possible to the fixture, appliance or equipment it serves.

♦ The end of the indirect waste pipe must be above the flood level rim of the receptor by at least *twice* the diameter of the drain it serves. For example, a 1-inch indirect waste pipe must have an air gap of 2 inches above the receiving fixture. Figure 8-2 shows the required separation.

Air Break Drainage

An air break is a physical separation, usually a low inlet into the indirect waste receptor.

There are two acceptable types of air break drainage systems. The one that connects to the drainage system beneath the floor is the most

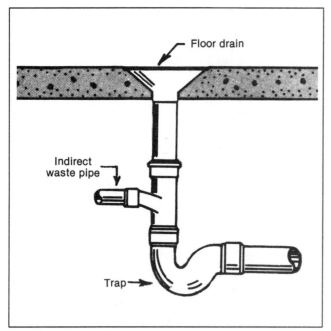

Figure 8-9   Air break waste pipe connection beneath floor

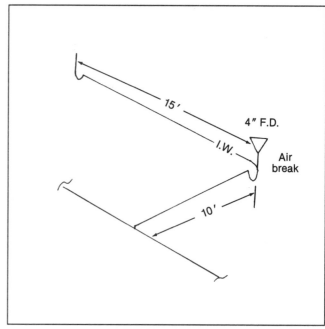

Figure 8-10   Air break waste pipe arrangement for isolated fixture

common. It's shown in Figure 8-9. It's a practical method that takes less labor and materials than above-floor installations.

Beneath-floor installations also make it easier to reach remote fixtures without venting. For example, the receptor of a 4-inch floor drain may extend up to 10 feet from its vent or a vented building drain. And the indirect waste pipe may extend another 15 feet (provided it's trapped) without venting. So you can serve an isolated fixture with indirect waste pipe up to 25 feet developed length without an individual vent. See Figure 8-10.

The second, and less common, air break system connects to the drainage system above the finished floor. The end of the indirect waste pipe can terminate below the overflow rim of the receiving fixture. Look at page 164 in the Glossary. For a system like this, get the building department to approve how far the indirect waste pipe outlet extends below the flood level rim of the receptacle.

When floor drains are required for cleaning walk-in refrigerators or food storeroom floors, here are the code requirements:

- ◆ The cooler floor must be at least 2 inches above the overflow rim of the receptacle.

- ◆ The cooler drain pipe must connect to the drainage system with an air break.

- ◆ The drain pipe must be at least 2 inches in diameter.

- ◆ The cooler floor must be protected from reverse flow by an accessible check valve. Figure 8-11 shows the arrangement.

The code accepts a drip pipe from a walk-in refrigerator or a cooler room refrigerator coil with either an air gap or an air break. A flap check valve isn't required in this case. See Figure 8-12.

Drinking Fountains

The code classifies the waste discharge from a drinking fountain as a *low rate flow*. Fountains have one fixture unit in most codes, 1/2 fixture unit in others. Their wastes contain little or no organic matter. If there are no partitions to conceal the waste and vent pipe, you can dis-

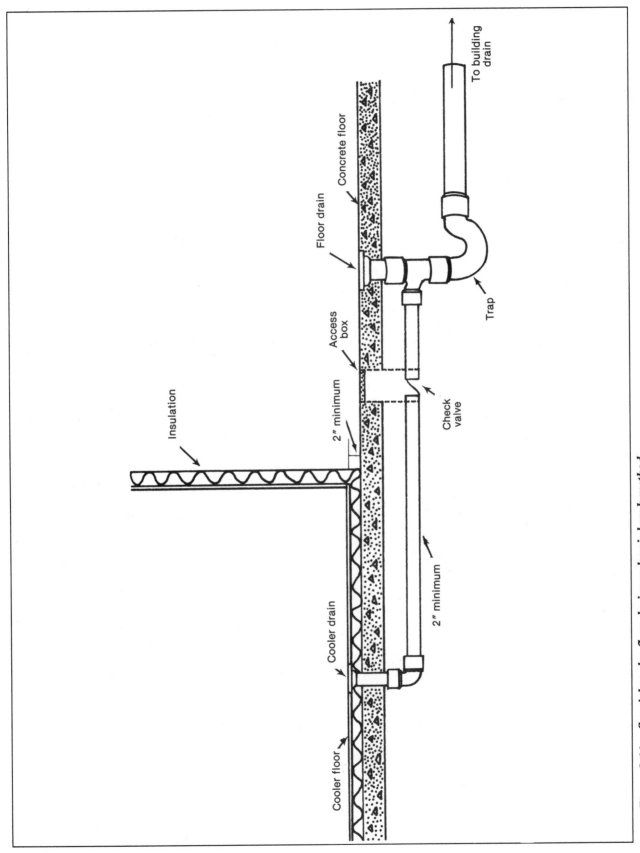

Figure 8-11 Special cooler floor drainage by air break method

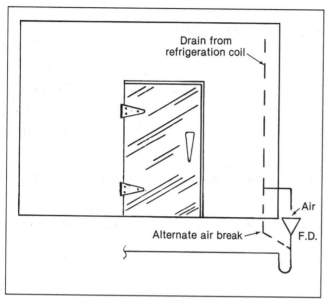

Figure 8-12   Air gap and air break connection for walk-in refrigerator

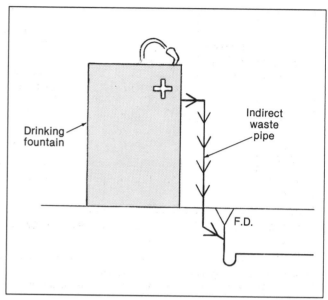

Figure 8-13   Air break connection for drinking fountain

charge their wastes indirectly into the building sanitary drainage system. The air break connection is more common, however. Figure 8-13 shows an air break installation.

Other Types of Special Waste

Swimming Pool Wastes

Commercial swimming pools, wading pools and spas have special objectionable wastes. That's because ordinary public sewer systems and treatment plants simply can't handle huge amounts of waste suddenly discharged into the system. The health department is also concerned about possible health problems caused by treating the wastes.

With advance approval, you can use any of these methods to dispose of backwash water and to empty the pool:

♦ An indirect connection to the building sanitary or storm water system.

♦ A disposal well.

♦ An open waterway, bay or ocean.

♦ A sprinkler system used for irrigation purposes.

♦ A soakage pit or drainfield designed for this purpose. See Figure 8-14 for specific design criteria.

Local authorities will usually permit *private* pool wastes to be puddled on private property. When it's allowed, these conditions apply:

♦ The disposal area must be big enough and graded to retain the waste water within the confines of the property.

♦ The percolation rate of the disposal area must not permit standing water to remain more than one hour after discharge.

♦ The disposal area must be a minimum of 50 feet from any water supply well.

The authorities will never accept the discharge of pool wastes into a sanitary drainage system connected to a septic tank. It could hurt both the septic tank and the subsoil leach field. Sudden flooding can create a reverse flow of wastes into the building drainage pipes. And the

Pool capacity (gallons)	Diameter S & G filter	Soil percolation rates (minutes/inch)											
		1		2		3		4		5		6	
		Sq. ft.	Gallons	Sq. ft.	Gallons	Sq. ft.	Gallons	Sq. ft.	Gallons	Sq. ft.	Gallons	Sq. ft.	Gallons
17,000	24"	53.5	2,000	96	3,590	130	4,860	158	5,910	182	6,800	202	7,560
17,000 to 26,000	30"	83	3,100	149	5,560	200	7,550	247	9,240	280	10,500	315	11,780
26,000 to 38,000	36"	120	4,490	215	8,050	292	10,910	358	13,400	408	15,290	452	16,900
38,000 to 52,000	42"	163	6,100	293	10,970	400	14,980	485	18,150	555	20,800	618	23,100

Note: Effective depth of soakage pits is 5'0".
Square feet refers to the area of the bottom of the pit.

*Figure 8-14 **Minimum area and volume of soakage pits for swimming pools***

chlorine in the pool water can destroy the bacterial process that makes the septic tank function.

Air Conditioning Condensate Drains

Air conditioning units also generate special waste. Check your local code for specifics, but most codes require these waste disposal methods:

♦ When air conditioning units are located on the roof, the waste may discharge onto the roof and into the roof drain. This is permissible only if the leader pipe discharges into a storm sewer, soakage pit or adequately-sized pervious area. You can't do it if the leader pipe discharges onto any paved or non-pervious area where wastes can become a health hazard or nuisance.

♦ When an air conditioning unit is centrally located below the roof of a building, it may indirectly connect to a rain leader pipe. Figure 8-15 shows a method that's accepted by most codes. But you can't use this method on a sanitary drainage, waste or vent system.

♦ Drainage from an air handling equipment room must be by indirect means. Always place the receptor outside of the equipment room. Look at Figure 8-16.

♦ The main condensate drain line in a multi-story building may receive the discharge from many air conditioning units. Each individual unit must be

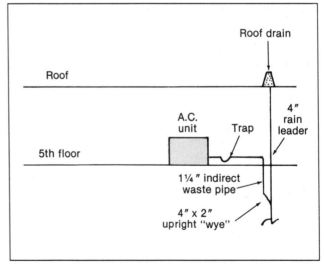

*Figure 8-15 **Indirect waste connection to inside rain leader***

107

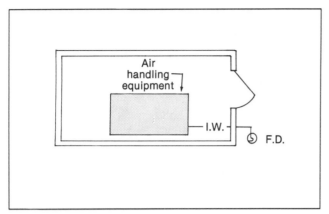

Figure 8-16   Indirect waste pipe connected to floor drain located outside of room

trapped. Some codes require a vent in the main drain line above the highest connection. The vent may extend up and through the roof independently or you can equip it with a perforated cap 2 feet above the highest connection. The condensate drain may discharge indirectly into the building sanitary drainage system or into a dry well. Figure 8-17 shows a typical connection.

♦ When air conditioning waste discharges into the drainage system, include this waste in sizing the building drainage system. The code says each gallon of flow per minute equals 2 fixture units, or 15 gallons.

♦ Find the total fixture units for the vertical and horizontal condensate drain pipes. Then use Figure 4-6 (back in Chapter 4) to size these drain pipes. Here's a restriction: Never use the condensate waste from an air conditioning unit to reseal the trap of any floor drain.

Other disposal methods— In some areas local authorities may approve these alternate methods of waste disposal.

♦ Air conditioning units up to 5-ton capacity may discharge their waste on a pervious area such as bare soil.

♦ Air conditioning units up to 10-ton capacity may discharge their waste into a buried pipe 10 inches in diameter and 24 inches long filled with crushed rock. No cover is required.

♦ The main condensate drain line from a unit or combined units exceeding 10 tons must discharge indirectly into the building sanitary or storm drainage system, or into a drainage well, soakage pit or drainfield.

Storm Drainage Systems

The storm drainage system carries rainwater to a legal disposal point. It includes roof drains, area drains, catch basins, gutters, leaders, building storm drains, building storm sewers and ground surface storm sewers.

Rainwater that's not properly collected can be a nuisance — even a health hazard. Storm

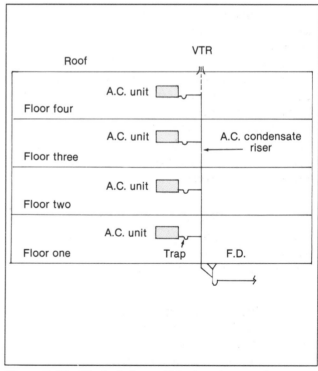

Figure 8-17   Typical air conditioning riser condensate drain connected to building drain by air break method

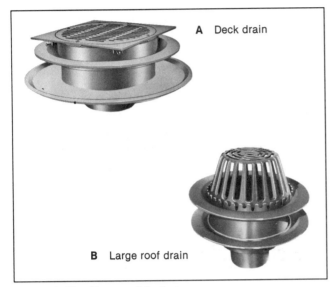

Figure 8-18   Two roof drain types

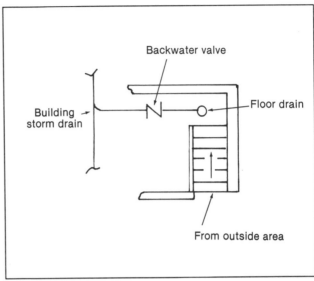

Figure 8-19   Areaway drain connection to storm drain

water from paved parking lots and large residential and commercial buildings can collect into stagnant pools of water. That's an ideal breeding ground for mosquitoes and offensive odors.

The codes recognize the importance of collecting and disposing of storm water from commercial properties. Many older cities near lakes, rivers or the ocean have used a combined sewer system to carry both storm water and partially treated or untreated sewage. They usually ended in outfall lines that dumped the waste into the water at a considerable distance from the city. But the situation is improving. Most such cities are trying to correct these environmental assaults by establishing stricter controls.

You'll probably need advance approval to tie any new construction into one of these old dual systems. Most local codes now require separate sewage and storm water collection systems.

Specify only approved durable materials for storm drainage systems. There are several approved materials available. *Except for rainwater pipes on the exterior of a building*, you can use the same materials, installation, protection and supports that are approved for sanitary drainage, waste vent systems. Refer back to Chapter 4.

Strainers

You must provide a strainer where roof surfaces drain into the inlet pipe of an inside leader. The strainer cover must extend at least 4 inches above the roof surface. The strainer itself must have an available inlet that's at least 1-1/2 times the area of the leader the drain connects to. (It's 2-1/2 in some codes.)

On sun decks, parking decks and other public areas, use flat deck drain strainers. They can be flat because their public exposure means they're more likely to be serviced and maintained. The available inlet area has to be at least 2 times the area of the leader to which the drain is connected. (Some codes require 2-1/2 times.) Figure 8-18 shows both types of roof drains.

Roof Drains and Special Drains

Roof drains must be made of cast iron, copper, lead, or some other approved *corrosion-resistant* material.

There are times when special drains are required to convey liquid wastes to a legal point of disposal. An *areaway drain*, placed at the foot of a stairwell, is shown in Figure 8-19. A *window well drain* (required where there's a flat surface be-

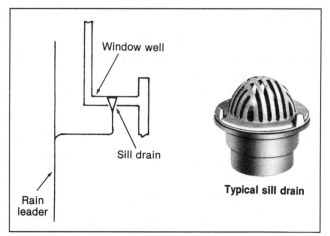

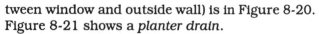

Figure 8-20   Sill drain connection to rain leader

Figure 8-21   Typical planter drain

tween window and outside wall) is in Figure 8-20. Figure 8-21 shows a *planter drain*.

Most codes require that these wastes discharge to the building storm drain, street gutter or curb. But where that's impractical, they'll almost always accept a properly-graded open area, an adequate soakage pit, a dry well or a drainfield designed for this purpose.

You must provide a backwater valve for any special drain connected to the building storm drain that's subject to backflow during heavy rains. Locate the valve where it's accessible for inspection and maintenance. Look at Figure 8-19 and page 166 in the Glossary.

Any floor drain that collects special liquid waste and connects to a storm drain should have a trap. Since these drains are subject to evaporation, some codes require them to have a minimum 5-inch water seal with a diameter of at least 2 inches.

Traps are *not* required for regular storm water drains connected to a storm drainage system.

You can't use leader pipes as soil, waste or vent pipes — or use soil, waste and vent pipes as leaders. Each must be independent of the other.

Rainwater drains that carry runoff from leaders discharging directly into soakage pits (not through a catch basin) must have overflow fittings. Extend the fittings at the base of rainwater drains to the exterior to avoid flooding the building. The overflow fitting must be the same size as the leader, up to 4 inches. See Figure 8-22.

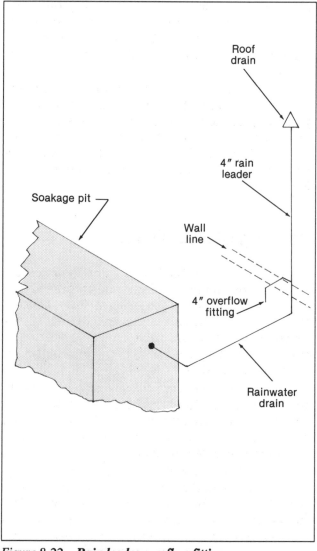

Figure 8-22   Rain leader overflow fitting

Sizing Storm Water Drainage Systems

Designing a storm drainage system might seem simple — but it actually takes considerable expertise to produce the best, most economical design. Let's take a look at some of the variables involved.

Rainfall intensity— The amount and rate of rainfall expected in the area is the most important factor. You can usually get precipitation data from your local code books or from the U.S. Department of Agriculture or Department of Commerce, Weather Bureau. I've included a sample table at the end of this chapter.

Your code requirements will reflect the maximum anticipated rainfall in any one hour. Rainfall can vary from less than 2 inches in one region to as much as 8 inches in another. Naturally, the greater the rainfall, the larger the pipe required.

When you've found the maximum anticipated rainfall and the square feet of roof surface, you can calculate the diameter of the storm water pipe from the tables in the code. I'm using tables from the Uniform Plumbing Code for my examples. Of course, you'll use the comparable tables in your local code.

Spacing of Roof Drains

Every code book has rainfall tables that indicate the diameter of vertical leaders (Figure 8-23) and horizontal piping (Figure 8-24) based on the roof area. But as the designer, you'll have to decide how many and what type of roof drains to use. Let's consider some general information on spacing roof drains.

Codes encourage the spacing of roof drains to eliminate puddling on the roof surface after a rainfall. Here's the statement from one code: *In no case shall the surface in the vicinity of the drain be recessed to create a reservoir.*

Although you'll be designing drainage systems for roofs that are relatively flat, their surface will always be somewhat uneven. Every roof will hold a little rainwater until it evaporates. It's your job to reduce it to a minimum. Here are a couple of general guidelines to consider. First, the more

Rainfall in inches	Size of drain or leader in inches					
	2	**3**	**4**	**5**	**6**	**8**
1	2880	8800	18400	34600	54000	116000
2	1440	4400	9200	17300	27000	58000
3	960	2930	6130	11530	17995	38660
4	720	2200	4600	8650	13500	29000
5	575	1760	3680	6920	10800	23200
6	480	1470	3070	5765	9000	19315
7	410	1260	2630	4945	7715	16570
8	360	1100	2300	4325	6750	14500
9	320	980	2045	3845	6000	12890
10	290	880	1840	3460	5400	11600
11	260	800	1675	3145	4910	10545
12	240	730	1530	2880	4500	9660

Table 9-2
Sizing of roof drains and rainwater piping for varying rainfall quantities are horizontal projected roof areas in square feet

From the Uniform Plumbing Code, © 1988, IAPMO

Figure 8-23   Sizing roof drains and rainwater piping

roof drains you use, the fewer puddles you'll have. Second, smaller roof drains and leader pipes are less expensive.

To begin your calculation, find the total square feet to be drained. Start with the area of the roof and add any vertical walls that permit storm water to drain onto the roof area. But review the vertical wall section of your code carefully. Depending on your location, you'll add from about 30 to 50 percent of the vertical wall area to the roof area. When you have to add vertical wall areas to the flat surfaces, it can dramatically increase the size of leaders and horizontal pipes.

Figure 8-25 suggests one way to arrange roof drains and size the storm water pipes for a typical roof with a vertical wall. You can follow this

Table 9-3					
Size of pipe in inches 1/8" slope	Maximum rainfall in inches per hour				
	2	3	4	5	6
3	1644	1096	822	657	548
4	3760	2506	1880	1504	1253
5	6680	4453	3340	2672	2227
6	10700	7133	5350	4280	3566
8	23000	15330	11500	9200	7600
10	41400	27600	20700	16580	13800
12	66600	44400	33300	26650	22200
15	109000	72800	59500	47600	39650
Size of pipe in inches 1/4" slope	Maximum rainfall in inches per hour				
	2	3	4	5	6
3	2320	1546	1160	928	773
4	5300	3533	2650	2120	1766
5	9440	6293	4720	3776	3146
6	15100	10066	7550	6040	5033
8	32600	21733	16300	13040	10866
10	58400	38950	29200	23350	19450
12	94000	62600	47000	37600	31350
15	168000	112000	84000	67250	56000
Size of pipe in inches 1/2" slope	Maximum rainfall in inches per hour				
	2	3	4	5	6
3	3288	2295	1644	1310	1096
4	7520	5010	3760	3010	2500
5	13360	8900	6680	5320	4450
6	21400	13700	10700	8580	7140
8	46000	30650	23000	18400	15320
10	82800	55200	41400	33150	27600
12	133200	88800	66600	53200	44400
15	238000	158800	119000	95300	79250

Figure 8-24 Sizing horizontal rainwater piping

example for draining any type or size roof. The main roof is 5,000 square feet with an attached 900-square foot vertical wall. Assume the code in this area calls for adding half of the vertical wall surface. So we'll add 450 SF to 5,000 SF for a total surface to be drained of 5,450 SF. Since it requires two leaders, each will drain 2,725 SF of area.

Use Figure 8-23 to size the rain leaders. The first column shows the rainfall in inches. Columns 2 through 8 show the maximum area in square feet that a certain pipe size can drain. The number at the top of each column is the pipe size in inches.

Assume the roof is in Los Angeles, a city with a maximum anticipated rainfall of 3.6 inches. You'll use the 4-inch line in the table. I've shaded that line so you can follow along easily. As you move from left to right on the shaded line, you see 720 and 2,200. Since we have 2,725 square feet to drain, those are both too small. We'll have to move to the next column, and use a leader large enough to drain 4,600 square feet. That's a 4-inch vertical leader pipe.

Now use Figure 8-24 for the horizontal rainwater pipes. The table is divided into three sections, for slopes of 1/8 inch, 1/4 inch and 1/2 inch. The greater the slope, the larger the area that can be drained by each pipe size. The left column shows the slope and the pipe size in inches. The other columns show the maximum area that can be drained by that size pipe during a rainfall of 2 to 6 inches per hour.

In Figure 8-25, the slope is 1/8 inch per foot, so we'll use the top section of the table. Note that the horizontal pipe in the drawing is divided into two sections, A and B. Section A carries the flow from only one leader, or 2,725 SF. Section B carries the flow for both leaders, or 5,450 SF. At 4 inches of maximum rainfall, you can specify a 5-inch pipe for Section A and an 8-inch pipe for Section B.

Combined Drainage Systems

I mentioned earlier that codes usually prohibit connecting a building storm drain with a building sanitary system. But some codes still include the criteria for that connection. Although

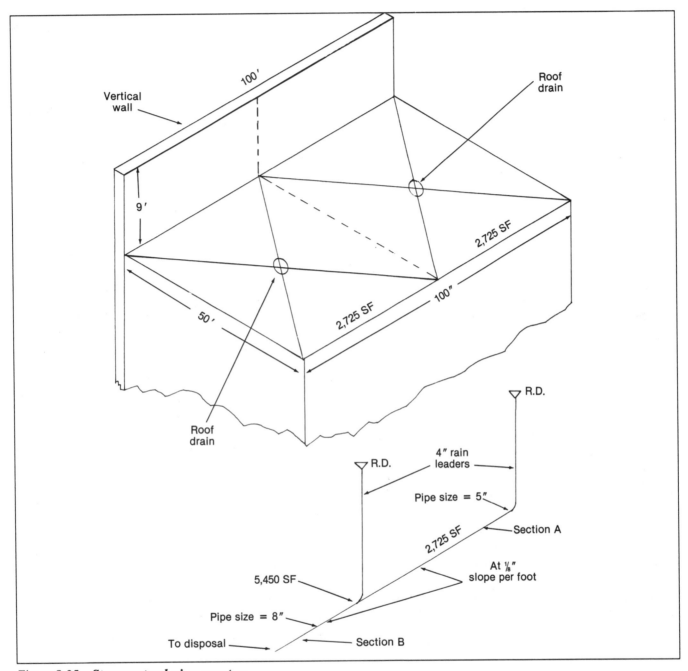

Figure 8-25 Storm water drainage system

you should know these requirements, remember that you always need prior approval for a combined system.

Leaders and storm drains that connect to the building sanitary drainage pipes must prevent the escape of sewer gases and objectionable odors. There are two ways to do this. First, you can provide a trap for the horizontal branch drain serving each leader before it connects to the building sanitary drain. Figure 8-26 shows the arrangement. Second, for a separate storm water collection system, provide a trap on the main storm drain before connecting to the sanitary drain. See Figure 8-27.

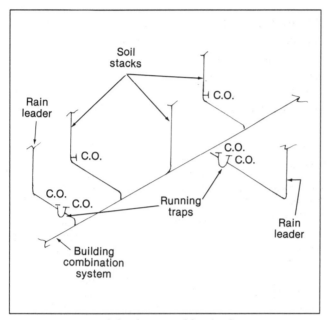

Figure 8-26 Each leader served by single trap

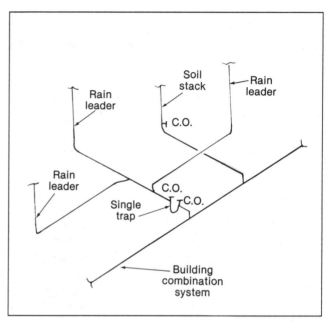

Figure 8-27 Single trap installed in main storm drain

Here's the rule: Each floor drain, area drain, or parking deck drain that connects to a combined system must be individually trapped. This is in addition to the main trap required for horizontal branch drains or main storm water drains we discussed earlier.

The required trap is always the same size as the pipe it serves. Running or house traps serving horizontal storm drains must have accessible cleanouts.

To avoid flow interference when combining the two systems, connect the storm drain in the same horizontal plane through a single wye fitting to the combined drain or sewer. Make the connection at least 10 feet downstream from any soil stack. You can't use a double wye fitting. See page 169 in the Glossary.

Sizing Combined System Building Drains

You need a formula for sizing the sanitary drain when storm building drains connect to sanitary building drains. Generally speaking, the flow in the storm building drains during maximum rainfall periods far exceeds the flow in the sanitary

building drains at peak load. So you have to size the combined building drain based on the storm drain pipe sizes listed in Figure 8-24. Then convert the sanitary drainage fixture unit load into the equivalent square feet of drained area.

Most codes accept this method for converting the fixture load units using a maximum rainfall rate of 4 inches per hour. For a total sanitary fixture load of less than 256 fixture units, use an equivalent drainage area of 1,000 square feet. If the fixture load exceeds 256 fixture units, add 3.9 square feet of drained area for each additional fixture unit.

To determine the load on the combined system, add the total equivalent drained area, based on the fixture units, to the actual drained area. Then just select the appropriate size of combined drain from Figure 8-24.

Let's work out an example. Assume 4 inches of rainfall per hour, and a building with 300 fixture units and 20,000 square feet of roof area. The pipe has a 1/8-inch slope. First, total the equivalent square feet.

20,000 SF + 1,000 SF + 171.6 SF = 21,171.6 SF to drain

Here's how we did it:

Original drainage area + SF equivalent of 256 F.U. + SF equivalent of the F.U. balance (44 x 3.9) = area to drain.

Now look at Figure 8-24. For 4 inches of rainfall, you need a 12-inch pipe. A 10-inch pipe can carry the drainage for only 20,700 square feet.

Figure 8-28 is the typical maximum rainfall table I promised you earlier in this chapter.

But what if there's more or less than 4 inches of rainfall? You can adjust the figures in the 2-inch rainfall column in Figure 8-24. Multiply the figure by 2, then divide by the maximum rate

Alabama:	Pensacola 9.4	**Louisiana:**	**Nebraska:**	Columbus 6.1	Del Rio 7.6
Anniston 7.2	Sand Key 6.6	New Orleans . 8.2	Lincoln 6.6	Dayton 6.0	El Paso 4.2
Birmingham . . .7.0	Tampa 8.4	Shreveport . . . 7.5	North Platte . . .6.0	Sandusky 6.2	Fort Worth . . . 6.6
Mobile 8.4	**Georgia:**	**Maine:**	Omaha 7.0	Toledo 6.0	Galveston 8.2
Montgomery . .7.0	Atlanta 7.7	Eastport 4.7	Valentine 6.3	**Oklahoma:**	Houston 8.0
Alaska:	Augusta 8.4	Portland 4.7	**Nevada:**	Oklahoma City 6.7	Palestine 6.6
Fairbanks 3.7	Macon 7.2	**Maryland:**	Reno 3.2	**Oregon:**	Port Arthur . . . 7.5
Juneau 1.7	Savannah 6.8	Baltimore 7.8	Tonopah 3.0	Baker 3.3	San Antonio . . 7.5
Arizona:	Thomasville . . .7.3	**Massachusetts:**	Winnemucca . .2.7	Portland 3.0	Taylor 7.7
Phoenix 4.3	**Hawaii:**	Boston 5.5	**New Hampshire:**	Roseburg 3.6	**Utah:**
Arkansas:	Honolulu 5.2	Nantucket 4.8	Concord 6.2	**Pennsylvania:**	Modena 3.8
Bentonville 7.4		**Michigan:**	**New Jersey:**	Erie 6.5	Salt Lake City . 3.4
Ft. Smith 6.2	**Idaho:**	Alpena 6.1	Atlantic City . . .6.2	Harrisburg 7.0	**Vermont:**
Little Rock 6.7	Boise 2.7	Detroit 6.4	Sandy Hook . . .7.0	Philadelphia . . 6.5	Burlington 5.4
California:	Lewiston 3.1	East Lansing . 6.1	Trenton 6.4	Pittsburgh . . . 6.4	Northfield 6.2
Eureka 2.7	Pocatello 3.7	Escanaba 5.4		Reading 6.5	**Virginia:**
Fresno 3.6		Grand Haven . 5.0	**New Mexico:**	Scranton 6.1	Cape Henry . . 7.4
Los Angeles . . .3.6	**Illinois:**	Grand Rapids . 6.0	Albuquerque . .3.7		Lynchburg . . . 6.0
Mt. Tamalpais .2.5	Cairo 6.6	Houghton 5.0	Roswell 5.4	**Puerto Rico:**	Norfolk 6.8
Pt. Reyes 2.4	Chicago 7.0	Marquette 6.0	Santa Fe 4.4	San Juan 5.7	Richmond 7.2
Red Bluff 3.8	Peoria 6.2	Port Huron . . . 5.3	**New York:**	**Rhode Island:**	Wytheville . . . 5.7
Sacramento . . .3.0	Springfield 6.6	Sault Ste. Marie 5.2	Albany 6.0	Block Island . . 5.3	**Washington:**
San Diego 3.3	**Indiana:**	**Minnesota:**	Binghamton . . .5.0	Providence . . . 4.8	North Head . . 2.8
San Francisco .3.0	Evansville . . . 6.0	Duluth 6.2	Buffalo 5.5	**South Carolina:**	Port Angeles . . 2.2
San Jose 2.0	Ft. Wayne 6.3	Minneapolis . . 6.6	Canton 5.6	Charleston . . .7.0	Seattle 2.2
San Luis Obispo 3.1	Indianapolis . . 6.3	Moorhead 5.8	Ithaca 6.0	Columbia 6.6	Spokane 3.1
Colorado:	Terre Haute . . 7.5	St. Paul 6.3	New York 6.6	Greenville 6.6	Tacoma 2.8
Denver 5.7		**Mississippi:**	Oswego 5.9	**South Dakota:**	Tatoosh Island 3.2
Grand Junction 3.0	**Iowa:**	Meridian 7.4	Rochester 5.4	Huron 6.2	Walla Walla . . 2.7
Pueblo 5.0	Charles City . 6.5	Vicksburg 7.5	Syracuse 6.3	Pierre 6.5	Yakima 2.6
Wagon Wheel	Davenport 6.4	**Missouri:**	**North Carolina:**	Rapid City 5.5	**West Virginia:**
Gap 3.6	Des Moines . . . 6.4	Columbia 7.0	Asheville 6.7	Yankton 5.8	Elkins 6.2
Conneticut:	Dubuque 7.4	Hannibal 6.5	Charlotte 7.0	**Tennessee:**	Parkersburg . . 6.7
Hartford 6.2	Keokuk 6.8	Kansas City . . 6.9	Greensboro . . .6.6	Chattanooga . . 7.2	**Wisconsin:**
New Haven . . .6.6	Sioux City 7.0	St. Joseph . . . 6.5	Hatteras 6.8	Knoxville 6.2	Green Bay . . . 5.1
District of	**Kansas:**	St. Louis 6.5	Raleigh 7.5	Memphis 6.8	La Crosse . . . 6.5
Columbia:	Concordia 7.5	Springfield . . . 7.0	Wilmington . . .7.0	Nashville 7.2	Madison 6.0
Washington . . .7.2	Dodge City . . . 6.3	**Montana:**	**North Dakota:**	**Texas:**	Milwaukee . . . 6.2
Florida:	Iola 8.4	Havre 4.3	Bismarck 6.7	Abilene 7.2	**Wyoming:**
Apalachicola . .7.3	Topeka 6.8	Helena 3.8	Devils Lake . . .6.8	Amarillo 6.8	Cheyenne . . . 5.6
Jacksonville . . .7.4	Wichita 6.9	Kalispell 3.3	Williston 6.5	Austin 7.4	Lander 3.7
Key West 6.6	**Kentucky:**	Miles City 7.0	**Ohio:**	Brownsville . . . 7.5	Sheridan 5.2
Miami 7.5	Lexington 6.0	Missoula 2.7	Cincinnati 6.5	Corpus Christi . 6.6	Yellowstone
	Louisville 7.0		Cleveland 6.9	Dallas 7.2	Park 2.5

Rates given are intensities for a **5 minute duration** and a **10 year return period**, from Technical Paper Number 25, Rainfall Intensity — Duration — Frequency Curves, U.S. Dept. of Commerce, Weather Bureau.

Figure 8-28 **Maximum rainfall rates in inches per hour**

of rainfall in inches per hour. Here are two examples:

For a 3-inch rainfall:

66,600 SF to be drained x 2 = 133,200

133,200 divided by 3 inches = 44,400 SF to drain

For a 6-inch rainfall:

66,600 SF to be drained x 2 = 133,200

133,200 divided by 3 inches = 22,200 SF to drain

Protecting Leaders or Conductors

Plan to protect all exposed rainwater leaders you install in parking garages, alleys, driveways or anywhere they could be damaged. The most common protection is a 3-inch galvanized steel pipe supported in a concrete base. You can protect fragile materials (sheet metal conductors or plastics) by installing a cast iron pipe boot on the lower 5-foot portion of the leader.

Chapter 9

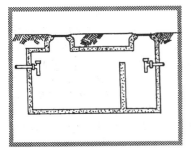

Private Sewage Disposal Systems

Not too many years ago people in the country and in many cities still used outhouses and cesspools to dispose of human waste. But those methods are grossly inadequate for our increasing population. Now there are model plumbing codes all over the country that outlaw these outmoded systems of waste disposal.

People in rural areas get their drinking water from open or closed wells that are vulnerable to contamination from sewage. In towns and cities, cross connections in the plumbing can also contaminate the drinking water. The lack of basic sanitary facilities was responsible for the plague that swept across Europe in the Dark Ages, killing nearly half the population.

In spite of its shortcomings, the common septic tank is still an acceptable method for sewage disposal in areas with no public sewers. Over 40 million people in the U.S. depend on septic tanks to treat and dispose of the sewage they generate. That makes septic tanks and disposal fields an integral part of the plumbing designer's work. You must know how to size and locate a septic tank system that meets code requirements.

How a Septic Tank System Works

A septic tank is simply a watertight receptacle for the sewage discharged by a building drainage system. It separates the solid from the liquid wastes before the treated liquid seeps into the ground. There's usually about 3/4 pound of solids in each 100 gallons of waste water. The heavier parts settle to the bottom of the tank while the lighter particles and grease rise to the top.

The tank should be large enough to hold approximately 24 hours of anticipated flow. This retention period gives the bacterial action time to digest the solids. That transforms the sewage into gases and harmless liquids. As new sewage enters the tank, it forces the gases up and through the drainage vent pipes where they're vented above the roof.

The new sewage entering the tank also forces an equal amount of treated liquid out through the outlet tee of the septic tank. This effluent enters a subsurface system of open-joint or perforated piping installed on a bed of washed rock. It's further nitrified through oxidation and evaporation as it seeps out of the perforated piping. Finally, the treated effluent returns to the soil outside the tank.

When the bacterial process is complete, the remaining solids settle to the bottom as sludge. Lighter undigested particles rise and form a scum on top of the liquid contents. Over a period of years, the sludge and scum build up and reduce the tank's efficiency. Periodic cleaning keeps it working effectively.

Septic Tank Construction

Choose a septic tank approved in the area where you're working. Some codes approve many kinds of septic tanks, ranging from precast concrete to the latest fiberglass tanks. Precast concrete or cast-in-place septic tanks are most common. They meet virtually all code requirements.

When you design a septic tank system, make sure that all the pertinent data shows on your plans. This includes all dimensions, reinforcing, structural calculations and site locations. The septic tank you design must produce a clarified effluent that meets local standards. It also needs to be large enough to accommodate the sludge and scum buildup.

Septic tanks must be made of solid, durable materials free from excessive corrosion or decay — and of course they have to be watertight. Block, brick, wooden or sectional tanks are prohibited. Figure 9-1 shows the design criteria that most codes require for septic tanks. Here are some of the details:

♦ Septic tanks must have at least two compartments (although some codes do accept one compartment). Look at Figure 9-1, details A and B.

♦ With two compartments, the inlet compartment must be at least two-thirds of the total tank capacity.

♦ The inlet compartment should retain a minimum of 500 gallons of liquid capacity. (The smallest approved tank size has a 750 gallon liquid capacity.)

♦ Septic tanks should be a minimum of 3 feet wide and 5 feet long, with a liquid depth of 2 feet 6 inches. The liquid depth should never exceed 6 feet. (Some code standards require a minimum depth of 4 feet.)

♦ In two-compartment tanks, the secondary compartment should have a minimum capacity of 250 gallons. It can't exceed one-third the maximum total capacity of the tank.

♦ The secondary compartment of a septic tank of 1,500 gallons or larger shouldn't be more than 5 feet long.

♦ A cover slab in removable sections is acceptable for cleaning a residential septic tank. See Figure 9-1, detail A.

♦ You'll need manholes brought to grade for access for cleaning commercial septic tanks or tanks installed under paving. One manhole must be located over the inlet tee and one over the outlet tee. Wherever a first compartment is more than 12 feet long, add an additional manhole over the baffle wall. Manhole sizes vary from 20 to 24 inches in diameter, depending on the code used. See Figure 9-1, detail C.

♦ A septic tank inlet and outlet pipe should never be smaller in diameter than the connecting building sewer pipe.

♦ The vertical legs of the inlet and outlet tees must be as large as the connecting building sewer pipe, at least 4 inches in diameter.

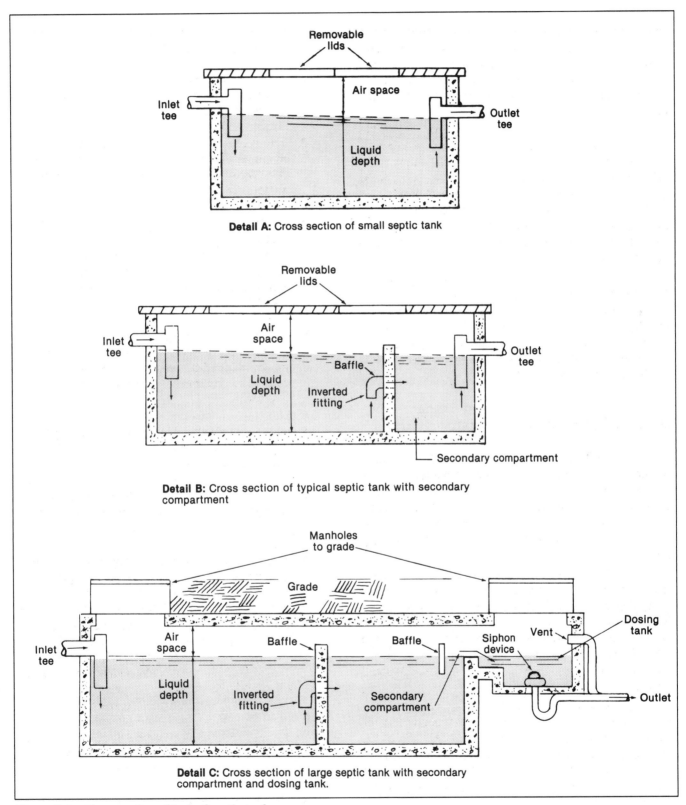

Figure 9-1   *Construction of typical septic tanks*

♦ When you use a baffle-type fitting, its cross-sectional area should be equivalent to that of the connecting building sewer pipe.

♦ The inlet and outlet pipe or baffle must extend at least 4 inches above and at least 12 inches below the liquid level of the septic tank.

♦ The inlet pipe should be at least 2 inches higher than the outlet pipe.

♦ The inlet and outlet pipe or baffle should allow free ventilation above the liquid level. This provides circulation of air from the disposal field and septic tank through the building drainage and vent system. All three details in Figure 9-1 show this.

♦ Provide at least a 9-inch air space above the liquid level of septic tank. (In some codes, it's 8 inches.)

♦ Partitions or baffles between compartments must be of solid, durable materials and extend 4 inches above the liquid level. To allow liquids to pass from the inlet to the secondary compartment, there's an inverted fitting midway in the liquid depth. (Some codes accept a slot.) The opening must be equivalent in size to the connecting building sewer (Figure 9-1, details B and C).

♦ Septic tanks must be strong enough to withstand all anticipated earth or other loads. Septic tank covers must be able to support an earth load of at least 300 pounds per square foot.

♦ For septic tanks in parking lots or other areas with vehicular traffic, provide a traffic cover acceptable to the building department.

Septic Tank Location

The code has placed a number of restrictions on septic tank locations. You can't place a septic tank within the *45-degree angle of pressure* transferred from the base of an existing structure to the sides of an excavation.

Here are other restrictions on septic tank location:

♦ It can't be located within 5 feet of any building.

♦ Don't place it within 5 feet of private property lines other than public streets, alleys or sidewalks.

♦ Put it at least 50 feet from any water supply well providing water for human consumption, bathing or swimming.

♦ It must be at least 50 feet from any stream or shoreline of open bodies of water.

♦ Allow at least a 5-foot separation from any seepage pit, cesspool or disposal field.

♦ Locate it at least 10 feet from established trees.

♦ Maintain a 5-foot clearance between the tank and on-site domestic water service piping.

♦ Keep a 10-foot clearance between the tank and a public water main.

Septic Tank Sizing

Your local code will specify septic tank sizes for your area. Each code has its own unique way of arriving at minimum tank capacity. The tables I'll use here are based on the Uniform Plumbing Code. Figure 9-2 outlines the minimum capacity requirements for septic tanks in normal residential use. The capacity is based on the number of bedrooms.

In a single family house, Figure 9-2 shows the required capacity for up to six bedrooms. For each bedroom over six, add 150 gallons to the six-bedroom capacity. For a seven-bedroom house, you'd need a 1,650-gallon tank.

For multiple dwelling units with one bedroom each, use column two for the number of units (up to 10) and column four for the septic tank size. Again, for each bedroom above *one per unit,* add 150 gallons to the minimum liquid capacity

Single family residences — Number of bedrooms	Multiple residential units — One bedroom each	Maximum fixture units for other uses per Figure 4-7	Minimum septic tank capacity in gallons
2 or less		15	750
3		20	1000
4	2 units	25	1200
5 or 6	3	33	1500
*	4	45	2000
	5	55	2250
	6	60	2500
	7	70	2750
	8	80	3000
	9	90	3250
	10	100	3500

*Single family residence: Extra bedroom, add 150 gallons each.

Multiple residential units: Extra units over 10, add 250 gallons each

Fixture units for other uses: Extra fixture units over 100, add 25 gallons per fixture unit

Figure 9-2   Capacity of septic tanks

in column four. A four-unit apartment building with a total of six bedrooms would need a 2,300-gallon tank.

For multiple dwelling units with more than ten units, add *250* gallons for each additional unit to the capacity listed in column four. A fourteen-unit apartment building (each apartment containing one bedroom) would need a 4,500-gallon tank. Then if any unit has more than one bedroom, add 150 gallons for each extra bedroom.

The septic tank sizes listed in Figure 9-2 include sludge storage capacity and allow for the use of garbage disposers.

Minimum septic tank capacities for normal *commercial use* are shown in Figure 9-3. It's based on an estimated sewage flow rate for various businesses. You'll run into many variables in sizing commercial tanks. You may have to adjust capacities in Figure 9-3 to fit a particular job. Always get advance approval from the building department before making changes.

The first column of Figure 9-3 shows the type of occupancy. The second column gives the estimated waste/sewage flow rates in gallons per day. The Uniform Plumbing Code recommends using these criteria when you've established the estimated flow rates:

♦ Waste/sewage flow, up to 1,500 gal/day x 1.5 = septic tank size.

♦ Waste/sewage flow above 1,500 gal/day x 0.75 + 1,125 = septic tank size.

Let's look at a couple of examples.

Example 1: Bowling alley with 10 lanes and a snack bar. The number of people isn't a factor.

Flow rate per lane   Septic tank size

75 gallons x 10 lanes x 1.5 =1,125 gallons

Types of occupancy	Estimated gallons per day	Types of occupancy	Estimated gallons per day
Airports	15 per employee 5 per passenger	Offices	20 per employee
Auto washers	Check with equipment manufacturer	Parks:	
		Mobile homes	250 per space
Bowling alleys (snack bar only)	75 per lane	Picnic parks (toilet only)	20 per parking space
Camps:		Recreational vehicles with out water hookup	75 per space
Campground with central comfort station	35 per person	with water and sewer hookup	100 per space
With flush toilets, no shower	25 per person	Restaurants, cafeterias:	20 per employee
Day camps (no meals served)	15 per person	Toilet	7 per customer
Summer and seasonal	50 per person	Kitchen waste	6 per meal
Churches:		Add for garbage disposal	1 per meal
Sanctuary	5 per seat	Add for cocktail lounge	2 per customer
With kitchen waste	7 per seat	Kitchen waste (disposal service)	2 per meal
Dance halls	5 per person	Schools:	
Factories:		Staff and office	20 per person
No showers	25 per employee	Elementary students	15 per person
With showers	35 per employee	Intermediate and high	20 per student
Cafeteria, add	5 per employee	With gym and showers, add	5 per student
Hospitals:		With cafeteria, add	3 per student
Kitchen waste only	25 per bed	Boarding, total waste	100 per person
Laundry waste only	40 per bed	Service stations:	
Hotels (no kitchen waste)	60 per bed (2 persons)	Toilets	1000 for first bay
Institutions:			500 for each additional bay
Resident	75 per person		20 per employee
Nursing home	125 per person	Stores:	
Rest home	125 per person	Public restrooms, add	1 per 10 SF floor space
Laundries:		Swimming pools, public	10 per person
Self-service (min. 10 hrs. /day	50 per wash cycle	Theatres:	
Commercial	Per manufacturer's specifications	Auditorium	5 per seat
Motels:		Drive-in	10 per space
No kitchen	50 per bed space	**NOTE:** **Uniform Plumbing Code recommended design criteria for priate sewage disposal systems.**	
With kitchen	60 per bed space		

Figure 9-3 Estimated sewage flow rates

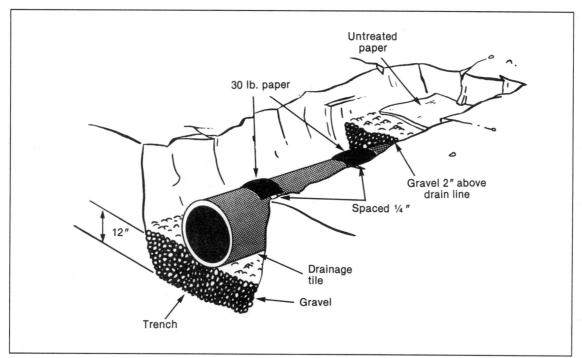

Figure 9-4   Tile drainage trench installation

Example 2: Office building with 150 employees. The number of clients doesn't matter.

Flow rate per person   Septic tank size

150 employees x 20 gallons x 0.75 + 1,125
= 3,375 gallons

Drainfield Construction

There are several approved materials you can use to distribute the effluent throughout the leaching area, but only two are in common use today. The first is clay tile, concrete block or cradle drain units laid with open joints. Second, there's perforated pipe made of clay, bituminous fiber, high density polyethylene, ABS or PVC.

We'll look at the installation method for each of these materials. The model codes differ in the spacing between distribution drain lines and the size and depth of filter materials. As always, check local code requirements before you begin your design.

Tile Drainfields

Drainfield tile must have a minimum inside diameter of 4 inches and slope no more than 3 inches per 100 feet. (Some codes say 1/2 inch per 10 feet.) Lay the tile pieces on a bed of 3/4-inch to 2-1/2-inch washed rock, gravel or slag. The filter material must be at least 12 inches deep under the drain line (6 inches in some codes) and extend 2 inches above the drain line. This gives an approximate total depth of 19 inches (12 inches in some codes) along the full width of the trench. Figure 9-4 shows a typical tile drainfield installation.

Lay the tile with a space of 1/4 inch between the tile ends. Cover the gaps with a strip of 4-inch by 16-inch 30-pound bituminous saturated paper to prevent sand from filtering into the openings.

Other codes require that you cover all the filter material with untreated paper or a 2-inch layer of straw. Figure 9-5 shows the details. Each trench must be from 18 to 36 inches wide.

No drain line can be more than 100 feet long. If you need more than one drain line, allow

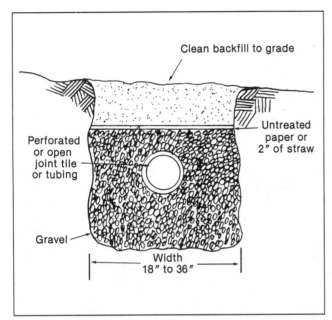

Figure 9-5   *Detail of absorption trench*

at least 4 feet between drain lines in trenches or leaching beds. Drain lines in leaching beds can't exceed 6 feet, center to center. Don't place the perimeter of the leach bed closer than 3 feet to the outside distribution drain line. Seal the end of each drain line with a cap. Figure 9-6 shows the recommended spacing.

Reservoir-Type Drainfield

Some codes accept block or cradle drain units. You'll usually use these drain units in single excavations based on the square foot rule (length times width) rather than in individual trenches. Each drain unit equals four square feet of leaching bed.

Install block or cradle drain units to slope not more than 1/2 inch per 10 feet. Lay them on a bed of washed rock, gravel, slag or other filter material sized from 3/4 inch to 2-1/2 inches. The filter material extends from 6 inches (12 inches in some codes) under the drain units to 8 inches (10 inches in some codes) above the bottom of the units. The filter material must extend the full width of the excavation.

Drain units with a fixed opening along the bottom to provide seepage may be butted tight

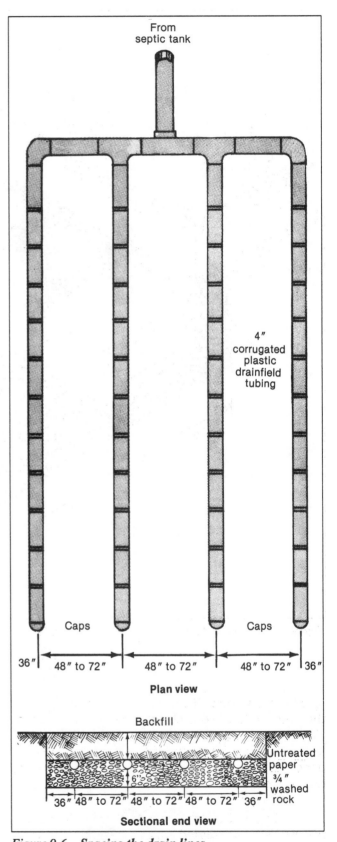

Figure 9-6   *Spacing the drain lines*

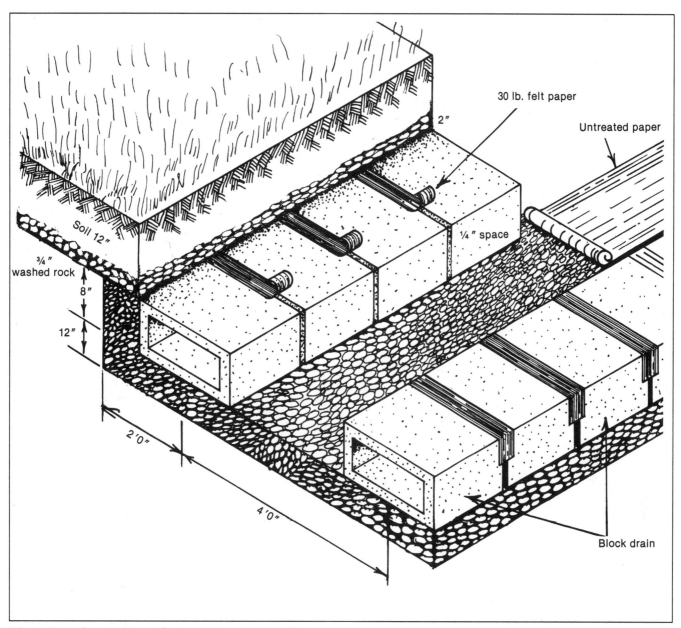

Figure 9-7   Cross section of reservoir-type drainfield

against each other. If there's no fixed opening, lay the units with a 1/4-inch space between the ends. Cover the 1/4-inch gap with a suitable length of 4-inch width, 30-pound bituminous saturated paper to protect the top seam. The paper must extend down 4 inches on each side of the units. Look at Figure 9-7.

Cover the entire area of drainfield filter material with untreated paper. That prevents sand and other small particles from filtering down and through the washed rock.

The centers of the distribution lines must not be more than 4 feet apart. The outside distribution line must be at least 2 feet from the excavated wall of the filter bed.

Distribution lines can't exceed 100 feet. If you use two or more lines, make them as near the same length as possible and connect them with a

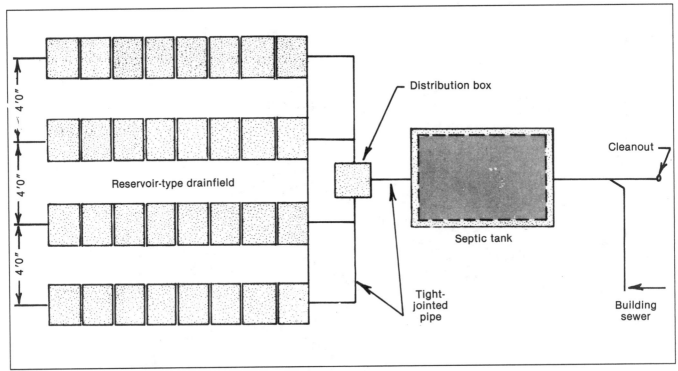

Figure 9-8   Detail of septic tank distribution box and drainfield

distribution box. That's a small container that receives the effluent from the septic tank and distributes it evenly to each drain line. You must connect the septic tank's outlet tee to the distribution box and the distribution box to the fixed reservoir distribution lines with a tight-jointed pipe. See Figure 9-8.

Perforated Distribution Drain Piping

The codes treat all perforated drain piping, regardless of material, the same way. You can use perforated piping for trench installations and for single excavations based on the square foot rule.

Perforated piping must have a minimum inside diameter of 4 inches and slope no more than 3 inches per 100 feet. (Some codes say 1/2 inch per 10 feet.) Provide a bed of 3/4 to 2-1/2-inch washed rock, gravel or slag at least 12 inches deep beneath the bottom of drain lines (6 inches in some codes) and 2 inches over the drain lines. That's a total depth of 18 inches (12 inches in some codes) for the full width of the excavation.

Since the drain pipe has fixed openings for seepage, all joints are tight. Cover the entire excavation area of filter material with untreated paper. Cap the ends of each distribution drain line.

Maintain a maximum distance of 6 feet (30 inches in some codes) between centers of the distribution lines. The outside distribution line must be at least 3 feet (15 inches in some codes) from the excavated wall of the filter bed. If you use two or more lines, they should be as near the same length as you can make them. You'll need a distribution box, except when you're connecting plastic tubing distribution lines together. You can use tees for that. Again, refer to Figure 9-6.

Location of Leaching Areas

Here are the code guidelines for locating the leaching area. The disposal field must be located at least:

♦   8 feet from any building or structure.

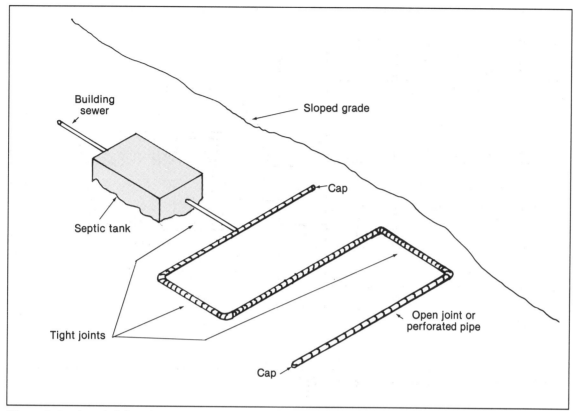

Figure 9-9   A serial distribution system installed on steep grades

◆ 5 feet from private property lines other than public streets, alleys or sidewalks.

◆ 100 feet from any water supply well which provides water for human consumption, bathing or swimming.

◆ 50 feet from a stream or shoreline of any open body of water.

◆ 5 feet from seepage pits or cesspools.

◆ 5 feet from a domestic water service line.

◆ 5 feet from the distribution box.

◆ 10 feet from any pressure public water main.

Special Types of Effluent Disposal

There are two factors that affect the soil absorption requirements: the topography and the absorption capacities of the soils. Codes vary in the type and size of drainfields, especially where unusual conditions require special design features for leaching areas.

Topography

In some areas, you'll encounter steep grades in the leaching area. The effluent could pass too quickly through the drain lines, without enough time to seep into the soil. In those regions, the code will probably require you to install stepped leach lines or leach beds.

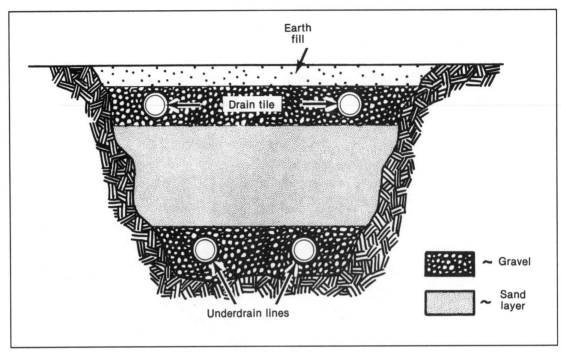

Figure 9-10   Sectional end view of underdrain installation

This usually means separate trenches, connected in series. The effluent flows from the septic tank into the first trench. As the first trench is filled, the effluent overflows into the next trench and the next until it fills the entire leach area. A typical serial distribution system built in an area of steep grade is shown in Figure 9-9.

Underdrains

What if you're building in impervious soil — predominantly sugar sand (fine sand), rock or clay? If the standard subsurface system can't absorb all the daily effluent, local authorities may approve underdrains. See Figures 9-10 (end view) and 9-11 (plan view).

Underdrains are open-joint drain tiles (Figure 9-4). There's a second set of drain lines installed about twice as deep as the regular distribution drain lines. The underdrains are a separate system, not connected to the regular subsurface drainage system. Space the underdrains about midway between the regular subsurface drainage lines (Figure 9-10). In areas with poor percolation rates, you can design an underdrain system with prior approval.

Seepage Pits

As a rule, seepage pits are acceptable where subsurface or underdrain systems are inadequate because the soils are impervious. Seepage pits always require prior approval. You can use them to supplement the regular subsurface drainage system (Figure 9-12) or alone to dispose of all the septic tank effluent (Figure 9-13).

If you're using multiple seepage pits in a regular subsurface drainage system, they must be served through a distribution box. Use tight-jointed pipes to connect seepage pits in series (Figure 9-13).

The amount of liquid waste and the character and porosity of the surrounding soil determine the capacity, number and depth of seepage pits. Look back to Figure 9-3, which shows estimated sewage flow rates. Figure 9-14 has the design criteria for five typical soils.

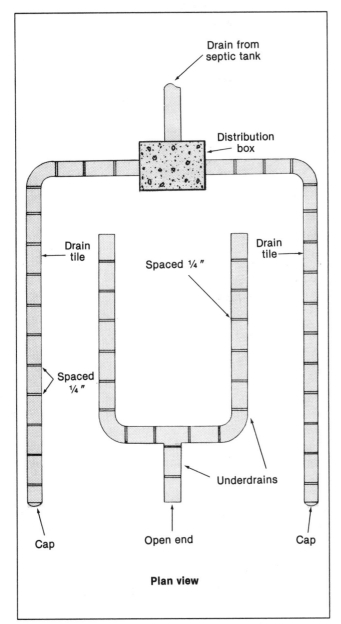

Figure 9-11   *Underdrains used with drain tile*

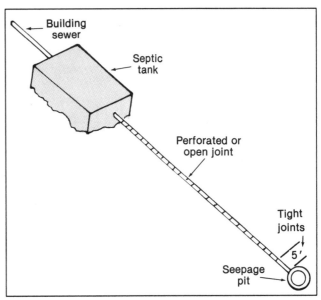

Figure 9-12   *Seepage pit to supplement regular subsurface drainage system*

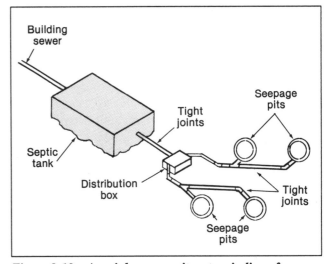

Figure 9-13   *A serial seepage pit system in lieu of subsurface drainage system*

Seepage Pit Construction

The code imposes strict construction requirements on seepage pits. As a designer, you have to understand these criteria:

♦ Seepage pits must be circular in shape, with a minimum depth of 4 feet and a maximum depth of 6 feet. The bottom may *not* penetrate the water table.

♦ They must be lined with new, hard-burned clay brick, concrete brick, concrete circular type cesspool blocks or other approved material.

Type of soil	Required SF of leaching area/100 gallons	Maximum absorption capacity gal/SF of leaching area for a 24 hour period
1. Coarse sand or gravel	20	5
2. Fine sand	25	4
3. Sandy loam or sandy clay	40	2.5
4. Clay with considerable sand or gravel	90	1.10
5. Clay with small amount of sand or gravel	120	0-.83

Figure 9-14   Design criteria of five typical soils

♦ The lining must be built on a circular footing to support the walls. The bottom is open.

♦ Place the lining materials tight together and lay them with joints staggered to permit effluent to pass out through the wall to the surrounding porous soil.

♦ The walls must be at least 4 inches in width.

♦ The annular space between the outside wall and excavation must be at least 6 inches and filled with 3/4 inch clean gravel or rock.

♦ Use only materials with a minimum compressive strength of 2,500 pounds per square inch.

♦ Seepage pits must have a minimum sidewall (not including the arch) of 10 feet below the inlet.

♦ Build the arch or dome of approved new, hard-burned clay brick or solid concrete brick or block with cement mortar joints or approved brick or block laid dry without mortar joints.

♦ The lid or cover must be made of reinforced concrete slab of 2,500 pounds per square inch. It must be at least 5 inches thick. Each cover must have a 9-inch inspection hole with a plug or cover.

♦ Place the cover a minimum of 18 inches or a maximum of 4 feet below the ground surface.

♦ Arrange vented inlet fittings to prevent the liquid inflow from damaging the sidewall.

Cesspools

A cesspool has a function that's quite different from a seepage pit. While a seepage pit receives effluent from a septic tank, a cesspool receives the raw sewage directly from the building. In effect, the cesspool serves as a septic tank *and* disposal field. It disposes of waste like an outhouse. Of course, many codes accept neither cesspools nor outhouses for disposing of human waste. But some codes still permit cesspools for limited, minor or temporary use. This is usually to avoid unnecessary hardship to property owners when a public sewer will be available within two years.

Cesspools, when they're allowed at all, can serve single-family homes and perhaps other limited uses with prior approval by the building department. They're built like seepage pits.

Commercial or Industrial Wastes

Liquid wastes containing excessive amounts of grease, garbage, flammable wastes, oil, sand or other objectionable waste material must be intercepted. Figure 9-15 shows a typical grease interceptor used with a septic tank. Interceptors must be an approved type and sized for the particular type of waste generated. Refer to Chapter 7.

After the interceptor has removed the objectionable waste, the discharge may connect to the building drain or sewer served by a septic tank. Or the interceptor may dispose of its wastes into

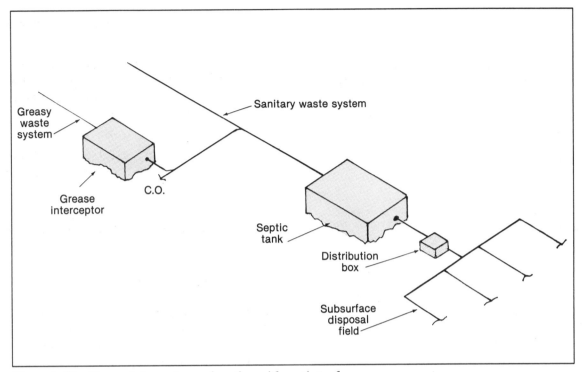

Figure 9-15   Grease interceptor conjunction with septic tank

a separate disposal system that consists of a second septic tank and disposal field. Some codes will accept just a disposal field if it's adequate.

Interceptors used with a septic tank must have at least two compartments. A sampling box may be required by some building departments. It's located in the secondary compartment and provides a way to test if all objectionable waste is being retained in the primary (first) compartment.

Seepage Pits and Cesspool Locations

All codes place basic restrictions on seepage pit and cesspool locations. You can *never* locate seepage pits and cesspools:

♦ within 8 feet of any building or structure.

♦ within 8 feet of property lines.

♦ within 150 feet of a water supply well which provides water for human consumption, bathing or swimming.

♦ within 100 feet of a stream or shoreline of open bodies of water.

♦ within 10 feet of any established tree.

♦ closer than 12 feet to another seepage pit or cesspool.

♦ within 5 feet of a disposal field.

♦ within 5 feet of an on-site domestic water service line.

♦ within 5 feet of any distribution box.

♦ within 10 feet of any public water main.

Sizing Disposal Fields

The soil in a disposal field must be able to absorb all the effluent from a septic tank. That's easy when the land is relatively flat and the soil is sand or gravel. In places with limited soil porosity, take a percolation test to find how long it takes for

Number of bedrooms	Required SF of leaching area	Linear feet block or cradle drain	Linear feet of 4" drain tile or tubing
2	100	25	40
3	125	32	50
4	150	38	60
5	175	44	70

Note: Some codes consider each linear foot of 4-inch drain tile or tubing to equal 1.5 to 3.0 SF, depending on trench bottom width in inches. Each LF of block or cradle drain units equals 4 SF of leaching area.

Figure 9-16   Disposal field conversion table (residential use)

water to be absorbed into the soil. That determines the size of the leaching area — and the cost. Naturally, the larger the leaching area, the more expensive it is.

Let's look at some disposal field sizing problems. We'll do two residential projects and two commercial, each with a different soil type. Use Figures 9-2, 9-3, and 9-14.

Residential Leaching Area

Let's assume we're sizing a drainfield for a four-bedroom, single-family house on a site with coarse sand. The first column in Figure 9-2 shows the number of bedrooms for a single family residence. Column four is the minimum capacity of the septic tank in gallons. For our four-bedroom house, it's 1,200 gallons.

Now look at Figure 9-14. The second column gives the minimum square feet of leaching area per 100 gallons for each soil type. Since we have coarse sand, it's 20 square feet. Here's how to size the drainfield. Multiply the required capacity by the required leaching area, then divide by 100 gallons:

$$\frac{1{,}200 \text{ gal. x } 20 \text{ SF}}{100 \text{ gal.}} = 240 \text{ SF total leaching area}$$

We need 240 square feet of total leaching area. Let's do one more sizing problem. We'll use the same four bedroom house, but this time the site is clay with considerable sand or gravel. That requires 90 square feet of leaching area for each 100 gallons.

$$\frac{1{,}200 \text{ gal. x } 90 \text{ SF}}{100 \text{ gal.}} = 1{,}080 \text{ SF total leaching area}$$

Commercial Leaching Area

You have to establish the sewage rate before you can size the leaching area for a commercial building. Look back at Figure 9-3. Column two shows the gallons-per-day flow rate for various commercial occupancies. Then use Figure 9-14 to size the leaching area per 100 gallons of flow rate.

For the first problem, assume an office building employing 100 people built on a site consisting of coarse sand. The table gives a figure of 20 gallons per employee per day for office buildings. So multiply 100 employees times 20 gallons times 20 square feet, and divide by 100 gallons.

$$\frac{100 \text{ employees x } 20 \text{ gal. x } 20 \text{ SF}}{100 \text{ gal.}} = \frac{400 \text{ SF total}}{\text{leaching area}}$$

Now let's do the same office building on sandy loam or sandy clay. The only difference is that you need 40 square feet of leaching area per 100 gallons instead of 20.

$$\frac{100 \text{ employees x } 20 \text{ gal. x } 40 \text{ SF}}{100 \text{ gal}} = \frac{800 \text{ SF total}}{\text{leaching area}}$$

Disposal Field Conversion

Sometimes disposal fields die — the soil can no longer absorb the effluent. How do you replace a lifeless drainfield? For a residence, use Figure 9-16. You can quickly calculate the square feet or linear feet of seepage area you need to replace a drainfield for houses up to five bedrooms.

For example, a three-bedroom house would require 125 square feet of leaching area (column 2). If you used block or cradle drain (column 3), 32 linear feet of block or cradle drain would be enough. But you'd need 50 linear feet of drain tile or tubing.

For commercial buildings, use Figure 9-3 to find the sewage flow rate. If you need a replacement for a commercial building that's not listed in Figure 9-3, this formula will help you. To find the daily sewage flow, simply check the water bill for the month. It'll show the amount of water used. Divide the monthly usage by the number of days covered by the bill (probably 30). When you know the daily usage, use this formula:

Daily sewage flow x 43.5 divided by 100 = required leaching area.

If you locate leaching areas under pavement, increase the absorption area by at least 10 percent if the percolation rate is good. If percolation rates are poor, check with the building department for the amount to increase the absorption area.

Chapter 10

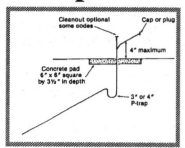

Mobile Home and RV Park Plumbing Systems

Throughout the country, the growing popularity of both mobile homes and recreational vehicles has forced local agencies to regulate the plumbing systems for mobile home parks. And sooner or later, you'll probably have to know the standards for fixtures, sewage collection and water distribution systems in these parks.

Recreational Vehicles and Motorized Homes

Recreational vehicles and motorized homes are usually defined by code as *dependent vehicles*. That means they don't have a plumbing system that can connect semi-permanently to the park sewage or water system. They're portable structures built on a chassis for travel.

Most modern motor homes and recreational vehicles are self-contained units, with bath facilities but not necessarily water closets. They

have a water storage tank to operate the plumbing fixtures and a holding tank for the waste water. They use mobile home park facilities to refill the storage tanks and empty the holding tanks. The code doesn't require recreational vehicle parks to provide individual water/sewer connections, but they do have to have a separate building with toilet facilities and a waste disposal station.

Mobile Homes

The code defines a mobile home as an *independent trailer coach* — a structure, transportable in one or more sections, that's at least 8 feet wide and 32 feet long. It's built on a permanent chassis and designed as a dwelling, with or without a permanent foundation. Most mobile home owners lease or buy space in a mobile home park. The park operator provides each space with water, electricity, gas and sewer connection — and is responsible for maintaining those services. It's up to the individual homeowners to keep their own plumbing and drainage systems in good operating condition.

Definitions

There are some plumbing terms and definitions, unique to mobile home and travel trailer parks, which you'll have to know to make your drawings accurate.

Air lock An entrapment of air in the flexible hose connection from the mobile home or trailer to the park sewer connection caused by a sag. Air that becomes trapped in such a manner slows or completely stops the flow of liquid waste or sewage.

Branch drainage pipe That portion of the drainage system extending from the park sanitary drainage system to the trailer site. Includes the terminal end which connects to the trailer drain hose.

Branch water pipe That portion of the water distribution system extending from the park service main to a trailer site. Includes the terminal end which connects to the trailer water supply pipe.

Dependent travel trailer Any motorized vehicle used as a temporary dwelling unit for travel, vacation and recreation. Usually has limited built-in sanitary facilities but not a plumbing system suitable for connection to the park sewage and water supply system.

Dependent travel trailer sanitary service station A trailer park location equipped for emptying intermediate waste holding tanks.

Drain connection An approved flexible hose that is easily detachable and used to connect the trailer drain to the park's sewer inlet connection.

Independent trailer coach Any trailer coach designed for permanent occupancy, equipped with kitchen and bathroom facilities and a plumbing system suitable for connection to the park sewage, water and gas supply system.

Inlet coupling The terminal end of the park's water system to each trailer site. The water service connection from the trailer coach is made by a swivel fitting or threaded pipe end.

Intermediate waste holding tank An enclosed tank mounted on a travel trailer for temporary retention of waterborne waste.

Mobile home lot Space in a mobile home park designed for the accommodation of one mobile home.

Mobile home, left side The side farthest from the curb when the mobile home is being towed or in transit.

Mobile home park A parcel of land designated and improved to accommodate one or more trailers. Such trailers may be used for temporary or permanent living quarters.

Mobile park sanitary drainage system The entire drainage piping system used to convey waterborne waste to a legal point of disposal.

Mobile park water service main That portion of the park's water-distributing system that extends from park's water supply source to each branch service line.

Service building A building in a trailer park with toilet and bathing facilities for men and women, as well as laundry facilities.

General Regulations

Plumbing systems installed in mobile home parks must meet local code requirements. Here are some basic components of most of those codes:

◆ Before working in mobile home parks, you have to file duplicate plans and specifications and get permits from the building department.

◆ The park plot plan must be drawn to scale, indicating elevations, property lines, driveways, existing or proposed buildings, and the sizes of mobile home sites.

◆ You'll have to provide complete specifications and piping layouts of proposed plumbing systems and sewage disposal systems or alterations to the existing systems.

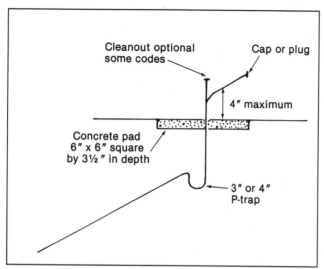

Figure 10-1   Trailer site connection properly supported with concrete pad

♦ Your plans and specifications must be clear enough to show that the proposed work will conform to local code regulations.

Materials

All drainage, waste and vent piping and fittings in a park drainage system must meet the material standards in Table A of the UPC. You can use any materials listed as approved for underground or above-ground use in Chapters 4 and 5 of this book.

Designing Park Drainage Systems

The park drainage system must connect to a public system if there's one available. If there isn't, you can use a private disposal system — *but you need approval before you complete your design work.*

Make sure your collection lines will have a velocity of 2 feet per second at full capacity. The system must have a minimum flow design of 150 gallons per day for each mobile home lot.

Provide a minimum 3-inch drain inlet to receive waste from vehicles equipped with water closets for each mobile home lot. To connect the mobile home water outlet to the park sewer inlet pipe, use materials that are semi-rigid, corrosion resistant, non-absorbent and durable. The inner surface must be smooth and all joints must be watertight.

The design must include provisions for plugging or capping each trailer connection when it's not in use. The rim of the park sewer inlet pipe can't be more than 4 inches above ground elevation. Some codes, however, specify 3 inches to 6 inches. Look at Figure 10-1.

Protect each drain inlet with a concrete pad to prevent movement. The pad must be at least 3-1/2 inches thick and extend at least 6 inches on all sides of the inlet pipe, as shown in Figure 10-1. (Some codes require an 18-inch square concrete pad that's 4 inches deep.)

Locate the park sewer inlet pipe within a 4-foot area in the rear third section of each mobile home lot on the left (road) side of the mobile home.

To design drain inlets for vehicles that aren't properly trapped or vented, follow the illustrations in Figure 10-2 or 10-3. Figure 10-2 is for codes that only accept wet vented systems. Some codes will accept the individually vented drain inlets shown in Figure 10-3. Always check with local code enforcement to find out which system is approved in your area.

For drain inlets for properly trapped and vented vehicles, you can omit the traps, as illustrated in Figure 10-4.

Individual vent pipes on sewage collection systems must be at least 10 feet from the property line and extend a minimum of 10 feet above ground level. Figure 10-5 shows the other dimensions. Where individual vents aren't permitted, you can vent the park drainage system with a combination drain and vent system (Figures 10-2 and 10-4).

Also look at Figures 10-2 and 10-4 for these vents:

♦ Install a 3- or 4-inch diameter vent no more than 15 feet downstream from the uppermost branch drainage pipe. You need

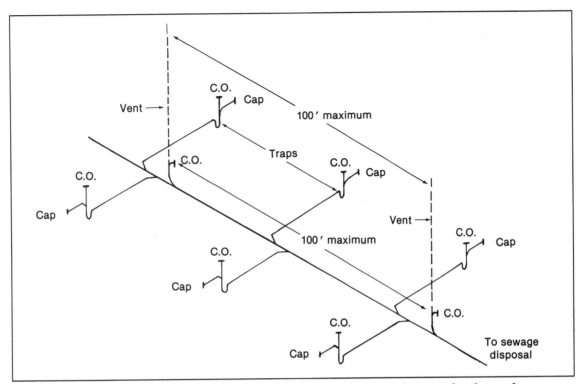

Figure 10-2   Wet vented sewage collection system for trailers not properly trapped and vented

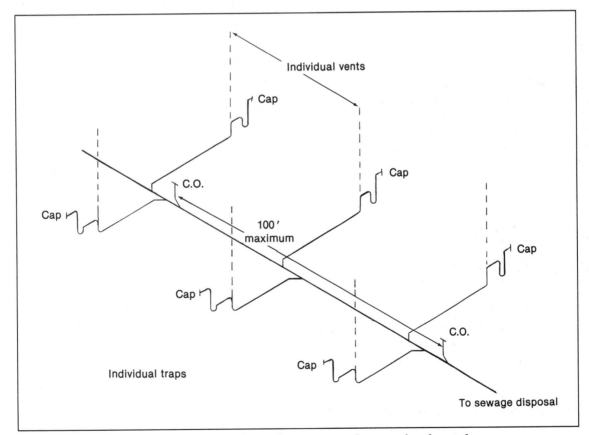

Figure 10-3   Individually vented system for trailers not properly trapped and vented.

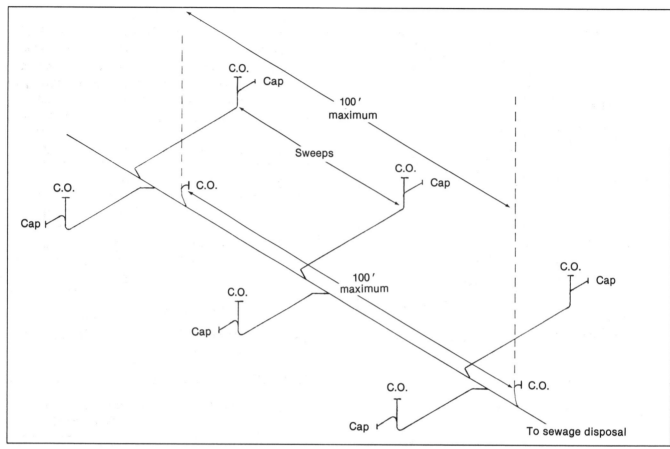

Figure 10-4   Wet vented sewage collection system for trailers properly trapped and vented

relief vents at 100 foot intervals or any portion of 100 feet.

♦ Three-inch wet vent drainage laterals can't be longer than 6 feet. Four-inch laterals can't exceed 15 feet.

You can't normally discharge a service building drain line into a wet vented drainage system. But under very unusual circumstances you may be able to get approval for this type of installation. If you do, you'll have to make the portion of the wet vented system that receives the discharge two pipe sizes larger than normal.

Install cleanouts like those for a conventional plumbing system, described in Chapter 6 of this book. See Figures 10-2, 10-3 and 10-4.

Sizing a Park Drainage and Vent System

There's a big difference between the fixture unit loads for a park drainage system and conventional buildings. In a building, each plumbing fixture is totaled separately. In a park, you can only estimate the number of fixture units. That's why most codes include two tables for sizing the park drainage system, based on the number of independent trailer lot drains in the system. Figure 10-6 lists the minimum size of drainage and vent piping for both individually vented and wet vented drainage systems. Figure 10-7 gives the minimum grade for each size pipe and maximum number of trailer drain inlets served.

Most codes assign a waste loading value of 6 fixture units for each trailer lot drain inlet. To size a wet vented system with traps (Figure 10-2)

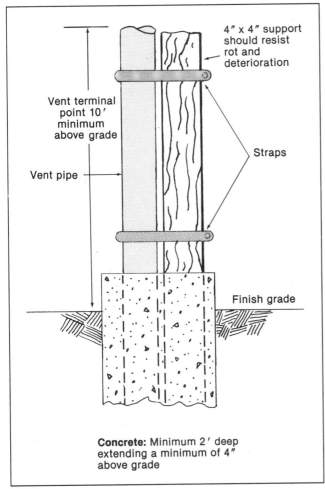

Figure 10-5   Individual vents properly supported for wet vent system

Size of drainage pipe (inches)	Maximum no. of fixture units, individually vented system	Maximum no. of fixture units, wet vented system	Terminal and relief vent, wet vented system (inches)
*2	8	4	2
3	35	14	2
4	180	35	3
5	356	180	4
6	600	356	4
*except 6 unit fixtures			

Figure 10-6   Drainage pipe sizes and number of fixture units served

Pipe size (inches)	Slope per 100 ft. (in inches)
2	25
3	20
4	15
5	11
6	8
8	4
10	3½
12	3

Figure 10-7   Minimum size and slope of drainage pipe

or without traps (Figure 10-4), use column 3 in Figure 10-6. To size an individually vented and trapped system (Figure 10-3), use column 2. Both wet vented and individually vented drainage systems must conform to Figures 10-6 and 10-7.

Toilet and Shower Facilities for Dependent Trailers

If your sites are approved for use only by *dependent trailers*, you have to include a service building with public toilet and bath facilities within 500 feet of the farthest trailer site. And you've got to equip the service building with an individual sewer connection. The table in Figure 10-8 shows the fixtures you need for both sexes in a park with 125 dependent trailer sites. The toilets have to be the elongated type with open front seats, installed in compartments with doors. Make the compartments at least 30 inches wide and

	Women	Men
__Toilets__ Four toilets required for first 28 sites and one toilet for each additional 25 sites	8	5
__Lavatories__ An equal number of lavatories up to 6 toilets. One lavatory for each 2 additional toilets	7	7
__Urinals__ 1/3 of required toilets may be replaced with men's urinals. One urinal may replace a toilet in minimum park facilities (28 sites, or 4 toilets).		3

Figure 10-8 Toilet facilites for 125 dependent trailer sites

provide a 30-inch clearance in front of the toilet. The dividing walls have to be at least 5 feet high and not more than 12 inches off the floor.

Some codes also require showers. If so, they have to be individual stalls, at least 30 inches by 30 inches, and screened from view. Include curbs to keep water from running into the dressing area.

Laundry facilities are also required by most codes. You'll have to put in an automatic washer or a laundry tray with hot and cold water for each 20 or 25 spaces. So you'd need five or six washers or trays for the 125 sites in our hypothetical park, depending on which code you followed.

Note that Figure 10-8 is from the Uniform Plumbing Code. Other codes vary widely in their minimum requirements. As always, check the local code before you design the system.

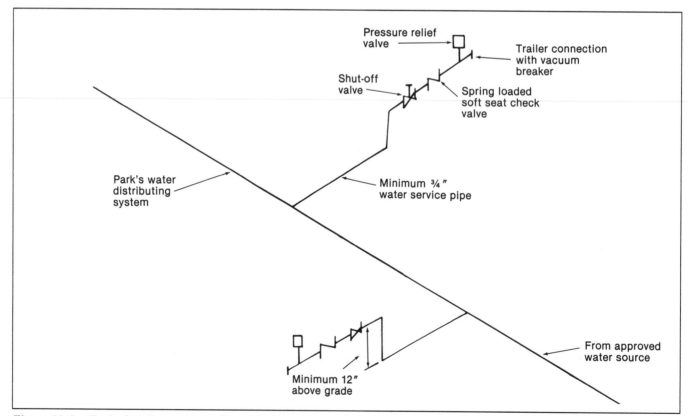

Figure 10-9 Typical trailer water service outlet with approved controls

Designing a Park Water Distribution System

You have to provide adequate, safe, and accessible water in every dependent and independent trailer park. The park must connect to a public water supply system if there's one available. If not, you can use a private well if you have prior approval from the building department.

A branch service line connected to the park's water main must provide potable water to each trailer site. The line has to terminate on the same side of the trailer site as the trailer sewer lateral.

The park's distributing system should provide a minimum pressure of 20 psi at each trailer site, from a 3/4-inch water service outlet. Make sure each trailer is connected to the park's water distributing system with a separate shutoff valve and a spring loaded, soft-seat check valve on the branch service line. Each valve must be located near the service connection. Look at Figure 10-9.

When you're required to install a backflow preventer at the water service outlet, include an approved pressure relief valve on the discharge side of the backflow preventer. Each manufacturer must ensure that pressure relief valves release pressure at a maximum 150 psi. The backflow preventer and pressure relief valve must be located at least 12 inches above grade (Figure 10-9).

Use a flexible connector at least 1/2 inch in diameter to connect the water service outlet and each trailer. The flexible connector may be made of copper tubing or other approved material and must be equipped with quick-disconnect fittings. It doesn't take any special tools or knowledge to install and remove these fittings.

Any piping materials you use in a park water distribution system must meet the same standards as other water systems and the material standards shown in Figure 3-1, back in Chapter 3.

Chapter 11

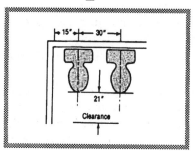

Drawing Your Drainage and Vent Systems

Y ou'll usually design drain, waste and vent systems based on plans prepared by an architect. To compile an accurate bid, a contractor or subcontractor needs a complete set of plans (for the location, components, and quantities required) and specifications (for the quality standards).

The building department may require an engineer's seal for complex buildings. On most large projects, the architect and engineer work closely together to lay out a plumbing system that will meet code specifications.

In residential or small commercial buildings that don't need an engineer's seal, the architect will probably draw the plumbing plans alone. And those plans will probably include the specifications. For more complex work, expect to find the specifications printed and bound separately.

The plans and the specs will be available to all contractors bidding the job. But know this: *Few plans and specifications are perfect when they leave the architect's office.* They don't have to be perfect — but they do have to be complete enough to guide the contractor in preparing a realistic (and complete) bid. In this chapter we'll look at what's included in a satisfactory bid set.

The Working Drawings

A typical blueprint consists of several drawing sheets, usually of uniform size, bound into one job set. They always begin with the lowest floor and work upward, usually in this order:

♦ The site plan and sometimes an index of the drawings

♦ Architectural details and the structural set

♦ Heating and air conditioning plans

♦ Plumbing plans

♦ Electrical plans

In the lower right-hand corner of each sheet, there's a title block which shows:

♦ The sheet numbers

    A (architectural)
    S (structural)
    M (mechanical — heating and air
       conditioning)
    P (plumbing)
    E (electrical)

♦ The number of sheets in each set (P-1 of 5, P-2 of 5, etc.)

♦ The date of the plan set, plus each revision date

♦ The initials of the person who drew and approved the sheet

Scale

For each drawing, you'll need to include a clearly identified scale in the title block or beneath each layout. The most common scale for plans and elevations is 1/8" = 1'0", and 1/16" = 1'0" for the plot plan.

Designers use a larger scale for complex areas that require more detail, like public toilet rooms. They're usually drawn to a 1/4" or 1/2" scale. Cabinet work requires even more detail and ranges from a 3/4" to 1-1/2" scale.

Drawings shouldn't be cluttered with notes which belong in the specifications. Sometimes a designer puts notes on drawings to alert his own draftsman or specifications writer. Make sure those notes don't survive into the final drawings.

What you'll find on the drawings and what's in the specifications will vary from job to job. There seems to be no legal precedent that one is more binding than the other. But if there are discrepancies between the notes on the plans and the specifications, the specs will usually govern. If you spot a discrepancy, ask the architect to issue a written statement (an addendum) to clarify the issue.

Let's look at example to see why this is so important. Suppose an architect puts the following note on a set of plans for his draftsman:

"Check sewage ejector location with me later."

But the draftsman forgets to check with the architect, and also fails to show the ejector on the plan. The specifications, however, do include the size and type of ejector required for the job. The plans go out for bids with this discrepancy. Even though the ejector isn't shown on the plans, the plumbing contractor should know that he has to include it. If he doesn't, the architect could later force him to furnish the ejector (with no increase in the contract price).

To avoid a possible legal hassle, the plumbing contractor should ask the architect to provide an addendum to the plans. That would clear up the discrepancy and identify the location of the ejector.

I recommend taking the sizes, quantities, design and location from the working drawings. Use the specifications for materials, quality, procedures and general requirements. Just remember this: A draftsman's oversight in omitting a piece of equipment from the drawings doesn't justify excluding it from your bid if it's listed in the specifications. Both the working drawings and specifications are important. Never rely solely on one or the other.

Job Specifications

Architects and engineers haven't come up with a standardized way to set up job specifications. As a rule, however, they divide plumbing into three groups: *General Provisions* (or *Scope*), *Materials*, and *Fabrication and Erection*.

Scope includes all the items the plumbing contractor will furnish and install, and any items furnished by others and installed by the plumbing contractor. This section also lists some general requirements — if shop drawings, samples and tests are required, for instance. But no matter how detailed it is, the Scope section can't include each and every item. Always check the working drawings against the Scope.

The *Materials* section lists the materials for a specific job. The format depends on what kind of specification it is:

1) The *closed specification* means that the contractor can only furnish and install a single trade name.

2) The *contractor's option specification*, known as *bidders' choice*, lists trade names the contractor may choose from.

3) The *substitute bid specification* may list several trade names that are acceptable, but the contractor can suggest a substitute when he submits the bid. If the alternate product costs less, he subtracts the difference from his bid.

4) The *or approved equal specification* lists a trade name but qualifies it by the phrase "or approved equal." This is the most widely-used type of specification and provides the widest competition. It rewards the contractor who knows his products, prices and sources. The architect, or the engineer in some cases, decides if the product is "equal."

5) The *product description specification* describes bulk materials and, particularly in government work, some manufacturers' articles. For example, you might include this statement about the selection of bulk materials for a water distribution: "Drainage piping and fittings shall be cast iron standard weight, hubless . . . ." Or you might detail the manufacturer's items for a particular job: "For kitchen in Building C, use WADE W-5100-XT, cast iron grease interceptor having a minimum grease capacity of 100 lb.

6) The *performance specification* doesn't usually describe the materials. Instead, it describes the job they're required to do, in terms of strength, mechanical ability or some other measurable result.

7) The *reference standards* refer to specifications published by national construction organizations. See Figure 4-1 in Chapter 4 (Table A in the Uniform Plumbing Code). Many architects and engineers will also refer to manufacturer's specifications that show installation procedures. They're available for your use along with the plans.

Fabrication and Erection defines the methods and quality of workmanship required. It sets performance standards for field work, and usually includes the manufacturer's installation instructions. There may be sections on protection, cleaning, guarantees, warranties, maintenance and operating instructions.

Floor Plans

Floor plans are an essential part of all working drawings. The floor plan shows the type, quantity and location of the plumbing fixtures and other parts of the plumbing system. The type of occupancy and the number of people using the facilities will determine the plumbing fixtures required by the code. But the model codes vary, especially for commercial use, so you'll need to refer to the code in your area.

Identifying Plumbing Fixtures and Components

Most architects and designers use standard symbols for plumbing components. They also use common abbreviations for fixtures, appliances, equipment and pipes on plans for residential and small commercial projects. You'll need to include a key with the abbreviations (not the words they represent) in alphabetical order. Figure 11-1 shows a typical list of plumbing fixture abbreviations. In the Appendix there's a more com-

Plumbing fixture	Abbreviation
Bidet	Bidet
Bar sink	BS
Bathtub	BT
Clothes washing machine	CWM
Dishwasher	DW
Food waster disposer	FWD
Hot water heater	HWH
Kitchen sink	KS
Lavatory	L or LAV
Laundry tray	LT
Shower	SH
Water closet	WC

Figure 11-1   Typical plumbing fixture abbreviations

Abbreviations		Fixture or Item		Legend (Description)
BD	building drain	P- 1	water closet	floor mounted, flushometer
BS	building sewer	P- 2	handicap water closet	floor mounted, flushometer
CO	cleanout	P- 3	urinal	wall mounted, flushometer
FCO	floor cleanout	P- 4	lavatory	countertop mounted
IWP	indirect waste pipe	P- 5	handicap lavatory	countertop mounted
VTR	vent through roof	P- 6	mop receptacle	3" bottom drain
WCO	wall cleanout	P- 7	electric water cooler	wall mounted
		P- 8	hand sink	wall mounted
		P- 9	glass sink	countertop mounted
		P-10	garbage grinder	
		P-11	coffee urn	
		P-12	sink	single compartment
		P-13	commercial dishwasher	undercounter type
		P-14	pot sink	three compartment
		P-15	ice machine	
		P-16	hot water heater	82 gallon, natural gas
		P-17	garbage can wash	3" drain with basket
		P-18	floor drain	3" drain with basket
		P-19	floor sink	3" drain with basket
		P-20	bar stool	
		P-21	grease interceptor	4,320 gal, 2 peak hr. periods

Figure 11-2   Key to drawing (Figures 11-3 and 11-4)

plete list of common industry abbreviations. Use them as a guide to standardize your drawings.

But for large commercial projects, there are probably "not so standard" plumbing items like mop receptacles, coffee urns, ice machines, lint interceptors and laboratory sinks. Most designers identify these with a code using the letter P (for plumbing) and a number. The key to drawings (on the first plumbing sheet) will explain this code. There's no limit to the number of items you can list and identify this way.

Look at Figure 11-2. It's the key to the drawings of a restaurant in Figures 11-3 and 11-4. You'll probably have to provide a key like this for any large project you design.

To use this system you'll need three columns. Column one, *Abbreviations*, includes the items identified by adding an abbreviation to the symbols. Column two, *Fixture or Item*, lists the codes beginning with the letter P used on the floor plans and isometrics. Column three, *Legend* (or *Description*), describes the fixtures listed in column two.

Some Pitfalls to Avoid

Some codes prohibit the use of fixtures made of pervious materials (such as Roman baths or shower baths built of tile or marble) whose waste outlets are designed to retain water. Check your local code.

Lack of adequate lighting or ventilation promotes unsanitary conditions. That's why all plumbing fixtures must be located in adequately lighted and ventilated rooms. If there aren't windows to provide natural ventilation, you have to build in mechanical ventilation.

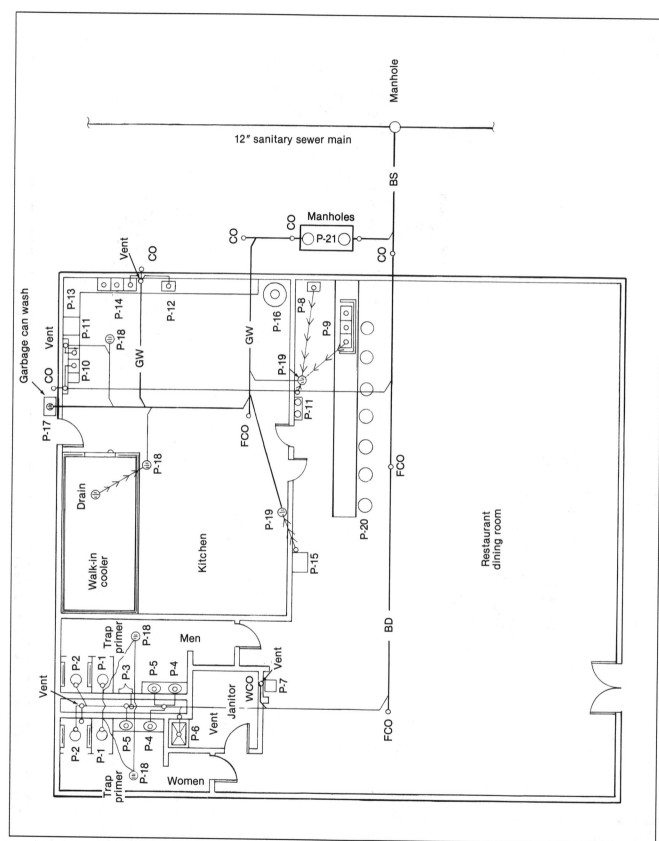

Figure 11-3 Plumbing floor plan (restaurant)

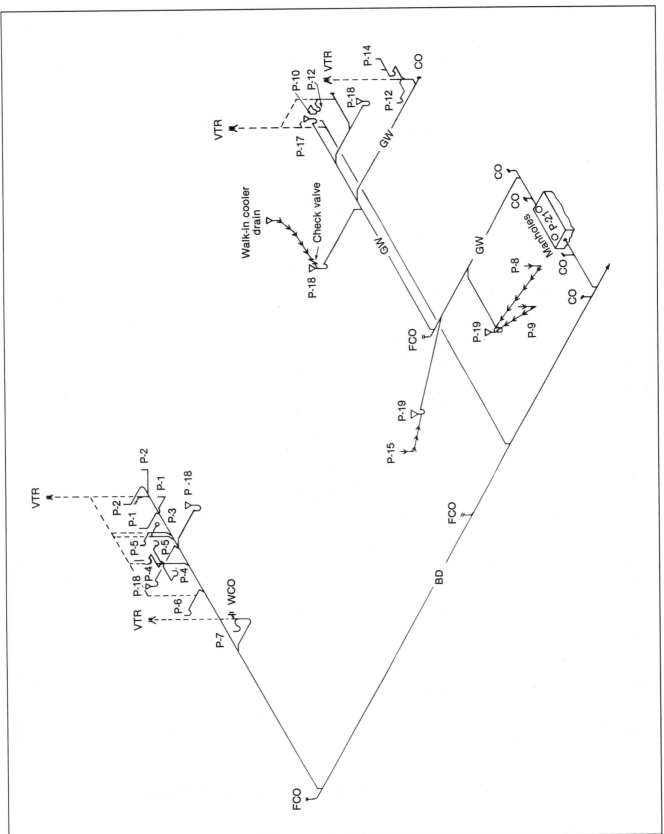

Figure 11-4 Plumbing isometric (restaurant)

Locate floor drains and floor sinks where they're accessible for inspection and cleaning. You can't place floor drains to receive indirect waste from food or drink storage rooms or appliances in toilet rooms or any inaccessible or unventilated closet or storeroom. And you can never locate any plumbing fixture (including floor drains) in a room that contains air handling equipment.

Don't put drinking fountains in a public toilet room or in any vestibule leading to one.

Water closets designed for public use (that's anyplace except a single-family home or apartment building) must have an elongated bowl and an open front seat.

If your design system includes a garbage can washer, remember that the waste can't discharge through a trap that serves any other device or fixture. The waste pipe must connect directly into the greasy waste line so that waste can discharge through a grease interceptor. See Figures 11-3 and 11-4.

Plumbing Fixture Clearance

The code has strict requirements for spacing plumbing fixtures. It's the designer's responsibility to lay out rooms large enough to accommodate the specified fixtures. Make sure every fixture has enough space around it to permit easy access for cleaning, repair and replacement, as well as the intended usage. Locate all plumbing fixtures, appliances and appurtenances where they're easily accessible for service or replacement. They may not be in a location where a permanent part of the building has to be removed to get to them. Figure 11-5 shows the minimum clearances observed in most codes.

Plumbing Fixtures for the Handicapped

Federal and state laws require all public and private buildings to have toilet facilities accessible to the physically handicapped. As a plumbing designer, you must know about these requirements. Only single-family and duplex homes, and buildings considered hazardous, are exempt from them. In large multi-story buildings, you must provide facilities for men and women on each floor.

In each required toilet room there must be one water closet, one lavatory and — in the men's room — one urinal which comply with standards created by the President's Committee on Employment of the Physically Handicapped and the American National Standards Institute, Inc. You can write to American National Standards Institute for a copy of the standards:

American National Standards
Institute, Inc.
1430 Broadway
New York, NY 10018

Here are some of the standards:

1) The bathrooms have to be large enough to allow people in wheelchairs to move around.

2) Each bathroom needs at least one toilet stall that's 3 feet wide, a minimum of 4 feet 8 inches (preferably 5 feet) deep, with a door that's 29 inches wide and swings outward.

It also needs 1-1/2-inch diameter handrails on each side, 33 inches high and parallel to the floor. The handrails must clear the wall by 1-1/2 inches and be securely fastened at each end and at the center.

The toilet seat must be 20 inches above the floor. It's best to specify a wall-mounted water closet with a narrow understructure that recedes sharply. If you specify a floor-mounted water closet, it shouldn't have a wide front that's perpendicular to the floor at the front of the seat. The bowl should be shallow at the front of the seat and turned backward more than downward. This design will permit the individual in a wheelchair to get the seat of the wheelchair close to the water closet.

3) All toilet rooms must have at least one lavatory with a narrow apron that people in wheelchairs can reach when it's mounted at standard height. It may be mounted higher when the design demands it, as long as it's accessible.

Make sure the drain pipes and hot water pipes are insulated or located where they can't burn a handicapped person without sensation.

4) Men's rooms must have at least one floor-mounted urinal (where code permits) that's level with the floor, or a wall-mounted urinal with a basin opening not more than 19 inches above the floor.

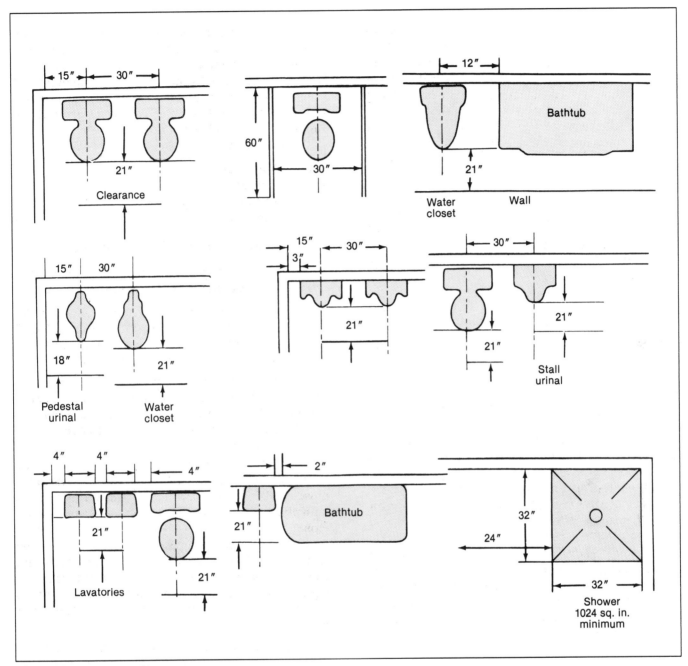

Figure 11-5 Fixture clearances

5) There must be an appropriate number of water coolers or fountains accessible to the physically handicapped. They must have up-front spouts and hand controls. People in wheelchairs can use floor-mounted water coolers if they're equipped with a small fountain mounted on the side of the cooler 30 inches above the floor. Both able-bodied and wheelchair occupants can use wall-mounted, hand-operated coolers that are installed 36 inches above the floor.

Fully-recessed water fountains aren't acceptable for handicapped use, unless they're recessed in an alcove that's wide enough (minimum 32 inches) to accommodate a wheelchair.

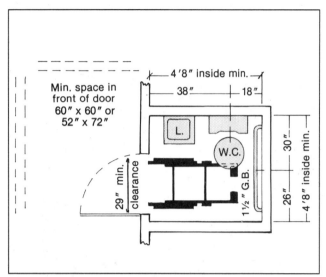

Figure 11-6   Toilet room with side approach to water closet

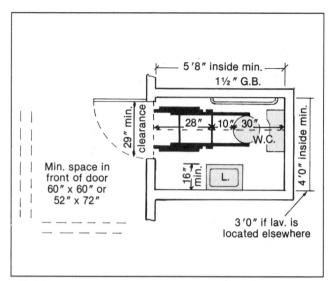

Figure 11-7   Toilet room with front approach to water closet

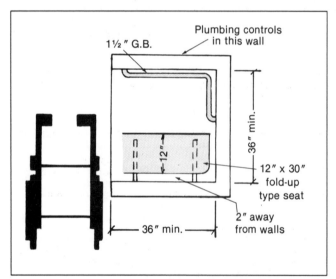

Figure 11-8   Minimum size shower for the handicapped person

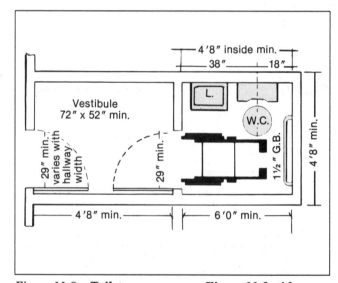

Figure 11-9   Toilet room, same as Figure 11-2 with minimum size vestibule

Figures 11-6 through 11-14 show minimum size toilet rooms and toilet room layouts acceptable for the physically handicapped. These layouts show the minimum space requirements for accessibility.

Isometric Drawings

Whether you're an experienced plumbing designer or working on your first plumbing plan, you know that lines on isometric drawings represent pipe and fittings. The functions of these various pipes are illustrated by solid lines (which identify drainage pipes and traps that receive liquid waste) and broken lines (which show the dry portion or vents).

Your plan must meet the intent of the code and be easy for the user to interpret. Some of you will admit that drawing good, clear isometrics is one of the more difficult parts of your job. If that's true for you, check the order form at the back of

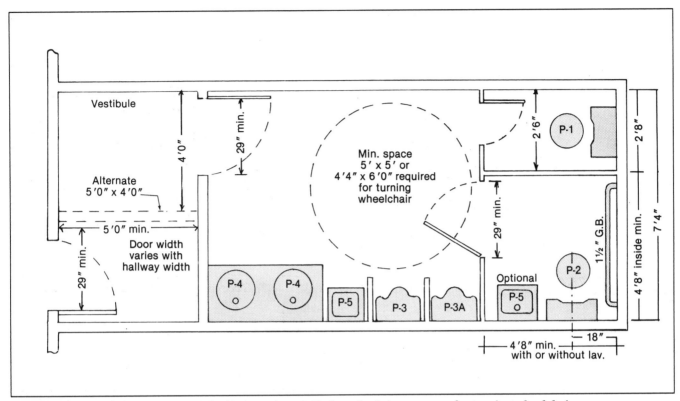

Figure 11-10 *Public toilet room with alternate size vestibule and minimum space for turning wheelchair*

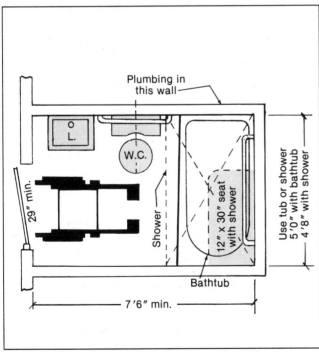

Figure 11-11 *Bathroom layout for hotels, motels and apartments, acceptable for handicapped use*

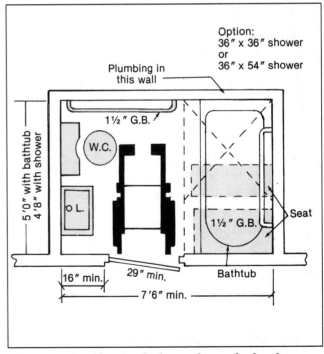

Figure 11-12 *Alternate bathroom layout for hotels, motels and apartments, acceptable for handicapped use*

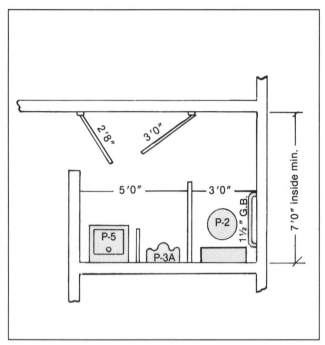

Figure 11-13   Minimum size toilet room designed with three fixtures

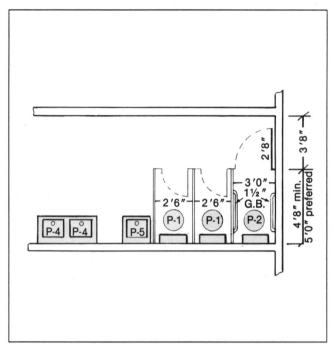

Figure 11-14   Multiple fixtured toilet room layout with minimum size

this manual. *Basic Plumbing with Illustrations*, by this author, is a good source to help you improve your isometric drawing skills.

I'm including two plumbing layouts with their respective isometrics in this chapter. I chose these particular drawings because you may not get many opportunities to work with some of the special items and designs in them.

One-Story Office Building

Anyone who designs plumbing systems needs to know how to read and make isometric drawings that meet the intent of the code. When you design commercial buildings, you may have to draw two or more separate drainage systems. All buildings include the standard sanitary DWV system, but some also have special waste systems for storm water drainage, greasy waste or acid waste. Identify the waste these special pipes carry on your drawings, and reference them in the key.

Figures 11-15 and 11-16 show the plumbing layout and isometric for a one-story dentist's

office. Notice that there are private toilet rooms for each office. According to code, they must be sized and designed for the handicapped.

The code also requires an interceptor trap (P-36) designed into the waste line of a drainage system where wax or other objectionable substances may enter, as in this dental sink (P-35). There will probably be damaging chemicals used in the laboratory sinks (P-33), so most codes require the installation of an approved dilution or neutralizing tank (P-34) in the laboratory drain line.

Construction must be of glass, earthenware, or other approved non-corrosive materials. And you'll need to design a controlled water supply so that harmful materials can be diluted to the point where they won't harm the plumbing system.

Specify that drainage pipes, fittings and vent pipes for corrosive waste must be made of duriron, glass, plastic or other approved non-corrosive materials. Identify this system with the abbreviation AW (acid waste).

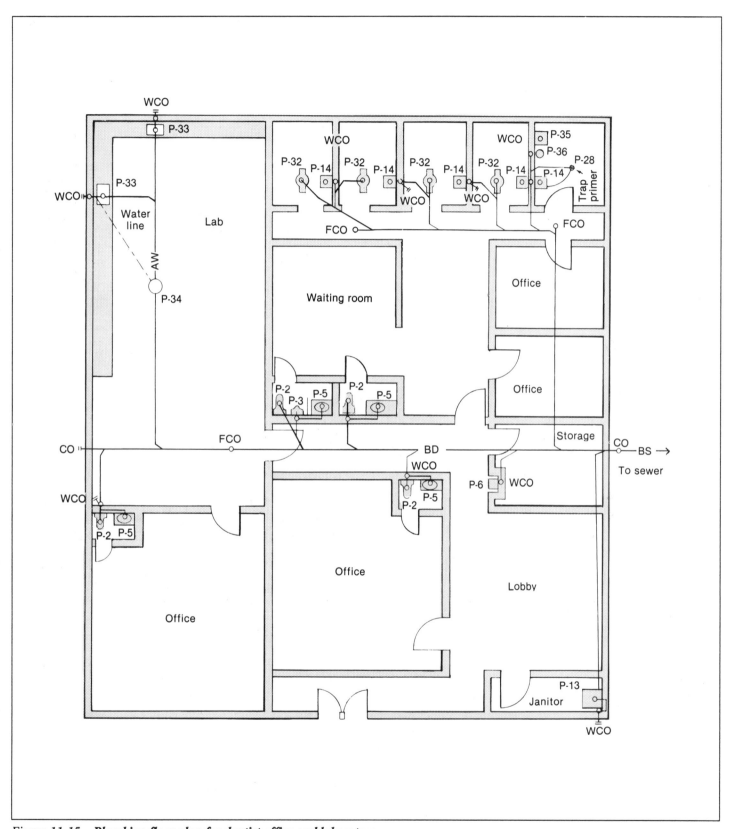

Figure 11-15   Plumbing floor plan for dentist office and laboratory

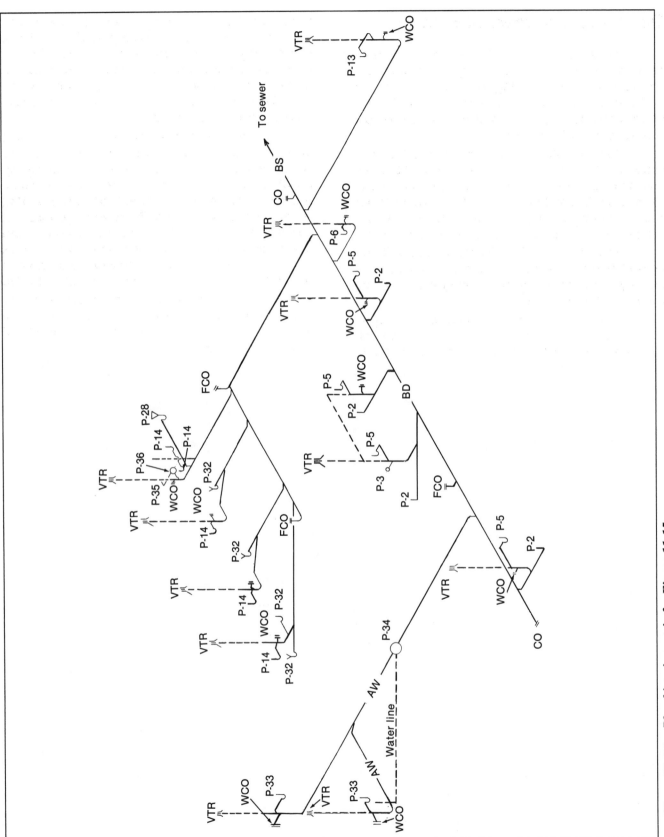

Figure 11-16   Plumbing isometric for Figure 11-15

Two-Story Commercial Building

Look at Figure 11-17 (the site and floor plan of the first floor of a typical commercial building — not to scale), Figure 11-18 (second floor of the same building), and Figure 11-19 (the isometric drawing for both floors) as you focus on the following special features.

Private toilet rooms are shown for each store and the doctor's office in Figure 11-17. Each one must be designed to provide for the handicapped. In Figure 11-18 the toilet room for Office 3 doesn't have to comply because there are handicapped toilet facilities in the public toilet rooms.

In Figure 11-17, a clear water sump (P-38) doesn't require a cover or vent. It must connect directly to the building drainage system as illustrated in Figure 11-19.

There's a commercial laundry in Figure 11-17. Since commercial laundries discharge solids such as lint, string and buttons with the liquid waste (which must enter the drainage system), you have to include a lint interceptor (P-30). Some codes categorize horizontal drainage pipe serving commercial clothes washing machines (P-37) as indirect waste pipe. If so, it doesn't need to be vented (as illustrated in Figure 11-19). Check local code for vent requirements.

When plumbing fixtures are installed below the building drainage pipes, as they are in the basement in Figure 11-17, they discharge by gravity into a receiving tank (P-39). Then the waste must be lifted and discharged into the building sewer or drain by ejectors. The receiving tank must be designed to retain a 30-minute peak flow. Pump discharge pipes must be provided with a check valve located as close as possible to the pump and on the pump side of a gate valve. See Figure 11-19.

The code requires a vent on the receiving tank. Minimum vent size for a sump receiving body waste can vary from 1-1/2 to 3 inches. Check local code for vent size.

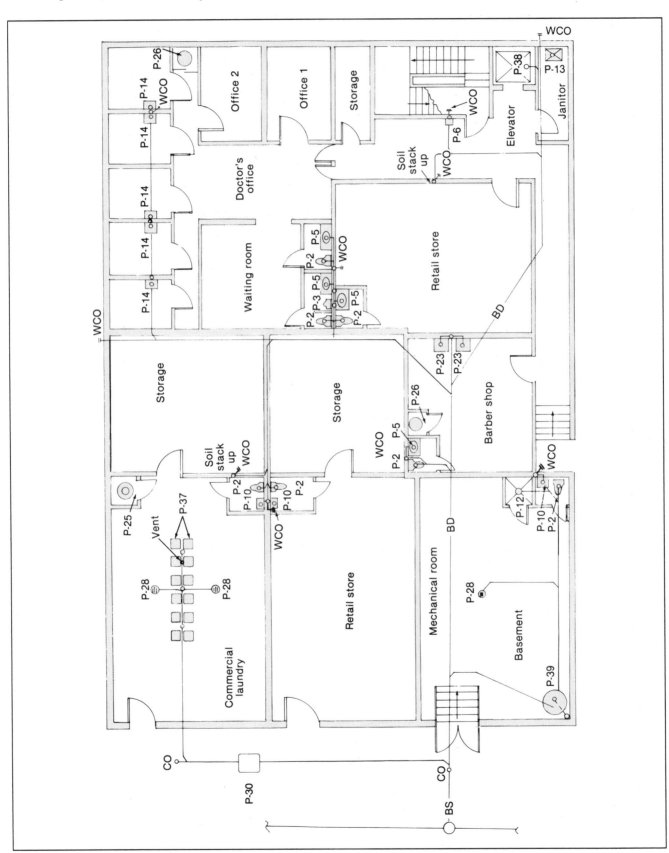

Figure 11-17   First floor plumbing plan

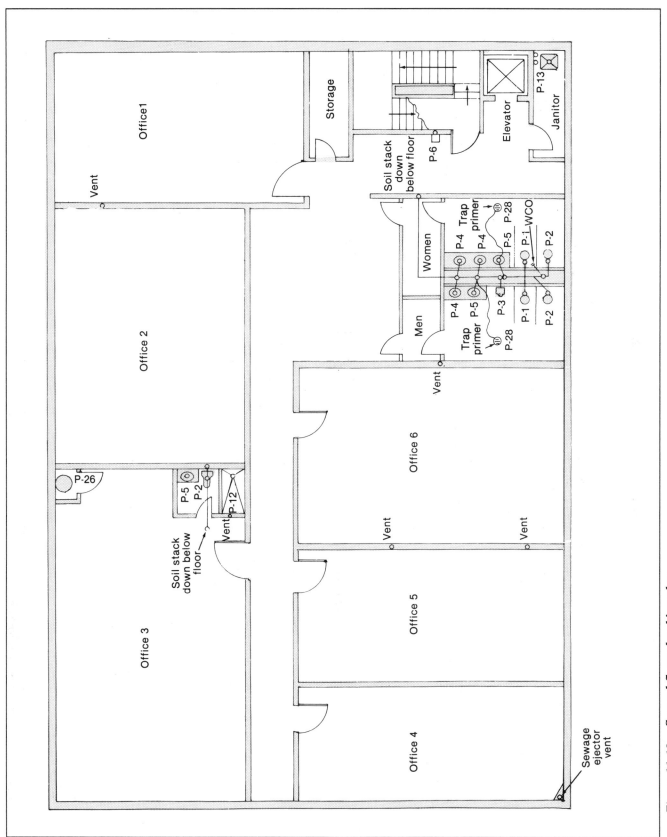

Figure 11-18   Second floor plumbing plan

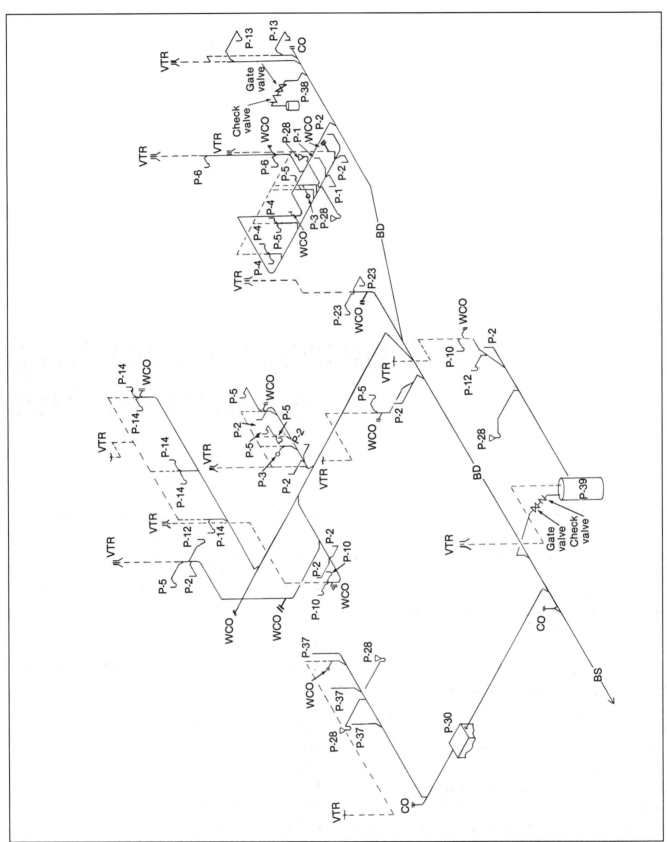

Figure 11-19   First and second floor plumbing isometric for Figures 11-17 and 11-18

Common Plumbing Abbreviations

A	air or area
ACC	access
AD	area drain
AFF	above finished floor
AGA	American Gas Association
AISI	American Iron and Steel Institute
AL	aluminum
ALT	alternate
AP	access panel
API	American Petroleum Institute
APX	approximate
ARCH	architect
ASA	American Standard Association
ASB	asbestos
ASC	above suspended ceiling
ASCE	American Society of Civil Engineering
ASHRAE	American Society of Heating, Refrigeration and Air Conditioning Engineers

ASME	American Society of Mechanical Engineers
ASSE	American Society of Sanitary Engineering
ASTM	American Society for Testing and Materials
AUTO	automatic
AVG	average
AWWA	American Water Works Association
B	bidet
B&S	bell and spigot
BBL	barrel
BEL	below
BET	between
BIT	bituminous
BLDG	building
BM	bench mark

BOCA	Building Officials Conference of America
BOD	biochemical oxygen demand
BOT	bottom
BRZ	bronze
BS	bar sink
BSMT	basement
BT	bathtub
BTU	British Thermal Unit
C	Centigrade or condensate
°C	degrees Centigrade
C to C	center to center
CB	catch basin
CFL	counterflashing
CFM	cubic feet per minute
CHT	ceiling height
CI	cast iron
CIPC	cast-in-place concrete
CIR	circle
CIRC	circumference
CISP	cast iron soil pipe
CISPI	Cast Iron Soil Pipe Institute
CK	caulk
CLG	ceiling
COL	column
CO	cleanout
CPR	copper
CS	cast steel
CS	Commercial Standard
CS	countersink
CT	ceramic tile
CTR	counter
CU IN	cubic inch
CU FT	cubic foot
CV	check valve
CW	cold water
CWM	clothes washing machine
D	drain
DEG or °	degree
DF	drinking fountain

DIA	diameter
DIAG	diagonal
DIM	dimension
DL	dead load
DRB	drainboard
DS	downspout
DT	drain tile
DW	dishwasher or dumbwaiter
DWG	drawing
E	east
E to C	end to center
EL	elevation
ELEC	electric
ELEV	elevator
EMER	emergency
ENC	enclose
EP	electrical panelboard
EQ	equal
EQP	equipment
ESC	escalator
EST	estimate
EWC	electric water cooler
EXCA	excavate
EXG	existing
EXH	exhaust
EXP	exposed
EXT	exterior
°F	degrees Fahrenheit
F	Fahrenheit
FA	fire alarm
FB	footbath
FD	floor drain
FDC	fire department connection
FE	fire extinguisher
FEC	fire extinguisher cabinet
FF	finish floor
FFE	finished floor elevation
FG	finish grade
FGL	fiberglass
FHC	fire hose cabinet
FHS	fire hose station

FIG	figure
FL	fire line
FLCO	floor cleanout
FLG	flashing
FLR	floor
FND	foundation
FP	fire plug
FRA	fresh air
FS	full size
FSP	fire standpipe
FTG	footing
FU	fixture unit
FUR	furred
FUT	future
FWD	food waste disposer
G	gas
GA	gage or gauge
GAL	gallons
GALV	galvanized
GB	grab bar
GD	grade
GI	galvanized iron
GKT	gasket
GP	galvanized pipe
GPD	gallons per day
GPM	gallons per minute
GS	glass sink
GV	gate valve
H	hydrogen
HB	hose bib
HD	head
HDR	header
HOR	horizontal
HR	hour
HT	height
HTG	heating
HVAC	heating/ventilating/air conditioning
HW	hot water
HWH	hot water heater
HWR	hot water return
HWT	hot water tank

IN	inch
IAPMO	International Association of Plumbing and Mechanical Officials
ICBO	International Conference of Building Officials
ID	inside diameter
INS	insulation
INT	interior
INV	invert
IPS	iron pipe size
IW	indirect waste
J	joist
JC	janitor's closet
JT	joint
KS	kitchen sink
KIT	kitchen
KW	kilowatt
L	length
L or LAV	lavatory
LAB	laboratory
LB	pound
LH	left hand
LT	laundry tray
M	meter
MAS	masonry
MAX	maximum
MC	medicine cabinet
MCA	Mechanical Contractors Association
MECH	mechanical
MFR	manufacturer
MGD	million gallons per day
MH	manhole
MI	malleable iron
MIN	minimum
MR	mop receptal
MS	mild steel
N	north
NAPHCC	National Association of Plumbing Heating and Cooling Contractors
NBFU	National Board of Fire Underwriters
NBS	National Bureau of Standards

NFPA	National Fire Protection Association		**SD**	storm drain
NPS	nominal pipe size		**SEC**	second
NTS	not to scale		**SH**	shower
			SPEC	specification
O	oil or oxygen		**SQ**	square
OD	outside diameter		**SP**	swimming pool
OZ	ounce		**SSK**	service sink
			SST	stainless steel
P	pressure		**ST**	steel
PAR	parallel		**STD**	standard
PCC	precast concrete		**STG**	seating
PCF	pounds per cubic foot		**STO**	storage
PD	planter drain		**STR**	structural
PE	porcelain enamel		**SV**	service
PED	pedestal		**SW**	service weight
PER	perimeter			
PFB	prefabricated		**T**	temperature
PLF	pounds per lineal foot		**TB**	towel bar
pH	hydrogen-ion concentration		**TC**	terra cotta
PK	parking		**TPD**	toilet paper dispenser
PL	plat or property line		**TPTN**	toilet partition
PP	pool piping		**TSL**	top of slab
PPM	parts per million		**U or URN**	urinal
PSF	pounds per square foot		**USASI**	United States of America Standards Institute
PSI	pounds per square inch			
QT	quart		**V**	vacuum cleaner line, velocity, vent or volume
R	riser		**VERT**	vertical
RA	return air		**VT**	vinyl tile
RAD	radius		**VTR**	vent through roof
RCP	reinforced concrete pipe			
RD	rate of demand or roof drain		**W**	waste or west
RED	reducer		**WC**	water closet
RL	roof leader		**WH**	wall hung, wall hydrant or water heater
RS	rate of supply		**WL**	water level
RWC	rainwater conductor		**WT**	weight
			WPOA	Western Plumbing Officials Association
S	south			
S&W	solid and waste			
SAN	sanitary			
SB	sitz bath			
SBCC	Southern Building Code Congress		**XH**	extra heavy

Glossary

A

Accessible Within physical reach. For example, a valve to control the flow of water to a battery of fixtures may be located in a partition. An access panel may have to be removed to make the valve accessible.

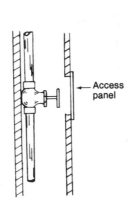

Accessible, readily Implies that the valve is physically accessible without necessitating the removal of an access panel or similar obstruction.

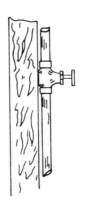

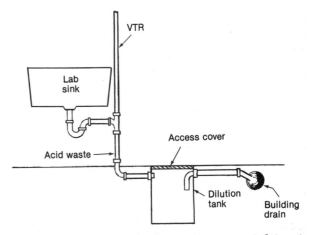

Acid waste Waste which requires special treatment before entry into the conventional drainage system.

Administrative authority The individual plumbing official, board, department, or other agency established and authorized by a state, county, city, or other political subdivision created by law to administer and enforce the provisions of the plumbing code as adopted or amended.

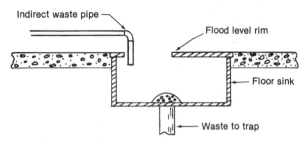

Air break (in a drainage system) An indirect piping arrangement in which a drain from a fixture, appliance or other device discharges indirectly into a waste receptor at a point below the flood level rim of the receptor.

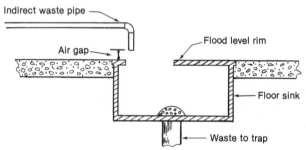

Air gap (in a drainage system) The unobstructed vertical distance through the free atmosphere between the lowest outlet of waste pipe and the flood level rim of the receptor into which it is discharging.

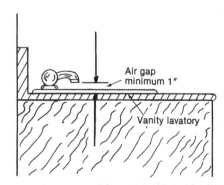

Air gap (in a water distribution system) In a water supply system: the unobstructed vertical distance through the free atmosphere between the lowest opening from any pipe or

faucet conveying water to a tank, plumbing fixture, or other device, and the flood level rim of the receptacle.

Air lock Air, gas or vapor entrapped between two liquid surfaces in a pipe or liquid container. The flow of liquid may be impeded, or stopped entirely, by the entrapped air, gas or vapor.

Anaerobic Living without free oxygen. Anaerobic bacteria found in septic tanks are beneficial in digesting organic matter.

Approved Accepted or acceptable under an applicable specification or standard stated or cited in the code, or accepted as suitable for the proposed use under procedures and powers of the administrative authority.

Approved testing agency A recognized agency established primarily to conduct tests to determine whether materials meet standards established by the administrative authority.

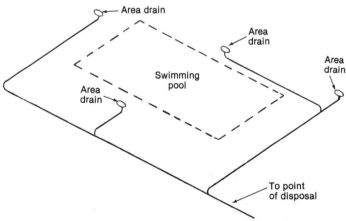

Area drain A receptacle designed to collect surface or rainwater from an open area.

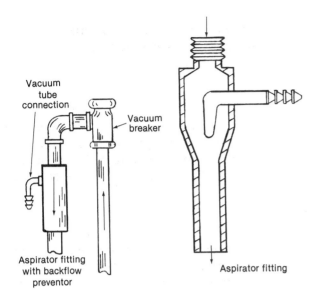

Note: Water operated aspirators, usually located in operating rooms, emergency rooms, delivery rooms and autopsy rooms are installed with approval of the health department. The waste from aspirators (blood, pus, or other fluids) must always connect **indirectly** to the drainage system

Aspirator A special fitting or device which may be supplied by water, or some other fluid under positive pressure, which passes through an integral orifice or constriction, causing a vacuum.

B

Backfill That portion of the trench excavation up to the original earth line which is replaced after the sewer or other piping has been laid.

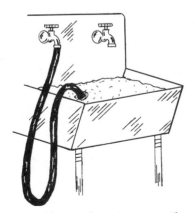

Backflow The flow of water or other liquids, mixtures, or substances into the distributing

pipes of a potable supply of water from any source other than its intended course (See *Back-siphonage*.)

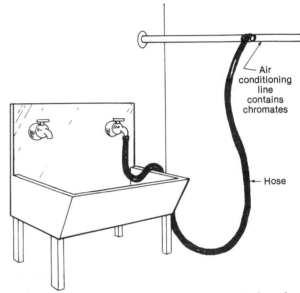

Backflow connection Any arrangement whereby backflow can occur.

Hose bibb vacuum breaker

Hose bibb vacuum breaker for frost-proof hydrants

Backflow preventer A device or means to prevent backflow into the potable water system.

Back-siphonage The flow of water or other liquids, mixtures or substances into the distributing pipes of a potable supply of water, or any other fixture, device or appliance, from any sources other than its intended course, due to a negative pressure in such pipe.

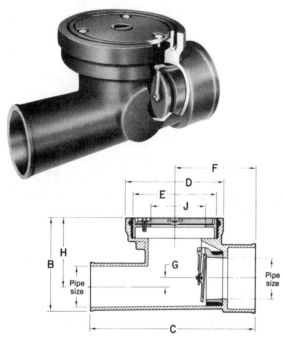

Backwater valve A special device installed in a drainage pipe to prevent backflow of liquid waste into a drainage system.

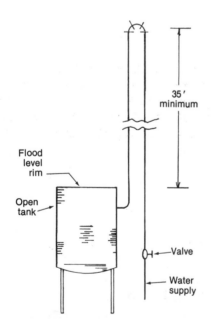

Barometric loop A loop formed from pipe and fittings, rising vertically some 35 feet above the highest fixture it serves to prevent back-siphonage into the potable water supply.

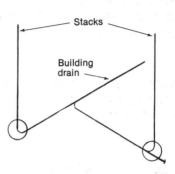

Base The lowest point of any vertical pipe

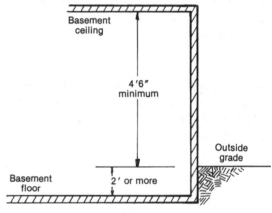

Basement The floor of a building which is 2 feet or more below outside grade and the ceiling of which is not more than 4 feet 6 inches above outside grade.

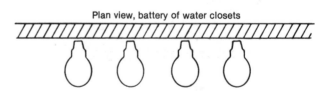

Battery of fixtures A group of two or more similar adjacent fixtures which discharge into a common horizontal waste or soil branch.

ceives individual fixture drains which are connected horizontally to a branch soil or waste pipe which is circuit or loop vented.

Bedpan steamer A special fixture designed and used for scalding bedpans or urinals by direct application of steam.

Bedpan washer A special fixture designed to wash bedpans and to flush the contents into the sanitary drainage system. The fixture may also provide for sterilizing the bedpan with steam or hot water.

Bedpan washer hose A special device, located adjacent to a water closet or clinic sink, supplied with hot and cold water, used for cleaning bedpans.

Boiler blow-off An outlet located on a boiler whose purpose is to permit emptying or discharge of water or sediment into a boiler blow-off tank.

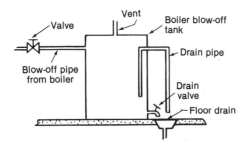

Boiler blow-off tank A tank designed to receive the discharge from a boiler blow-off outlet. Its purpose is to cool the water to an acceptable temperature for safe discharge into the drainage system.

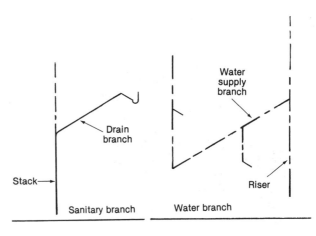

Branch Any part of the piping system other than a main, riser or stack.

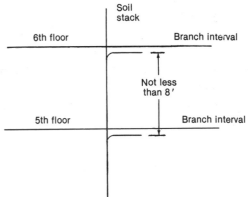

Branch interval A length of soil or waste stack (vertical pipe), generally one story in height (approximately 9 feet but not less than 8 feet) into which the horizontal branches from one story of a building are connected to the stack.

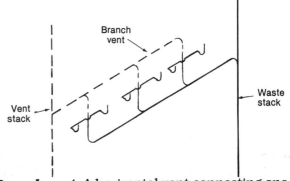

Branch vent A horizontal vent connecting one or more individual fixture vents to a vent stack or stack vent.

Brazed joint The joining of metal parts with alloys having a melting point higher than 800 degrees F, but lower than the metal parts to be joined.

Building Any structure built, erected and constructed of component parts intended for supporting or sheltering any use or occupancy.

Building classification The arrangement in local codes for the designation of buildings into classes based on use and occupancy. Note: Classification determines the required type and number of plumbing fixtures necessary to meet minimum fixture requirements.

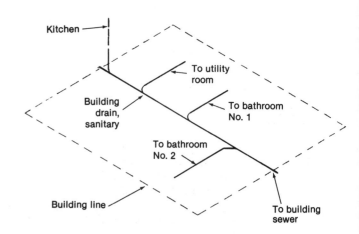

Building drain, sanitary The main horizontal sanitary collection system, inside the wall line of the building, which conveys sewage and other liquid waste from stacks and other drainage pipes (excluding storm water) to the building sewer, beginning 2 feet (more in some codes) outside the building wall. Note: *Most codes prohibit the entry of storm water into a building sanitary drainage system.*

Note: Most codes prohibit this installation.

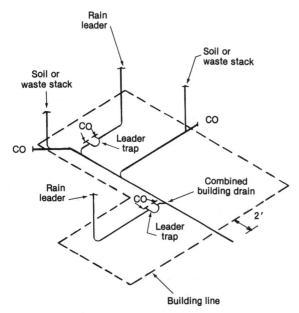

Building drain, combined The main horizontal collection system which conveys sewage, waste liquids and rainwater. Prohibited by most codes.

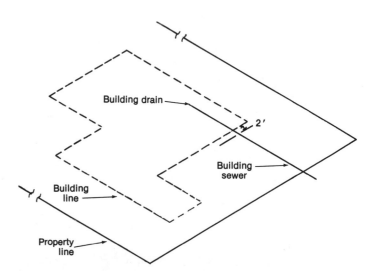

Building sewer That part of the horizontal piping of a drainage system which connects to the end of the building drain and conveys the contents to a public sewer, private sewer, individual sewage disposal system or other legal point of disposal.

Note: Most codes prohibit the use of a combined building sewer.

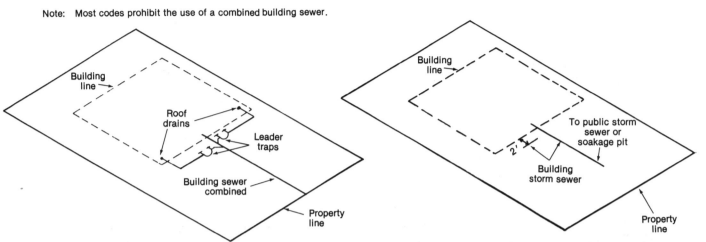

Building sewer, combined A building sewer pipe which conveys sewage, rainwater or other drainage. Note: *Most codes prohibit combined sewers.*

Building storm sewer A sewer which connects to the end of the building storm drain to receive and convey the contents to a public storm sewer, combined sewer (if approved), soakage pit, or other approved point of disposal.

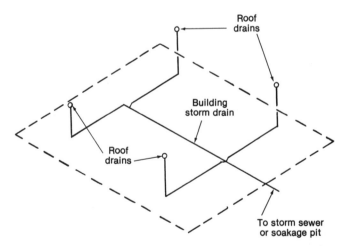

Building storm drain A drain used to receive and convey rainwater, surface water, ground water, subsurface and other approved clear water waste, and discharge these waste products into a building storm sewer or a combined building sewer (if approved), beginning 2 feet (more in some codes) outside the building wall.

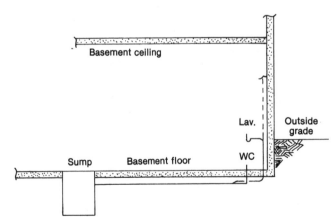

Building subdrain Any portion of a drainage system which cannot drain by gravity into the building sewer.

Building supply The pipe which carries potable water from the water meter or other approved source (private well) to a building. It is also known as a water service.

Note: Most codes prohibit the use of building traps (house traps)

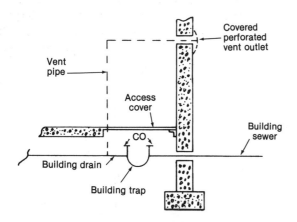

Building trap A special fitting or assembly of fittings installed in the building drain to prevent circulation of air between the drainage system of the building and the building sewer. *Most codes prohibit the use of a building trap in a drainage system today.*

C

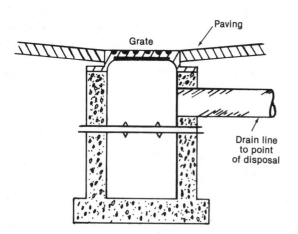

Catch basin A manufactured receptacle (sometimes job-constructed) in which rainwater and other approved liquids are retained for a sufficient time, preventing sand and other sediment from entering the storm drainage system.

Caulking Any approved method for rendering a joint watertight and gastight. For cast iron pipe and fittings with hub and spigot joints, the term refers to caulking the joint with lead and oakum.

Cesspool A lined and covered pit for the reception of domestic sewage or other organic waste from a drainage system. It's designed to retain organic matter while permitting the liquids to seep into the surrounding soil through the bottom and sides. *Not viewed favorably by most jurisdictional authorities.* Generally approved for limited time only, under conditions when a more acceptable way is not available.

Check valve A special valve designed to close automatically to prevent the flow of liquid in a reverse direction.

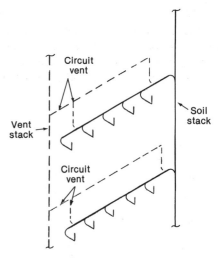

Circuit vent A vent branch that serves two or more traps and extends from between the last two fixture connections of a horizontal branch to the vent stack.

Cleanout A plug joined to an opening in a pipe, which can be removed for cleaning purposes.

Clear water waste Principally, the cooling and condensate drainage from refrigeration and air-conditioning equipment, or the cooled condensate from steam heating systems and similar liquid discharge.

Clinic sink A fixture designed to receive waste from bedpans, having the same flushing and cleansing characteristics as a water closet.

Code Regulations and their subsequent amendments or any emergency rule or regulation lawfully adopted to control the plumbing work by the administrative authority having jurisdiction.

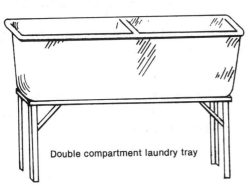

Double compartment laundry tray

Combination fixture A fixture combining a kitchen sink and laundry tray into a single unit. Also a two- or three-compartment sink or laundry tray combined into a single unit.

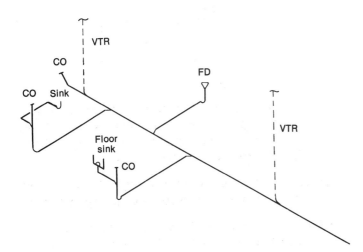

Combination waste and vent system, horizontal (permitted by some codes) A specially-designed waste piping embodying the horizontal wet venting of one or more sinks, floor sinks or floor drains by means of a common waste and vent pipe, adequately sized to provide free movement of air above the flow line of the drain. Generally used in restaurants.

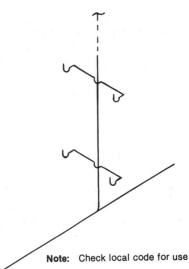

Note: Check local code for use

Combination waste and vent system, vertical (permitted by some codes) A specially-designed waste piping embodying the vertical wet venting of special low-rated fixtures (for example: sinks, lavatories and showers, but no water closets or pressure discharge type fixtures). Fixtures must be located in a direct vertical line on two or more floors, requiring no offset in vertical pipe. Pipes of limited length must be adequately sized to provide free air movement. Generally used in residential buildings.

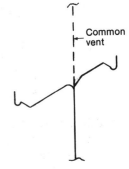

Common vent

Common vent A vertical vent connecting at the junction of two fixture drains installed at the same level in a vertical stack serving as a vent for both fixtures.

Condensate A liquid which separates from a gas due to a reduction in temperature.

Conductor See *Leader*.

Continuous vent A vertical pipe that is a continuation of the drain pipe to which it connects.

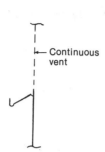

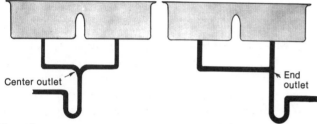

Two-compartment sinks and one trap approved

Center outlet

End outlet

Continuous waste A drain connecting a single fixture with more than one compartment or other permitted single fixtures (battery) to a common (single) trap.

Corrosion A gradual deterioration of piping, fittings and other materials brought about by chemical action, induced by certain soil, water and sewage characteristics, or by electrolysis.

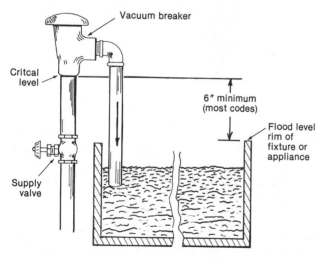

Vacuum breaker

Critcal level

6″ minimum (most codes)

Flood level rim of fixture or appliance

Supply valve

Critical level (in the plumbing code) A point on a backflow prevention device or vacuum

breaker (usually stamped on the device by the manufacturer) to indicate the minimum elevation the device may be installed above the flood level rim of the fixture or receptacle it serves. If a backflow prevention device is not so stamped, the bottom of the device shall constitute the critical level.

Cross connection Any physical connection or arrangement between two separate piping systems, one containing potable water and the other either water of unknown safety or questionable safety (such as steam, gas, chemicals, polluted or contaminated water).

D

VTR

CO

Dead end

Sink

2′ or more

Dead end A branch leading from a soil, waste, or vent pipe, building drain or building sewer which is terminated by a plug or other closed fitting (blind plug) at a developed length of 2 or more feet. Also defined as an extension for future connections, or as an extension of a cleanout for accessibility.

Deep-seal trap A trap having a water seal of 4 inches or more. Generally refers to interceptor or separator type trap.

Developed length The length as measured along the centerline of the pipe and fittings.

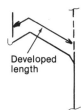

Diameter The nominal diameter of a pipe or fitting as designed commercially, unless specifically stated otherwise, based on the inside diameter.

Domestic sewage The waterborne wastes derived from ordinary living processes, free from industrial wastes, requiring no special separation or treatment.

Downspout See *Leader*.

Drain Any pipe which carries waste water or other waterborne wastes in a building drainage system to an approved point of disposal.

Drainage system All the piping within public or private premises which conveys sewage, rainwater, or other liquid wastes to legal point of disposal.

Drainage well Any drilled, driven or natural cavity which taps the underground water and into which surface waters, waste waters, industrial waste or sewage is placed. *Requires approval from administrative authority having jurisdiction.*

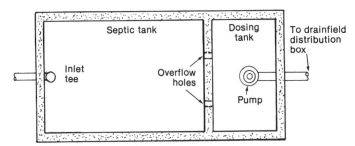

Dosing tank A watertight tank connected to the outlet pipe of a septic tank, located between the septic tank and drainfield distribution box, equipped with an automatic pump designed to discharge effluent intermittently to a disposal field.

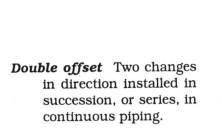

Double offset Two changes in direction installed in succession, or series, in continuous piping.

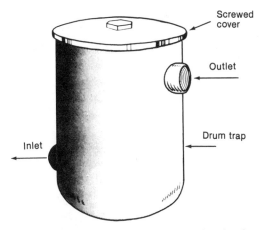

Drum trap A trap consisting of a cylinder having a removable cover for cleaning purposes, whose minimum diameter is 4 inches, with smaller size inlet and outlet. *Its use is prohibited or limited by many codes.*

Durham System An all-threaded waste pipe system of rigid construction, using recessed drainage fittings to correspond to the types of piping being used.

E

Effective opening The minimum cross-sectional area of the diameter of a circle at the point of water supply discharge.

Effluent The liquid waste as it flows from the septic tank outlet pipe and into the drainfield.

F

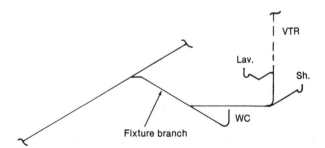

Fixture branch A waste pipe connecting several fixtures to any other drain pipe. Some codes refer to a fixture branch as being part of the water supply system.

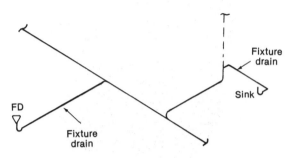

Fixture drain The drain from the trap of a fixture to the junction of another drain pipe.

Fixture supply A pipe supplying water to a fixture and connected to a branch water supply pipe, or directly to a main water supply pipe.

Fixture unit A design factor to determine the load-producing effects on the plumbing system of different kinds of plumbing fixtures. The unit flow rate from fixtures is determined to be 1 cubic foot, or 7.5 gallons of water per minute (GPM).

Flood level rim The top edge of a fixture or other receptacle from which water or other liquids will overflow.

Flooded The rise of the liquid in a fixture or receptacle to the flood level rim.

Floor drain A receptor located at approximately floor level connected to a trap to receive discharge from indirect waste pipes and provide floor drainage.

Floor sink A receptor designed to receive discharge from indirect waste pipes.

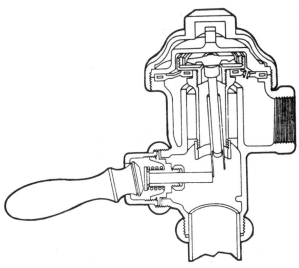

Flushometer valve A device actuated by direct water pressure which discharges a predetermined quantity of water to fixtures for flushing purposes.

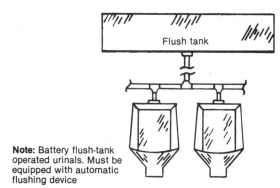

Note: Battery flush-tank operated urinals. Must be equipped with automatic flushing device

Flush tank A tank connected to the top of a water closet bowl or above a battery of urinals or similar fixtures designed for the purpose of flushing the useable portion of the fixture.

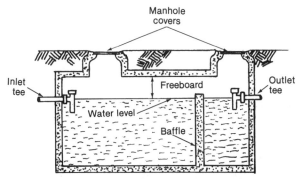

Freeboard A term used in plumbing to define the vertical distance (air space) between the maximum liquid level in a septic tank and the top of the septic tank.

G

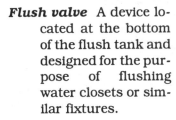
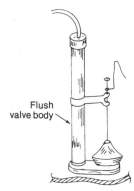

Flush valve A device located at the bottom of the flush tank and designed for the purpose of flushing water closets or similar fixtures.

Grade The slope or pitch, known as the *fall*, usually expressed in drainage piping as a fraction of an inch per foot.

Grease interceptor A tank of at least 750 gallon capacity, located outside of building, designed and sized to serve one or more fixtures.

Grease trap A device designed to retain small quantities of grease, generally located inside the building.

H

Hangers See *Supports*.

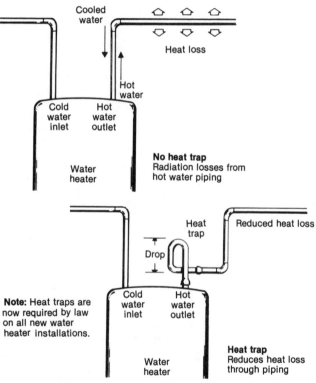

Note: Heat traps are now required by law on all new water heater installations.

Heat trap A device designed to prevent automatic circulation of heated water (and thus heat loss) in the outlet pipe of a water heater.

Horizontal branch drain A drain pipe extending laterally from a soil or waste stack or building drain to receive the discharge from one or more

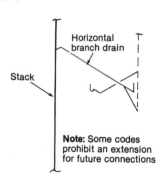

Note: Some codes prohibit an extension for future connections

fixtures. May or may not have vertical sections or branches.

Horizontal pipe Any pipe or fitting which makes an angle of not more than 45 degrees with the horizontal.

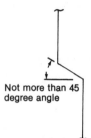

Not more than 45 degree angle

Hot water Water heated to a temperature of not less than 120 degrees Fahrenheit.

Hot water return A piping system designed to cause circulation of the heated water.

House drain See *Building drain*.

House sewer See *Building sewer*.

House trap See *Building trap*.

I

Impervious Having a smooth surface resistant to absorption. (Plumbing fixtures must *not* be constructed of materials that will absorb liquids or odors.)

Indirect waste pipe A pipe charged to convey liquid wastes (other than body wastes) not connected directly with the building drainage system. It discharges through an air break or air gap into a plumbing fixture or receptacle such as a floor drain or floor sink which is directly connected to the building drainage system.

Individual vent A pipe installed to vent a single fixture drain; may connect with the building vent system above the fixture served, or terminate outside the building into the open air.

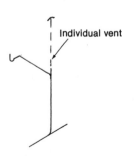

Individual vent

Industrial waste Liquid waste, free of body waste, resulting from the processes used in industrial and commercial establishments.

Insanitary A condition existing which is contrary to sanitary principles or injurious to health.

Interceptor A device designed and installed to separate and retain deleterious, hazardous, or undesirable substances from normal wastes and permit normal sewage or liquid wastes to discharge into the building drainage system or sewer by gravity.

L

Labeled Equipment or materials bearing the label of a listing agency accepted by the administrative authority.

Leader (Sometimes referred to as *conductor* or *downspout*.) The vertical rainwater conductor from the roof to the building storm drain, combined building sewer, or other approved means of disposal.

Liquid waste The discharge from any fixture, appliance or appurtenance which does not contain body waste.

Load factor The percentage of the total connected fixture unit flow rate which is likely to occur at any point, with the probability factor of simultaneous use. It varies with the type of occupancy and the code being used. (See *Fixture unit*)

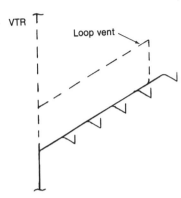

Loop vent A vent connecting a horizontal drainage branch or individual fixture drain to a common vent looped back and connected to a stack vent of the originating waste or soil stack.

Lot A single lot or individual parcel or area of land on which is situated a building or buildings, or which is the site of any work regulated by code. It shows the yards, courts and unoccupied spaces, with their dimensions. It must show the source of water and sewage disposal facilities and other facets relating to any plumbing required or not required by code.

M

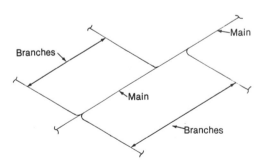

Main The principal artery of any system of continuous piping to which branches may be connected.

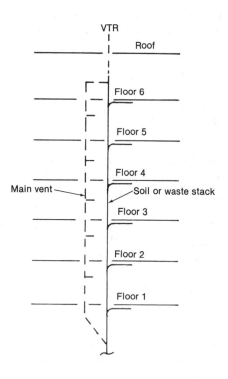

Main vent The principal pipe of the venting system, to which vent branches may be connected.

May As used in the plumbing code, it's a permissive term. You may do it, or you may not. It's optional.

Mezzanine An intermediate floor constructed in any story or room. When the total area of any such mezzanine floor exceeds 33-1/3% of the total floor area in that room or story, it's considered by code as constituting an additional story, rather than a mezzanine.

N

Non-potable water Water of unknown or questionable safety, not considered safe for drinking or for personal or culinary use.

Nuisance Obnoxious, inconvenient, or insanitary. (Any public nuisance known at common law or in equity jurisprudence; i.e., whatever building, structure, or premise is not properly ventilated, sewered, drained, cleaned or lighted, and whatever renders the air or human food or drink or water supply unwholesome in violation of the plumbing code.)

O

Offset A combination of elbows or bends which brings one section of pipe out of line but into a parallel line with the other section of pipe.

P

Pipe A cylindrical conduit or conductor, the wall thickness of which is sufficient to receive a standard pipe thread, thus conforming to the particular dimension commonly referred to as "pipe size." May be installed plain ended or threaded.

Pitch See *Grade*. Also referred to as *slope*.

Plumbing The business, trade or work having to do with the installation, removal, alteration, or repair of plumbing and drainage systems.

Plumbing appliance A special class of plumbing fixture whose operation and/or control may be dependent upon one or more energized components, such as motors, controls, heating elements or pressure or temperature sensing elements. The appliance may be manually adjusted or controlled by the user. It is designed for a specific purpose and not generally indispensable to the operation of the plumbing system. (Example: a dishwasher)

Plumbing appurtenance A manufactured device, or a prefabricated assembly of component parts, which is an adjunct to the basic plumbing system. Requires no additional water supply and contributes no additional load to the drainage system. It presumably serves some useful function in the operation, maintenance, or safety of the plumbing system.

Plumbing contractor A person who has been qualified as a master plumber by an examining board, who contracts on predetermined terms to provide labor, materials and knowledge, and to be responsible for work installed under his supervision to comply with established practices and specifications.

Plumbing fixtures Receptacles, devices, or appliances which are supplied with potable water or which receive or discharge liquids or liquid-borne wastes and discharge such wastes directly or indirectly into the building drainage system. (Industrial or commercial tanks, vats, or similar processing equipment are *not* plumbing fixtures; but they may be connected to, or discharged into, approved traps or plumbing fixtures.)

Plumbing inspector A trained person qualified to pass judgment on plumbing installations.

Plumbing official The chief administrative officer charged with the administration, enforcement and application of the plumbing code and all amendments thereto.

Plumbing system The drainage system, water supply, water distribution pipes, plumbing fixtures, traps, soil pipes, waste pipes, vent pipes, building drains, building sewers, building storm drain, building storm sewer, liquid waste piping, water treating, water-using equipment, sewage treatment, sewage treatment equipment, and relative appliances and appurtenances, including their respective connections and devices, used within the private property lines of a premises. Sometimes fire protection systems and equipment, chilled water piping in connection with refrigeration, and gas piping systems are excluded from the legal meaning of plumbing. Sometimes all or some of these are included, depending upon a particular code.

Potable water Water which is satisfactory for drinking, culinary and domestic purposes, and which meets requirements of the jurisdictional health authority.

Private (or private use) In relation to plumbing fixtures: in residences and apartments, to private bathrooms in hotels and similar installations where the fixtures are intended for the use of a family or an individual. (Some codes include toilet rooms in commercial establishments as being private, for the use of a family or an individual, and may exclude use by the general public.)

Private property All property except streets or roads dedicated to the public, and easements (excluding easements between private parties).

Private sewage disposal system A septic tank discharging the effluent into a subsurface disposal field into one or more seepage pits or into a combination of both.

Private sewer A sewer privately owned and not directly controlled by public authority.

Private water supply Any approved water supply other than a public water supply which serves one or more buildings.

Public (or public use) In relation to plumbing fixtures: in commercial and industrial establishments, in restaurants, bars, public buildings, comfort stations, schools, gymnasiums, railroad stations or places to which the public is invited or which are frequented by the public without special permission or special invitation, and other installations (whether paid or free) where a number of fixtures are installed so that their use is similarly unrestricted. In other words, plumbing fixtures located in buildings or structures that are not defined by code as private or for private use.

Public sewer A common sewer directly controlled by public authority.

Public swimming pool A pool together with its building and appurtenances where the public is allowed to bathe or which is open to the public for bathing purposes by consent of the owner.

R

Readily accessible See *Accessible, readily.*

Receptor An approved plumbing fixture or other device adequately designed to receive the discharge from indirect waste pipes.

Relief vent A vent, the primary function of which is to provide additional circulation of air between drainage and vent systems, other than regular vent pipes.

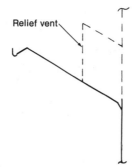

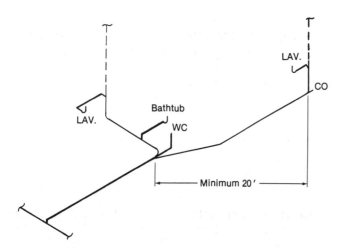

Remote fixture A single fixture installed more than 20 feet from the upper end of the branch line.

Rim In code usage, an unobstructed open edge at the overflow point of a fixture.

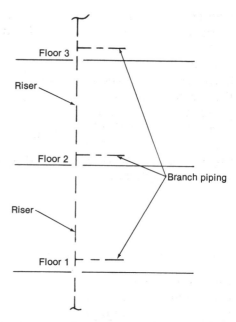

Riser A water supply pipe extending vertically one full story or more to convey water to branch piping or plumbing fixtures.

Rock drainfield Rock generally used in disposal field, consisting of 3/4-inch rock, 100% passing a 1-inch screen, a maximum of 10% passing a 1/2-inch screen.

Roof area The area on the building roof bounded by barriers, thus creating a drainage surface.

Roof drain An outlet fitted with a strainer to receive rainwater collecting on the surface of a roof which discharges the contents into the leader, downspout or conductor.

Courtesy: Tyler Pipe

Roughing-in The installation of all parts of the plumbing system which can be completed prior to the installation of plumbing fixtures; includes hot and cold water piping, drainage, waste and vent piping, and gas (some codes) and the necessary fixture supports.

Running trap A fitting constructed of cast iron, 4 inches or larger, in which the inlet and outlet are a horizontal straight line; however, between these two points the water way is depressed below the bottom side tangent of either the inlet or outlet, forming a water seal trap in the building drain or sewer. *Prohibited in many codes.*

Courtesy: Tyler Pipe

S

Saddle fitting A fitting attached with clamps to the outside of a pipe, sealed to the pipe with a gasket, located over an opening drilled or cut through the pipe wall, to create a change in direction, or to create a branch. *Prohibited in many codes.*

Tee saddle w/ bolts

Y saddle w/ bolts

Courtesy: Tyler Pipe

Safe pan (Sometimes referred to as a *drain pan* or *shower pan*.) A collector (receptacle) placed beneath a water heater located above first floor level to catch leakage and dispense it safely to an approved point of disposal. Also used to waterproof shower stalls.

Sand interceptor A device installed in a drainage pipe to prevent sand and other gritty material from entering the building drainage system.

Sanitary sewer A pipe which conveys sewage and excludes storm, surface and ground water.

Second hand A term applied to material or plumbing equipment which has been installed and used or removed from its first installation.

Seepage pit A covered and lined pit with open-jointed walls and bottom through which the effluent from a septic tank may seep into the surrounding soil.

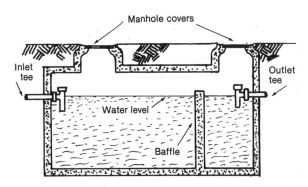

Septic tank A watertight receptacle which receives the discharge of a drainage system or part thereof, so designed and constructed as to separate solids from liquids by bacterial action, digest organic matter through a period of detention, and allow the liquids (effluent) to discharge into the soil outside the tank through a subsurface system of open-joint or perforated piping, or other approved methods.

Sewage Any liquid waste containing animal, mineral or vegetable matter in suspension or solution. May include liquids containing chemicals in solution; i.e., the used-water supply of a building.

Sewage ejector A device that operates automatically, designed for lifting and discharging sewage.

Shall A mandatory term. If the code says something *shall* be done, you have to do it, whether you like it or not.

Size of tubing See *Diameter.*

Slip joint An adjustable tubing connection in which the joint is made tight with a compression nut and compression ring, or a gasket, or a washer, or an O-ring.

Slope See *Grade*.

Soil pipe Any pipe which conveys the discharge of water closets or fixtures having similar functions, with or without the discharge from other fixtures, to the building drain or building sewer.

Soldered joint The act of joining copper tubing or copper tubing and fittings. An alloy of tin and lead which melts at a temperature below 800 degrees F. and above 300 degrees F.

Special wastes Wastes which require special handling before entry into the building drainage system or to a legal point of disposal, including, but not limited to: oil, sand, grease, glass and storm water.

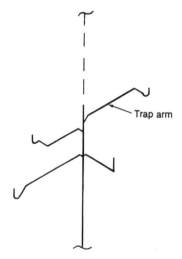

Stack vent The extension (dry portion) of a soil or waste stack above the highest horizontal drain connected to the stack.

Stack The vertical pipe of a system of soil, waste or vent piping.

Stack venting A method of venting one or more fixtures through the soil or waste stack.

Standpipe system A system of piping installed for fire protection purposes having a primary water supply constantly or automatically available at each hose outlet.

Storm sewer A pipe located outside of building wall line for conveying rain and/or surface water.

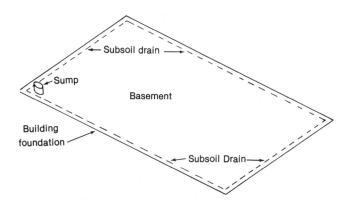

Subsoil drain A drain which collects only subsurface or seepage water and conveys it to a place of disposal.

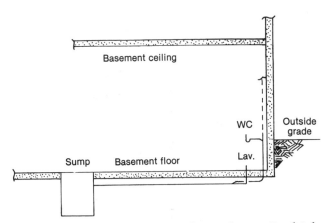

Sump An approved watertight tank or pit which receives sewage or liquid waste, located below normal grade of the gravity system and which must be emptied by mechanical means.

Supply well Any artificial opening in the ground designed to conduct water from a source bed through the surface when water from such well is used for public, semipublic or private use.

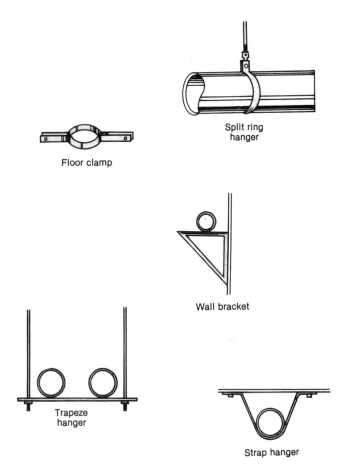

Supports Devices for supporting and securing pipe and fixtures to walls, ceilings, floors or structural members.

T

Trap A fitting or device so designed and constructed as to provide a liquid seal which will prevent the back passage of sewer gases into the building without materially affecting the flow of sewage or waste water through it.

Trap arm The drain from the trap of a fixture to the junction of that drain with the vent pipe. See *Fixture drain.*

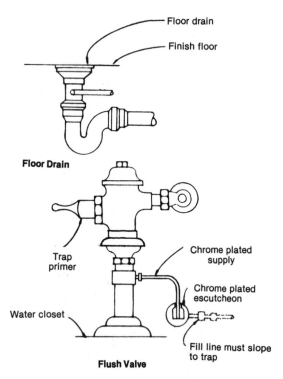

Floor Drain

Flush Valve

Trap primer A device to maintain automatically a water seal in a trap. (Example: a floor drain)

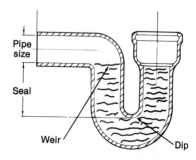

Trap seal The maximum vertical depth of liquid that a trap will retain, measured between the crown weir and the top of the dip of the trap.

V

Vacuum breaker See *Backflow preventer*.

Vent stack A vertical vent pipe installed primarily for the purpose of providing circulation of air to and from any part of the drainage system.

Vent system A pipe or pipes installed to provide a flow of air to or from a drainage system or to provide a circulation of air within such system.

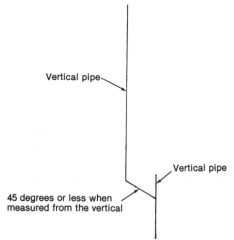

Vertical pipe Any pipe or fitting which is installed in a vertical position or which makes an angle of not more than 45 degrees with the vertical

W

Waste See *Liquid waste*.

Waste pipe Any pipe which receives the discharge of any fixture, except water closets or fixtures of similar functions, and conveys it to the building drain or to the soil or waste stack.

Water-distributing pipe A pipe which conveys water from the water service pipe (building supply pipe) to the plumbing fixtures, appliances and other water outlets.

Water main A water supply pipe installed for public or community use.

Water outlet As used in connection with the water-distributing system, the discharge opening for the water (1) to fixture, (2) to atmospheric pressure (except into an open tank which is part of the water supply system), (3) to a boiler or heating system, (4) to any water-operated device or equipment requiring water to operate, but not a part of the plumbing system.

Water service The supply of potable water from the water meter or other approved source (private well) to a building. It is also known as a *building supply*.

Water service pipe The pipe from the water main or other source of water supply to the building served. Also referred to as *building supply*.

Water supply system The water service pipe, the water-distributing pipes, and the necessary connecting pipes, fittings, control valves, and all appurtenances in or on private property.

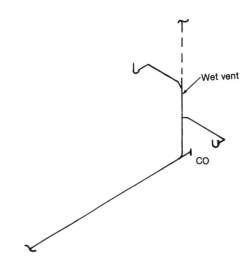

Wet vent A pipe which serves to vent and convey waste from fixtures other than water closets or similar fixtures.

Y

Yoke vent A pipe connecting upward from a soil or waste stack to a vent stack for the purpose of preventing pressure changes in the stacks. Generally used in high-rise buildings.

Index

Other Plumbing References

Estimating Plumbing Costs

Offers a basic procedure for estimating materials, labor, and direct and indirect costs for residential and commercial plumbing jobs. Explains how to interpret and understand plot plans, design drainage, waste, and vent systems, meet code requirements, and make an accurate take-off for materials and labor. Includes sample cost sheets, manhour production tables, complete illustrations, and all the practical information you need to accurately estimate plumbing costs. **224 pages, 8-1/2 x 11, $17.25**

Plumbers Handbook Revised

This new edition shows what will and what will not pass inspection in drainage, vent, and waste piping, septic tanks, water supply, fire protection, and gas piping systems. All tables, standards, and specifications are completely up-to-date with recent changes in the plumbing code. Covers common layouts for residential work, how to size piping, selecting and hanging fixtures, practical recommendations and trade tips. This book is the approved reference for the plumbing contractor's exam in many states. **240 pages, 8-1/2 x 11, $18.00**

Planning and Designing Plumbing Systems

Explains in clear language, with detailed illustrations, basic drafting principles for plumbing construction needs. Covers basic drafting fundamentals: isometric pipe drawing, sectional drawings and details, how to use a plot plan, and how to convert it into a working drawing. Gives instructions and examples for water supply systems, drainage and venting, pipe, valves and fixtures, and has a special section covering heating systems, refrigeration, gas, oil, and compressed air piping, storm, roof and building drains, fire hydrants, and more. **224 pages, 8-1/2 x 11, $13.00**

Plumber's Exam Preparation Guide

Lists questions like those asked on most plumber's exams. Gives the correct answer to each question, under both the Uniform Plumbing Code and the Standard Plumbing Code — and explains why that answer is correct. Includes questions on system design and layout where a plan drawing is required. Covers plumbing systems (both standard and specialized), gas systems, plumbing isometrics, piping diagrams, and as much plumber's math as the examination requires. Suggests the best ways to prepare for the exam, how and what to study and describes what you can expect on exam day. At the end of the book is a complete sample exam that can predict how you'll do on the real tests. **320 pages, 8-1/2 x 11, $21.00**

Audiotape: Plumber's Exam

These tapes are made to order for the busy plumber looking for a better paying career as a licensed apprentice, journeyman or master plumber. Howard Massey, who developed the tapes, has written many of the questions used on plumber's exams, and has monitored and graded the exam. He knows what you need to pass. This two-audiotape set asks for over 100 often-used exam questions in an easy-to-remember format. This is the easiest way to study for the exam. **Two 60 minute audio tapes, $19.95**

HVAC Contracting

Your guide to setting up and running a successful HVAC contracting company. Shows how to plan and design all types of systems for maximum efficiency and lowest cost — and explains how to sell your customers on the designs you propose. Describes the right way to use all the instruments, equipment and reference materials essential to HVAC contracting. Includes a full chapter on estimating, bidding, and contract procedure. **256 pages, 8-1/2 x 11, $24.50**

Remodeling References

Manual of Professional Remodeling

This is the practical manual of professional remodeling written by an experienced and successful remodeling contractor. Shows how to evaluate a job and avoid 30-minute jobs that take all day, what to fix and what to leave alone, and what to watch for in dealing with subcontractors. Includes chapters on calculating space requirements, repairing structural defects, remodeling kitchens, baths, walls and ceilings, doors and windows, floors, roofs, installing fireplaces and chimneys (including built-ins), skylights, and exterior siding. Includes blank forms, checklists, sample contracts, and proposals you can copy and use. **400 pages, 8-1/2 x 11, $19.75**

Remodeling Kitchens and Baths

This book is your guide to succeeding in a very lucrative area of the remodeling market: how to repair and replace damaged floors; how to redo walls, ceilings, and plumbing; and how to modernize the home wiring system to accommodate today's heavy electrical demands. Show how to install new sinks and countertops, ceramic tile, sunken tubs, whirlpool baths, luminous ceilings, skylights, and even special lighting effects. Completely illustrated, with manhour tables for figuring your labor costs. **8-1/2 x 11, 384 pages, $26.25**

Paint Contractor's Manual

How to start and run a profitable paint contracting company: getting set up and organized to handle volume work, avoiding the mistakes most painters make, getting top production from your crews and the most value from your advertising dollar. Shows how to estimate all prep and painting. Loaded with manhour estimates, sample forms, contracts, charts, tables and examples you can use. **224 pages, 8-1/2 x 11, $19.25**

Remodeler's Handbook

The complete manual of home improvement contracting: Planning the job, estimating costs, doing the work, running your company and making profits. Pages of sample forms, contracts, documents, clear illustrations and examples. Chapters on evaluating the work, rehabilitation, kitchens, bathrooms, adding living area, re-flooring, re-siding, re-roofing, replacing windows and doors, installing new wall and ceiling cover, repainting, upgrading insulation, combating moisture damage, estimating, selling your services, and bookkeeping for remodelers. **416 pages, 8-1/2 x 11, $23.00**

Electrical References

Home Wiring: Improvement, Extension, Repairs

How to repair electrical wiring in older homes, extend or expand an existing electrical system in homes being remodeled, and bring the electrical system up to modern standards in any residence. Shows how to use the anticipated loads and demand factors to figure the amperage and number of new circuits needed, and how to size and install wiring, conduit, switches, and auxiliary panels and fixtures. Explains how to test and troubleshoot fixtures, circuit wiring, and switches, as well as how to service or replace low voltage systems. **224 pages, 5-1/2 x 8-1/2, $15.00**

Residential Wiring

Shows how to install rough and finish wiring in both new construction and alterations and additions. Complete instructions are included on troubleshooting and repairs. Every subject is referenced to the 1987 National Electrical Code, and over 24 pages of the most needed NEC tables are included to help you avoid errors so your wiring passes inspection — the first time. **352 pages, 5-1/2 x 8-1/2, $18.25**

Electrical Blueprint Reading

Shows how to read and interpret electrical drawings, wiring diagrams and specifications for construction of electrical systems in buildings. Show how a typical lighting plan and power layout would appear on the plans and explains what the contractor would do to execute this plan. Describes how to use a panelboard or heating schedule and includes typical electrical specifications. **128 pages, 8-1/2 x 11, $13.75**

Estimating Electrical Construction

A practical approach to estimating materials and labor for residential and commercial electrical construction. Written by the A.S.P.E. National Estimator of the Year, it explains how to use labor units, the plan take-off and the bid summary to establish an accurate estimate. Covers dealing with suppliers, pricing sheets, and how to modify labor units. Provides extensive labor unit tables, and blank forms for use in estimating your next electrical job. **272 pages, 8-1/2 x 11, $19.00**

Construction Estimating Guides

Estimating Home Building Costs

Estimate every phase of residential construction from site costs to the profit margin you should include in your bid. Shows how to keep track of manhours and make accurate labor cost estimates for footings, foundations, framing and sheathing finishes, electrical, plumbing and more. Explains the work being estimated and provides sample cost estimate worksheets with complete instructions for each job phase. **320 pages, 5-1/2 x 8-1/2, $17.00**

Construction Estimating Reference Data

Collected in this single volume are the building estimator's 300 most useful estimating reference tables. Labor requirements for nearly every type of construction are included: site work, concrete work, masonry, steel, carpentry, thermal & moisture protection, doors and windows, finishes, mechanical and electrical. Each section explains in detail the work being estimated and gives the appropriate crew size and equipment needed. **368 pages, 8-1/2 x 11, $26.00**

Cost Records for Construction Estimating

How to organize and use cost information from jobs just completed to make more accurate estimates in the future. Explains how to keep the cost records you need to reflect the time spent on each part of the job. Shows the best way to track costs for site work, footing, foundations, framing, interior finish, siding and trim, masonry, and subcontract expense. Provides sample forms. **208 pages, 8-1/2 x 11, $15.75**

Electrical Construction Estimator

If you estimate electrical jobs, this is your guide to current material costs, reliable manhour estimates per unit, and the total installed cost for all common electrical work: conduit, wire, boxes, fixtures, switches, outlets, loadcenters, panelboards, raceway, duct, signal systems, and more. Explains what every estimator should know before estimating each part of an electrical system. **416 pages, 8-1/2 x 11, $25.00. Revised annually**

Estimating Tables for Home Building

Produce accurate estimates in minutes for nearly any home or multi-family dwelling. This handy manual has the tables you need to find the quantity of materials and labor for most residential construction. Includes overhead and profit, how to develop unit costs for labor and materials and how to be sure you've considered every cost in the job. **336 pages, 8-1/2 x 11, $21.50**

National Construction Estimator

Current building costs in dollars and cents for residential, commercial and industrial construction. Prices for every commonly used building material, and the proper labor cost associated with installation of the material. Everything figured out to give you the "in place" cost in seconds. Many time-saving rules of thumb, waste and coverage factors and estimating tables are included. **544 pages, 8-1/2 x 11, $19.50. Revised annually**

Building Cost Manual

Square foot costs for residential, commercial, industrial, and farm buildings. In a few minutes you work up a reliable budget estimate based on the actual materials and design features, area, shape, wall height, number of floors and support requirements. Most important, you include all the important variables that can make any building unique from a cost standpoint. **240 pages, 8-1/2 x 11, $14.00. Revised annually.**

Berger Building Cost File

Labor and material costs needed to estimate major projects: shopping centers and stores, hospitals, educational facilities, office complexes, industrial and institutional buildings, and housing projects. All cost estimates show both the manhours required and the typical crew needed so you can figure the price and schedule the work quickly and easily. **304 pages, 8-1/2 x 11, $30.00. Revised annually**

Carpentry References

Stair Builder's Handbook

If you know the floor to floor rise, this handbook will give you everything else: the number and dimension of treads and risers, the total run, the correct well hole opening, the angle of incline, the quantity of materials and settings for your framing square for over 3,500 code approved rise and run combinations — several for every 1/8-inch interval from a 3 foot to a 12 foot floor to floor rise. **416 pages. 5-1/2 x 8-1/2, $15.50**

Carpentry Estimating

Simple, clear instructions show you how to take off quantities and figure costs for all rough and finish carpentry. Shows how much overhead and profit to include, how to convert piece prices to MBF prices or linear foot prices, and how to use the tables included to quickly estimate manhours. All carpentry is covered; floor joists, exterior and interior walls and finishes, ceiling joists and rafters, stairs, trim, windows, doors, and much more. Includes sample forms, checklists, and the author's factor worksheets to save you time and help prevent errors. **320 pages, 8-1/2 x 11, $25.50**

Building Layout

Shows how to use a transit to locate the building on the lot correctly, plan proper grades with minimum excavation, find utility lines and easements, establish correct elevations, lay out accurate foundations and set correct floor heights. Explains planning sewer connections, leveling a foundation out of level, using a story pole and batterboards, working on steep sites, and minimizing excavation costs. **240 pages, 5-1/2 x 8-1/2, $11.75**

Rafter Length Manual

Complete rafter length tables and the "how to" of roof framing. Shows how to use the tables to find the actual length of common, hip, valley and jack rafters. Shows how to measure, mark, cut and erect the rafters, find the drop of the hip, shorten jack rafters, mark the ridge and much more. Has the tables, explanations and illustrations every professional roof framer needs. **369 pages, 5-1/2 x 8-1/2, $15.75**

Roof Framing

Frame any type of roof in common use today, even if you've never framed a roof before. Shows how to use a pocket calculator to figure any common, hip, valley, and jack rafter length in seconds. Over 400 illustrations take you through every measurement and every cut on each type of roof: gable, hip, Dutch, Tudor, gambrel, shed, gazebo and more. **480 pages, 5-1/2 x 8-1/2, $22.00**

Wood-Frame House Construction

From the layout of the outer walls, excavation and formwork, to finish carpentry and painting, every step of construction is covered in detail with clear illustrations and explanations. Everything the builder needs to know about framing, roofing, siding, insulation and vapor barriers, interior finishing, floor coverings, and stairs. Complete step-by-step "how to" information on what goes into building a frame house. **240 pages, 8-1/2 x 11, $14.25. Revised edition**

Contractor's Guide to the Building Code Revised

Explains in plain English exactly what the Uniform Building Code requires and shows how to design and construct residential and light commercial buildings that will pass inspection the first time. Suggests how to work with the inspector to minimize construction costs, what common building shortcuts are likely to be cited, and where exceptions are granted. **544 pages, 5-1/2 x 8-1/2, $24.25**

Carpentry for Residential Construction

How to do professional quality carpentry work in homes and apartments. Illustrated instructions show you everything from setting batter boards to framing floors and walls, installing floor, wall and roof sheathing, and applying roofing. Covers finish carpentry, also: How to install each type of cornice, frieze, lookout, ledger, fascia and soffit; how to hang windows and doors; how to install siding, drywall and trim. Each job description includes the tools and materials needed, the estimated manhours required, and a step-by-step guide to each part of the task. **400 pages, 5-1/2 x 8-1/2, $19.75**